A Duty to Serve

TONBRIDGE SCHOOL
AND THE 1939–45 WAR

A Duty to Serve

TONBRIDGE SCHOOL
AND THE 1939–45 WAR

DAVID WALSH

THIRD MILLENNIUM
PUBLISHING, LONDON

This book is dedicated to Tonbridge School and to all Tonbridgians in memory of those Old Tonbridgians and Masters who gave their lives and of all those who at the call of duty, enduring hardship and facing death, strove to maintain the right ...

... and also dedicated to my mother and her indomitable generation.

A Duty to Serve: Tonbridge School and the 1939–45 War

© Tonbridge School and Third Millennium Information Ltd
First published in 2011 by Third Millennium Publishing Limited, a subsidiary of Third Millennium Information Limited.

2–5 Benjamin Street
London EC1M 5QL
United Kingdom

www.tmiltd.com

ISBN 978 1 906507 60 2

Written by David Walsh
Designed by Matthew Wilson
Editorial Direction by Christopher Fagg and Neil Burkey
Production by Bonnie Murray
Reprographics by Studio Fasoli, Italy
Printed by Printer Trento, Italy

Picture credits

Every attempt has been made to locate and credit copyright holders for all images. All images used in this book are © Tonbridge School unless otherwise noted below:

Tony Banham, 'Hong Kong War Diary': 79; Reymie Bousfield: 107; Bill Brown: back cover, 102, 103, 115, 116, 117, 128; Neil Burkey: cover (contemporary); Katharine Campbell: 53, 100; Commonwealth War Graves Commission: 97, 113; Chris Compton: 148; Corbis: 25, 77; *Daily Telegraph:* 16; Peter Doresa: 90, 91(left); Dulwich Archives: 13; Walter Eberstadt: 149; Michael Engelbach: 114; Major-General Roger Ephraums: 72(right); Fleet Air Arm Museum: 63; Graham Pitchfork Collection: 142, 145; Gurkha Museum: 88; Philip Harvey: 41; Richard Hide, 'Escape from Hong Kong': 80; John Hoare: 138(l); Photo restoration by Don Holtz: 78(l); Imperial War Museum: cover (planes), 40, 43, 49, 52, 60, 70, 91(r), 96(r), 108, 110(l), 140, 155; Jacquie Isaac: 125, 126; James Leahy: 68; Robin Lind: 122, 123; Robin Lucas: 48; Andrew Musson: 101; National Archives: ; Miriam Nicholls: 57, 59; Geoffrey Oswald: 92, 96(l), 133; Chris Passmore: 72(l); John Powell: 146; Nicholas Prowse: 134(bottom); RE Library: 138(r); Tim Read: 111, 112; William Rouse: 132; Royal Engineers: 54; Richard Scott: 61; Smythe Library: 65; John Sowrey: 129, 130; Peter Stainforth: 143, 144; Peter Steer: 29(l), 36; Tim Thomas: 46, 47; WGGP: 82, 84, 98, 141(r); Dennis Williams: 83(x2).

CONTENTS

INTRODUCTION

To be ignorant of what occurred before you were born is to remain always a child. For what is the worth of human life unless it is woven into the life of our ancestors by the records of history?

– Cicero

History is above all a story passed on from one generation to the next. The story of the Second World War and the part played in it by Tonbridgians is historical drama on a grand scale. In researching this book, I was struck by the sheer breadth and diversity of Tonbridgian war experience in what was a truly global conflict. Boys just out of school found themselves facing life-threatening danger at home and across the world, and the kind of responsibility few would be prepared to shoulder today.

I was lucky enough to be born into the first generation in three not to be swept up into a world war. From my father's and grandfather's generations I learned something about those wars

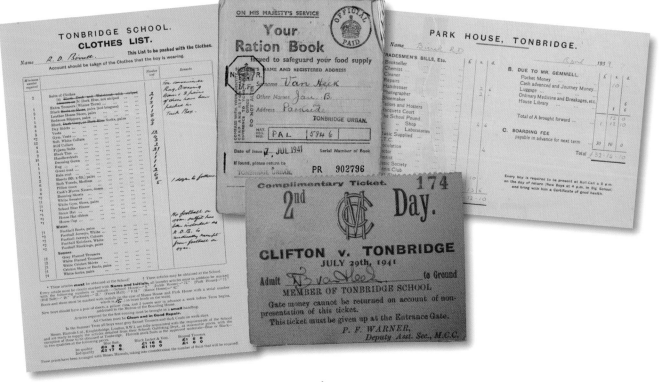

but, as with so many others, I have lived to regret not trying to find out more while they were still alive. As the number of Second World War veterans dwindle, so their experiences become increasingly special; we can still touch the war through them and find inspiration from their heroism and the strong moral cause for which they fought. This book therefore brings together some of the stories of that Tonbridge generation which was born in the shadow of the Great War and whose coming of age coincided with the next maelstrom.

Tonbridge has never been a particularly military school in terms of numbers going into the regular forces, but virtually every boy who came to the School between the 1880s and 1939, well in excess of 5,000, was involved in some form of service in the two world wars. The toll of lives lost, 415 in 1914–18 and 301 in 1939–45, had a huge impact on a school which, within those years, averaged only about 400 pupils in any given year. There is no more exciting and significant period in the 460-year history of the School.

I once came across some appropriate words on a village war memorial: 'These were ours in the days of their boyhood. Their names have become our heritage.' This book is about our heritage, Tonbridge boys who took the path of duty and endured more than our contemporary imagination can comprehend. It records stories of those who perished in the war, those who survived but have since passed on and those few who are still with us, and also draws on a well of memories about the School itself in the war years. It has been an immense privilege to hear from so many of those who fought in the war or were at school in those years, although the passage of time has undoubtedly prevented many other interesting and gallant stories from coming to light. That generation which fought in the war should not be forgotten, not now while some still live nor in the future when they are gone. Above all the book should evoke a very strong sense of pride in what it means to be a Tonbridgian.

David Walsh

FOREWORD

It is now 72 years since I left School House on the eve of war in July 1939. My last act as a schoolboy was to attend a special camp for public school air sections at Norton Priory near RAF Tangmere. I remember during that camp seeing Spitfires and Hurricanes drawn up for our inspection, and thinking that life was pretty exciting.

Five years at Tonbridge in the late 1930s proved to be a suitable preparation for the war whose coming became increasingly certain. We lived in the shadow of the Great War, passing every day into Chapel through the Gate of Remembrance. Many of our teachers had served in that war, including Gilbert Hoole, Tom Staveley, and the redoubtable RSM Sturgess, men due the greatest respect from us because of what they had endured on the Western Front, and we had OTC parades twice a week. We were proud too

Bill Brown recalls names on the 1939–45 War Memorial in Chapel, June 2011.

The Duke of Kent inspects the OTC in 1936 before opening the new Art and Biology building.

of our British Empire, so that service to it was very much an expectation. Even the spartan living conditions of our daily lives at school prepared us for the hardships to come – the lack of heating, the primitive washing and toilet facilities, the fierceness of Matron's 'cures' and the strict discipline wielded by the praes.

My own war allowed me to fulfil that dream of flying which had gripped me as a schoolboy. The RAF sent me to learn to fly in the Mojave Desert of California, my instructor a Hollywood stunt pilot of instinctive ability. I became an instructor myself at RAF Croughton, converting newly qualified pilots to the harsher rigours of operational aircraft, and then teaching the glider pilots of the Airborne Division the skills which they executed so gallantly in Normandy and at Arnhem. I finally escaped from instructing in 1944 to begin operations with the Pathfinder Force, flying the unique Mosquito bomber over Germany.

I was lucky to survive when 301 other Tonbridgians did not. On my visits to the School in my latter years I am always heartened by the interest of the young in what are now far-off days. I am therefore pleased that David Walsh should be telling the story of some of the inspiring ways Tonbridgians contributed to the war effort and how the School itself was affected. I am immensely grateful to Tonbridge for the start it gave me in life and I believe that all those of my generation who have passed on would also be very proud of what their school has become.

Bill Brown

CHAPTER 1:

THE FIRST YEAR OF WAR

Schools only reluctantly allow external events to intrude into their world. 'September,' records the 1938 School Letter. 'We met under the shadow of black political clouds, which well-nigh broke in thunderstorm; also in a meteorological drought which prohibited football.' The Munich Crisis of that September was the first serious intimation of coming war and came just a week or so after the start of the new school year. Earlier that year the housemasters had protested when the Governors suggested that it was for staff to take whatever steps they thought necessary for air raid precautions. Munich, however, created a new sense of urgency and the Governors then agreed to pay for an ARP programme, which initially included a single bomb-proof shelter under the Upper Hundred to house the whole school. This expensive and impractical suggestion was opposed vigorously by Ferdie Eames, housemaster of Hill Side, who demanded extra slit trenches

Above: 'Gas mask inspection in Manor House prep room'. Holly Leaves MH magazine, 1939.

Right: OT Society Dinner, Hotel Cecil, July 1929, F.O. Streeten presiding.

for his boys, and so it was decided that the Works Staff under Mr R. Werren would build separate house shelters. Gas masks were also distributed, necessitating a small cottage industry within the school to produce small cardboard boxes for them.

By January 1939 it had become impossible to ignore what was happening in Europe. In a school debate on government foreign policy, Gilbert Hoole strongly criticised the neglect of rearmament, especially in respect of the army, but a majority of the house still supported Chamberlain's policy. The British pledge to maintain Polish independence in March made louder the drumbeat of war, but Tonbridge boys were more concerned with their Athletics Sports, held in pouring rain and won by Welldon. In early April the Government announced the introduction of conscription, which would affect that summer's leavers. One of them, Bill Brown, regarded the likely coming of war with a youthful sense of excitement, but his parents showed more concern.

Summer term began in early May, an altogether more relaxed affair than nowadays, with School Certificate starting in mid-July and lasting just a week. The coming change of Headmaster, as Harold Sloman started his last term before retirement, was the main topic of school conversation, but the success of the 1st XI was also a cause for pride. In June the OTC was formally inspected by Brigadier Hughes, who commented on the excellence of the drill and the turnout. OTC Camp in August was cancelled by the War Office for the first time since 1914 but cadets took part in the National Service Parade, and the newly formed Air Training Section sent some boys to a public schools' camp at Tangmere.

On 5 July the annual OT Dinner, chaired by Rupert de la Bere (PS 1907), Conservative MP for Evesham, was held at the Café Royal, the last such occasion for seven years. One of the diners was General Sir Edmund Ironside, recently appointed Inspector-General of Overseas Forces, who visited Churchill at Chartwell later that month. They

talked until five in the morning and Ironside noted in his diary: 'I keep thinking of Winston Churchill down at Westerham, full of patriotism and ideas for saving the Empire. A man who knows you must act to win. Winston must be chafing at the inaction.'

On Skinners' Day, 29 July, the Captain of the School, John Dew (PS), made topical reference in his Latin speech to 'the underground fortifications for avoiding missiles hurled from airborne machines'. Sloman's speech catalogued the usual school achievements and made passing reference to the international situation by mentioning 'the various domed mounds of earth, ARP shelters', to be seen in the grounds, but the day resembled an oasis of calm as the storm clouds gathered, and Ironside, fresh from his sombre dinner with Churchill, must have been tempted to warn of what was coming. When the academic prizes were awarded, the prizewinners must have been one of the most distinguished groups to have graced the school. Bobby Robins (PS 1935) won the Gold Pen and another prize-winner was Maurice Wiles (WH 1936), both to become fellow code-breakers at Bletchley Park and distinguished academics: Robins Professor of Linguistics at London and Wiles Professor of Divinity at Oxford. John Fage (HS 1934), Smythe Exhibitioner for History, later became Britain's leading historian of African history, while Sidney Keyes (HS 1935), poet, scooped a wealth of prizes across the humanities.

A fine win over Clifton at Lord's sent the School happily home for a seven-week holiday on 2 August. *The Tonbridgian* of July 1939 might bemoan 'the perpetual state of international tension' but that was not likely to concern young schoolboys free from school obligations, while boys from the Tonbridge School Club in St Pancras came down to their usual camp on the school grounds. The leisurely summer days came abruptly to an end on 1 September, when Germany invaded Poland,

Eric Whitworth, a portrait by Edmund Nelson.

and on 3 September, when Britain declared war. All over the country young OTs were summoned back to their military units and Ironside was appointed Chief of the Imperial General Staff, the most senior job in the Army. Seven OTs rushed to marry that week before war dragged them apart, including Flying Officer Ted Wolfe (PH 1924), who would find himself in the thick of the Battle of Britain a year later.

Eric Whitworth, the Headmaster elect, was holidaying with his wife Evelyn in Devon, intending to move to Tonbridge in the second week of September. Whitworth had won an MC for gallantry with the South Wales Borderers in 1917 and had been Headmaster of Bradfield since 1928, where he had increased the numbers substantially, a strong factor in his favour when the Governors met at Skinners' Hall in April 1939 to choose Sloman's successor. Numbers at Tonbridge had worryingly dropped from 470 to 400 in the previous three years, a source of concern to the Governors. Whitworth thought he might be considered too old at 50 but the Governors liked his war record and his experience of headmastering another school, and saw him as the man to restore confidence in Tonbridge, which some prep school heads considered to have grown slack. There was not much time after his appointment for Whitworth to get to know Tonbridge, but he and his wife paid one brief visit in June, meeting staff and reviewing their living accommodation.

On 2 September Whitworth received a telegram from Colonel Latham, the Secretary, asking him to return immediately. He set out in his Austin Seven along roads now crammed with cars, mostly coming out of London, and stayed at the Rose and Crown while his own accommodation at School House was prepared. On 8 September he summoned a housemasters' meeting, the first of three before term started. The housemasters were impressed by his grip on the situation as they considered urgent questions of the black-out, gas masks and use of air raid shelters. David Somervell wrote of the encouragement he felt from 'the quiet confidence with which Whitworth faced the unknowable future of a school he had not yet begun to rule'.

To compound his difficulties, Whitworth had to deal with the consequences of an agreement made by Sloman that Dulwich College would be evacuated to Tonbridge if war came. Now, in the holidays and with little prior warning for Whitworth, who already had his hands full with Tonbridge issues, their evacuation began. Over 650 Dulwich boys and staff arrived to be housed

Dulwich College lesson at Tonbridge, October 1939.

in those Tonbridge boarding houses where there were vacancies, and in billets in the town. Their surreal day involved rugger after breakfast and lessons in the afternoon, the former being unpopular for digestive reasons and the latter creating problems of groping their way back to billets through a blacked-out Tonbridge. A Dulwich boy remembers it as 'a strange box-and-cox existence, and we were all rather glad when it was over.' A proper financial agreement had not been worked out and Dulwich complained at the size of the bill the Skinners' Company presented for the accommodation, while Tonbridge landladies complained at the low rate of the government allowance: six shillings and sixpence a week for small boys and ten and six for older ones. Twenty-four Dulwich boys were put up at Somerhill, now the home of Yardley Court, where Sir Osmond D'Avigdor Goldsmid made clear that the guests would have to do their own valeting. The arrangement lasted for just one term, to the relief of both schools, as Dulwich decided that the decision to evacuate was unnecessarily cautious. *The Tonbridgian* described it as 'Dulwich devacuated', agreeing prophetically with the decision 'for who would send his son to a deracinated and disorganised school picnicking somewhere in Kent?'

It would be hard to imagine any more difficult circumstances for a new Headmaster when term began on 22 September. Thirty anxious parents had withdrawn their sons during the summer, either taking them abroad or moving them to schools in safer areas. The Tonbridge numbers were therefore down to 370, the lowest since 1891, and clearly there were difficult financial decisions looming. After an initial flurry of ARP activity, term settled into the calmer waters of the 'phoney war'. For a time gas masks were carried, but they were soon discarded. A vegetable growing scheme was started in Clare House garden and many of the staff did duty in the evenings as air raid wardens or special constables. Leslie

Wright (JH 1938) remembers laughter when his housemaster, David Somervell, supervising junior prep, solemnly took four knitting needles and a partially finished khaki sock out of a bag, and proceeded to knit as his contribution to the war effort. As term came to an end, the rugby match on the Fifty against Dulwich attracted over 2,000 spectators and fierce but friendly partisanship, Tonbridge winning by 13 points to 6 with Charles Pillman having a particularly good game. Judde and School then fought out a close senior house match final, ending in a three–all draw. The final act was a production of *Hamlet* in which Denis Brown gave a memorable performance in the title role, while Keith Osborne achieved an uncharacteristic villainy as Claudius, and Sidney Keyes made an admirable Polonius. Seven of the cast would not see the end of the war.

The only real sadness in Whitworth's first term was Tonbridge's first war casualty. Thane

Cast of Hamlet, *December 1939. Sidney Keyes second row from the back, second from right, playing Polonius.*

Ladefoged (MH 1932) was a signalman in the armed trawler HMT *Sedgefly*, based in Hull; on patrol off Tynemouth on 16 December *Sedgefly* struck a mine and sank with the loss of all aboard. Thane's younger brother Anthony (Sc 1935) died two years later in the RAFVR, one of 17 sets of brothers to be killed in the war. It was a foretaste of what Whitworth could expect, but he was helped by his strong Christian faith, which led him to take personal responsibility for Chapel, appointing Harry Gripper (PS 1924) as Chaplain to help him. At his final Chapel service before retirement in 1949, Whitworth preached about the corporate life with its sense of mutual responsibility and shared affection, his text from Corinthians: 'Whether one member suffereth all the members suffer with it, or one member be honoured all the members rejoice with it.' It would have been an appropriate text for Christmas 1939 as school and nation geared itself for the ordeal to come.

The year 1940 began relatively quietly. Whitworth was beginning to make his presence felt with improved discipline and a noticeably greater sense of purpose about the place. Dulwich had returned to London and on the war front nothing much was happening. At a housemasters' meeting it was sufficiently quiet for agreement that shelters should be used by day but not at night. Some boys volunteered to man the town's dust carts to pick up scrap metal and paper, and pocketed some lurid discarded novels. The main feature of the term was the incredibly hard winter. Snow and frost lasted well into February and *The Tonbridgian* reported that 'we were snowed up for fully a third of the term, so that athletic activities were at a standstill; we have also been swept by icy winds, battered by hail and soaked with rain.' One consequence of this was an extensive flu epidemic which led, among other things, to the cancellation of the Cras. Donald Birrell, a 15-year-old in Hill Side, recorded in his diary on 9 February that 'the flu epidemic is still continuing unabated. I am twelfth senior person in the house now.' In April Whitworth took the decision to close Park House, whose numbers had declined to just 18 boys in January 1940 (Ferox with 26 boys was not in much better shape). Parental anxiety about the war, tighter finances and the obvious difficulty in recruiting new boarders to a school in such a potentially vulnerable position meant that costs had to be cut.

One week after the start of the Summer Term, on 10 May, Germany attacked in the west and Churchill became Prime Minister. By 25 May, when the Tonbridge 1st XI was winning its first match, the British Expeditionary Force (BEF) had been forced back to the coast and the seven-day Dunkirk evacuation had begun. Just 100 miles from school, therefore, dramatic and potentially disastrous events were unfolding. The most senior Tonbridge officer killed in this campaign was Lieutenant Colonel Eric Fraser (DB 1908), commanding 1st Suffolk. Fraser, a veteran of the Great War, was badly wounded as the army retreated, ironically close to where he had been wounded in 1914, and died on 23 May on a hospital ship. He was brought back to be buried at Leigh. Twelve other Tonbridgians were also killed, and many inevitably became prisoners for five long years. One of these was Lieutenant Colonel Geoffrey Kennedy (MH 1910), winner of the MC in 1918, who now commanded 4th Ox and Bucks in a gallant rearguard action round Cassel, for which he was awarded the DSO in 1945.

Another POW was Peter Allan (PS 1931), who was captured at St Valery with most of the 51st Highland Division. After tunnelling out of a camp at Laufen, Allan was recaptured six days later and sent to Colditz Castle in late 1940, the only Tonbridgian known to have been imprisoned there. In May 1941, fluent in German, he made an audacious escape from Colditz by hiding in some laundry being taken out on a lorry, and was at

CALAIS DEFENDERS IN LONDON

Four of the men who took part in the defence of Calais telling their story last night. Top, Maj. E. Williams, of King's Royal Rifle Corps, (left) and Maj. D. Talbot, of the Queen's Own Royal West Kent Regiment. Below, Rifleman Hosington, K.R.R.C., (left) and L./Cpl. N. Illingworth, Queen Victoria's Rifles.

Major Dennis Talbot at press conference after escape from Calais, June 1940.

(FH 1925) held the crucial position at Bergues with his Loyals' battalion in the final desperate rearguard action, and was one of the last to the beaches. Here he found a rowing boat and was picked up from mid-Channel by a French ship. Major Dennis Talbot (DB 1922), Brigade Major of 30 Infantry Brigade, organised the doomed defence of Calais for four crucial days. He was captured but escaped from a column of marching prisoners with two other officers. For nine days they walked by night and hid by day until they reached the coast, where they met some French soldiers with an old motor-boat. After various mechanical problems and nearly 24 hours at sea, they were picked up in the Channel and Talbot was given an audience with King George VI.

Against this dramatic background the life of the School somehow went on, with just the censored newspapers and BBC to provide news. Prayers for the deliverance of the Army were offered at Sunday Chapel on 26 May when Ironside, seeking solace from his heavy responsibilities as Chief of the Imperial General Staff (CIGS), told his son's housemaster, Hoffy Arnold, that there was little hope of saving much of the BEF. On the following Sunday Walter Oakeshott (JH 1917), High Master of St Paul's, was the preacher. Field Day was predictably cancelled, as was the Henley Regatta, but school fixtures continued on a limited basis. The Secretary of the Tennis Club apologised for having only one fixture, which he put down to the 'evacuation of opponents to places beyond our reach'.

Day boys had more freedom to explore the town and see stark evidence of the relentless intrusion of the war into school life. Troop trains, passing through Tonbridge from the Channel

large for a month, mainly walking, without papers, money or compass. At one point he hitched a lift in a car containing SS officers and, 'sweating a bit', managed to convince them he was an engineering student from Hamburg. He somehow reached Vienna, where he was cruelly turned away from the US Consulate, and then, starving and broke, fell asleep in a park and woke up to find himself arrested and returned to Colditz.

Other Tonbridgians escaped from France only with difficulty. James Carson (DB 1929), a subaltern in the Kent Yeomanry, made it back via the Channel Islands. Captain John Stares

Tonbridge High Street, June 1940.

ports, brought home exhausted BEF soldiers, who would sometimes throw out letters to be sent to their families. Boys who could speak French were asked to go to the station to help with French soldiers, while others handed out cigarettes, biscuits and cups of tea to haggard men, some in blood-soaked bandages or blinded by medical dressings. If more confirmation was needed of the unfolding crisis, Tonbridge itself now became heavily fortified. The River Medway would be the first significant barrier after the coast to any invading army, and the 'Medway Line' was therefore designated as a key line of defence, where heavy fighting would certainly have followed any invasion. Concrete pill-boxes and gun emplacements appeared all along the river and in the town, together with anti-tank obstacles. One such pillbox still lurks in the bushes by Dry Hill House. Barbed wire stretched the length of the High Street, concrete road blocks and armed guards were put at all the entrances to the town, road signs were taken down and an anti-tank ditch was dug across the Upper Hundred and along the edge of Martins. On open spaces around the School barbed wire and concrete blocks were laid to deter glider and parachute landings. The Home Guard came into existence in June with staff and senior boys helping to guard vital points around the town.

In these extraordinary circumstances came heightened parental anxiety about their sons' presence in what might rapidly become a war zone. Raids began in June, with boys being shepherded at night to sit in stuffy shelters, leaving them weary the next day. Donald Birrell's diary on 20 June noted: 'There was another air raid alarm at 11.15 last night. It lasted for five hours. We had breakfast at 9.45am and only two morning periods'. Gradually housemasters were allowed to use more discretion about sleeping arrangements. Hoffy Arnold responded firmly to one concerned Manor parent with an interesting piece of boy psychology. 'Although maximum bodily safety is secured by going directly to a shelter on hearing an alarm,' he wrote, 'continued rousing of boys from their beds may have a disastrous effect on their nerves. I propose therefore to leave boys in their beds when an alarm goes at night and only send them to the shelter when I think the acuteness of the situation warrants it.'

Whitworth feared both an increase in bombing of the Medway Line or nearby airfields but also being ordered to make a sudden and dangerous evacuation of the School in the event of invasion. With the safety of the boys as his paramount concern and to counter parental anxiety, he had therefore begun to make plans for evacuation as early as 31 May, writing to parents:

> The Governors are now taking action to find alternative accommodation for the School to which it could be immediately moved should the occasion arise. I shall inform parents as soon as any arrangements have been made.

He wrote initially to several headmasters to seek help. The only favourable response was from the Warden of St Edward's School Oxford, who offered shared use of his school if living accommodation could be found in colleges or private billets. Whitworth and Gilbert Hoole therefore travelled to Oxford in early June to search for billets. They received provisional promises from several

colleges of accommodation but only until the end of that term. Whitworth, however, still wanted to finish the term at Tonbridge, partly because of the School Certificate exams starting on 15 July, although exams cancelled by invasion would have been the ultimate schoolboy dream. Evacuation, especially a hurried one, would certainly have been a desperate undertaking of securing transport, packing necessary equipment and even mothballing school buildings, and Whitworth was also aware from the Dulwich experience of the great difficulties in managing an evacuated school. But many schools, including King's Canterbury at the Carlyon Bay Hotel in Cornwall, had already decamped to safer accommodation elsewhere, which not only created pressure from parents for

Crashed Heinkel bomber, October 1940, near the Old Barn, Hildenborough.

their time on farm work. An air raid warning disturbed afternoon tea, but the day finished with the traditional Gilbert and Sullivan, *The Pirates of Penzance*, and two days later term ended.

By now the Battle of Britain had begun, as the Luftwaffe sought to achieve mastery of the air over southern England as a necessary prelude to invasion. On Skinners' Day itself, just as afternoon tea was ending, 41 Squadron, led by Squadron Leader Dick Hood (DB 1923) was scrambled from Hornchurch to intercept raiders over Dover. This escalating drama was to be played out over Kent during the school holidays, watched and heard by staff and many local boys. By the time the School eventually re-assembled on 1 October, the battle was largely over and the threat of invasion had receded, but in that summer holiday of August/ September 1940, the fate of school and nation became dramatically intertwined.

During August aerial activity over Tonbridge greatly increased. It was on the direct route taken by German bombers heading for London but also close to several airfields, including Biggin Hill and Kenley. Many bombs fell in the vicinity, mostly jettisoned by fleeing German aircraft, and there was heightening tension about the possibility of invasion as southeast England swarmed with military activity. Whitworth was therefore forced again in late August to consider evacuating the School to a safer place. This time the Headmaster of Shrewsbury offered use of his school, and Whitworth travelled there towards the end of the month. Sharing Shrewsbury for work and games was not a problem, but billeting 400 boys and staff privately in the area was more difficult, and it was clear that they would be widely scattered. Whitworth feared not only the difficulty of keeping the school together as

Tonbridge to take this safety-first route but would make it more difficult to find suitable premises.

In mid-June Whitworth went to see Ironside, who gave him 30 minutes of his valuable time at Home Forces HQ. 'Have everything ready to go at 24-hours' notice,' Ironside told him, 'but don't go; and if I have any reason to change my mind, I will let you know'. Whitworth returned to Tonbridge to prepare that 24-hour readiness, but the need never came and evacuation to Oxford was ended as a possibility in July with the Ministry of Health claiming the earmarked accommodation for civil servants. On Skinners' Day, 27 July, Whitworth paid tribute to the work of the staff as Air Raid Wardens, Special Constables and Home Guard, and to the boys who had given up much of

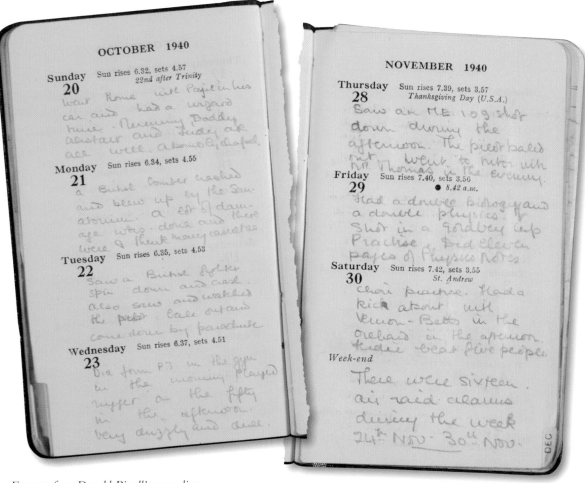

Excerpts from Donald Birrell's 1940 diary.

a community but the virtual impossibility of attracting new boys.

On 2 September Whitworth wrote to all parents, stressing that the school would stay put unless the Ministry of Health, responsible for the evacuation of schools, decided otherwise, but he alerted them to the invitation from Shrewsbury if it became impossible to remain at Tonbridge. In that first week of September the aerial battle intensified and on 7 September came the most serious invasion alert to date. That night more than 200 German bombers passed over Tonbridge to attack London and begin the Blitz, killing or injuring more than 2,000 people. Donald Birrell, from his home in Sanderstead, wrote in his diary

for 8 September: 'a large fire was visible during last night. Enemy planes dropped hundreds of bombs on the docks and London'.

The consequence of all this growing danger was another letter from Whitworth to parents on 13 September, a week before term was due to start. He wrote:

In my letter of September 2nd I informed parents that provisional arrangements had been made to move the school to Shrewsbury if evacuation from Tonbridge became necessary: the earliest date Shrewsbury could receive us in view of the opening of their term, September 26th, would be October 1st: in these circumstances I have decided to postpone the opening of the Christmas term until October 1st.

It was against this background that the final decision on evacuation had to be made. It was an agonising two weeks for Whitworth and for parents, with the fate of the School in the balance. He held three housemasters' meetings in September to consider all the issues. Arnold, the senior housemaster, was adamantly opposed to evacuation under any circumstances, but others stressed the risk to life in staying. One suggested splitting the school, with boarders going to Shrewsbury and day boys staying, but this would have been disastrous for the School's future. Whitworth received letters from many parents offering conflicting advice. One boarder parent, a Brigadier, greatly angered him by suggesting he had financial motives in not ordering immediate evacuation as 'the Skinners can pay'. Day boy parents were torn between trying to ensure the safety of their sons and not wanting them to move north away from home. Whitworth met them in Big School to gather their views and they voted by a large majority for the school to stay, accepting his assurance that assemblies and Chapel would not be held during raid warnings. Finally Whitworth met on 23 September with the Governors, the invasion threat receding but that of bombing still very much remaining. The responsibility was awesome, the tension in the meeting palpable, but the decision was taken to stay. Whitworth therefore announced to parents that term would begin at Tonbridge on 1 October and reassured them that every precaution would be taken to keep boys safe during air raids.

When the School reassembled, a return to normality was hardly possible, as German bombers passed over most nights, the railway line guiding them to London and back. Many boys, particularly boarders from London, had already endured air raids throughout the holidays. On 2 October there were six separate air raid warnings, and this became commonplace, causing a disrupted school schedule, many disturbed nights

Minutes of Housemasters' Meeting, 11 September 1940.

and an established routine for boarding houses. Judde boys in their dressing gowns would troop over to sit on benches in their stuffy shelter across the road at Clare House, while Somervell sometimes reclined outside in a deck chair, until he decided that the danger did not merit such discomfort. They were therefore allowed to stay in bed during warnings, Somervell supervising them from an empty top floor dormitory. Should the house be bombed, he told them, he would want to share their fate!

On clear nights a red glow could be seen in the sky to the north as London burned. Instruction was given on dealing with incendiary bombs while staff and senior boys took their turn fire-watching each night. The closest shave was when a bomb landed very close to the Chapel on 20 October, just 15 yards from where Leslie Wright was talking to his House Matron. The soft ground negated the force of the explosion, which shattered all the windows in the Chapel block classrooms and caused Matron a bout of hysteria, but miraculously left the Chapel structure and windows intact. Such excitements punctuating school routine became the norm for the term, but Tonbridge had survived the crisis and was carrying on. On 28 November Donald Birrell wrote in his diary: 'Saw an ME109 shot down during the afternoon. The pilot baled out. Went to tutor with Mr Thomas in the evening.'

Donald Birrell's diary, listing air raids in September–October 1940.

Eric Whitworth's letter to parents.

THE SCHOOL HOUSE,
TONBRIDGE.

13th September, 1940.

In my letter of September 2nd I informed parents that provisional arrangements had been made to move the school to Shrewsbury if evacuation from Tonbridge became necessary: the earliest date that Shrewsbury could receive us in view of the opening of their term on September 26th, would be October 1st: in these circumstances I have decided to postpone the opening of the Christmas Term until October 1st. We hope that evacuation will not be necessary and unless you hear to the contrary the term will open at Tonbridge on that day.

This postponement may also enable us to see more clearly how the situation is going to develop here in reference to Air Raid action, and in the interval we are making some alterations in the Air Raid shelters, so that if necessary the boys could gain adequate sleep if it were necessary to make more use of the shelters at night.

I am sorry for any inconvenience which the postponement of term may cause to parents, but up till now we have been fortunate in that the war has caused no interference with the life of the school, and if it is thought advisable and circumstances are favourable it will be possible to increase the length of the Easter Term.

E. E. A. WHITWORTH,
Headmaster of Tonbridge.

FIELD MARSHAL LORD IRONSIDE OF ARCHANGEL (1880–1959)

William Edmund Ironside (DB 1893) held for the first year of the war the most senior job in the British Army as Chief of the Imperial General Staff. He was brought up in Scotland by his mother, as his father, a Surgeon-Major in the Indian Army, died when he was only one. She moved to Kent and he entered Tonbridge in 1893, playing rugby at a good level but, by his own words, not benefiting much from the teaching. At six foot four and 16 stone, he was an imposing figure, earning him the nickname 'Tiny'. He served in the Boer War and was three times wounded, then undertook intelligence work in German South-West Africa (now Namibia), which supposedly made him the inspiration for John Buchan's character 'Richard Hannay'.

He was the first British officer to land in France in August 1914, finishing the war as a Brigadier-General. He was awarded the DSO in 1915 and mentioned in dispatches six times during a wartime career which ended with the command of 99th Brigade in 1918. Later that year he was sent to Archangel in northern Russia to command British forces in what became the chaotic Russian Civil War. For a year Ironside co-ordinated the British intervention against the Bolsheviks and then evacuated his force without serious loss when British political resolve ended. By now a Major-General, he was knighted on his return to England.

During the inter-war years Ironside held staff appointments in England and India, including Commandant of the Army Staff College. In April 1936 he became General Officer Commanding (GOC) Eastern Command. His diaries for this period are critical of the government's lack of proper financial provision for the training and equipment of the Army, as the international situation grew bleaker and the other two services received a greater share of the defence budget.

During this period he was a strong supporter of Tonbridge. He unveiled the Gate of Remembrance in 1925 and inspected the OTC on several occasions. He served on the committee of the OT Society and was President in 1947. The pages of *The Tonbridgian* in these years proudly tell of his every promotion. His son entered Manor in 1938, bringing him regularly to Skinners' Day and Sunday Chapel during the war.

On 1 July 1939 he was made Inspector-General of Overseas Forces, believing that he would soon be appointed to command the planned field force in France, a post which, to his great disappointment, went to Viscount Gort. He was however appointed CIGS on 3 September. 'I am

Maj-Gen. Sir Edmund Ironside (right) and Harold Sloman at Tonbridge, 10 October 1925.

General Sir Edmund Ironside (left) in France on 13 January 1940, with, from left to right: Gen. Georges, Winston Churchill, Gen. Gamelin and Gen. Viscount Gort.

bitterly disappointed that I am not to command the army in the field,' he wrote in his diary. 'My great ambition. I am not suited in temperament to such a job as CIGS but my whole life has been based on doing what I am told and there it is.'

This was a stressful period, as the under-strength army prepared itself for action in France. Frustrated by what he saw as the dithering of Chamberlain's government, Ironside tried to galvanise the country into action. He played the role of Kitchener in 1914 by raising 32 new divisions, but found himself having to acquiesce in the subordination of the BEF to flawed French strategy. In a reported aside to Whitworth that winter, he cast doubts on the willingness of the French to fight. He also made frequent visits to troops in France, but his relationship with War Minister Hore-Belisha was difficult and his diary entries about him often incandescent. On 2 December he wrote: 'then I went to the War Office and found Belisha. I told him how angry everyone in the BEF was at his criticisms of frontier defences in France.'

The disaster in Norway in April 1940 brought the fall of Chamberlain and fresh criticism of Ironside, and the subsequent defeat in France further undermined him. Churchill, on becoming Prime Minister, was keen to find new men at the top, so Ironside was moved from CIGS to become Commander-in-Chief (C-in-C) Home Forces on 27 May 1940, with the urgent task of preparing defences against German invasion, which he tackled with great energy. But Brooke and other BEF commanders disagreed with some of his plans, and on 19 July, aware that Churchill had decided against him, he resigned, being rewarded with a Field Marshal's baton and elevation to the peerage, but receiving no further military appointments.

Ironside was a great Tonbridgian and faithful servant of his School. History has not treated him that kindly because he had the misfortune to hold the highest office at the nadir of Britain's fortunes, but as a leader of men he had proved himself in South Africa, the Western Front, and Archangel. He was a much sharper and more creative military thinker than given credit for, but found himself frustrated by the failure of successive governments in the 1930s to recognize the importance of the Army, and then unfairly received the blame for the defeats of 1940.

CHAPTER 2:

DIGGING AND DOODLEBUGS

In his first Headmaster's Annual Report presented to the Governors on 16 September 1940, a date incidentally when he had many other worries, Eric Whitworth offers us a snapshot of the Tonbridge he took over. He described a school which catered well for the able boy, with six Oxbridge scholarships won that year, but only moderately for those of lesser ability, with just two thirds of School Certificate candidates passing in 1939–40. The 1937 Inspection Report had similarly concluded that 'the intellectual training received by the able boy is high', but pointed out that only 40 per cent of Tonbridge leavers reached even the Lower VIth. Whitworth drew attention to what he saw as a lack of drive in the Lower School, where 'boys who want to be idle can get away with it,' in part due to a lack of any formal syllabus in some departments and an uneven quality of classroom teaching.

Whitworth's main concern however was falling numbers. The public schools had recovered well in the 1920s from the war, but the Depression of the 1930s affected all schools. In 1934 Tonbridge had a full school of 485 boys, but numbers then started to slide – 468 in 1936, 410 in 1938 and 404 the term war broke out. The falling demand for the School was also shown by entry registrations, made at least a year before a boy came to Tonbridge, dropping from 209 in 1935 to 117 in 1939. Tonbridge was therefore in trouble even before the war, a fact blamed on Sloman's lack of energy in promoting the School to parents and prep schools. There was also a feeling within the staff that Sloman was happy to rely on them to keep the ship on course and did little to suggest changes or new ideas. Whitworth noted that Sloman did not meet prospective parents, leaving entry matters to the School Secretary, Colonel Latham, and he was also concerned at the narrowness of the Tonbridge clientele, too few sons of professional men and only one son of a clergyman. His oft-quoted remark about the spiritual home of Tonbridgians being the Stock Exchange was not just made in jest.

The war and the potential danger of Tonbridge's position greatly exacerbated Whitworth's problems of recruitment. In 1939–40, 60 boys were withdrawn for reasons directly due to the war, particularly affecting the boarding houses. Park House had to be closed in early 1940 and by that autumn there were only 225 boarders compared with 364 four years previously, a huge financial hit to the School which necessitated the further closure of Ferox Hall in December 1941. Whitworth, helped by the boarding housemasters, gradually succeeded in rebuilding the numbers, cultivating the prep schools (a difficult job since many had been evacuated) and creating the

Gas mask parade at Judde.

perception of a well-run and purposeful school. The gradual lessening of danger from bombing also helped. Boarding numbers dipped to their lowest point of 208 in January 1941 (with overall school numbers only 306) but thereafter steadily improved until they reached 312 boarders and a total of 415 at the end of the war.

Whitworth realised Tonbridge was in need of reform and rejuvenation, but this was an impossible task in war, when pragmatism ruled. That he surmounted the difficulties so effectively was due to his grasp of practical problems, while his commitment and modesty inspired a quiet and enduring confidence. These problems covered not just falling numbers, but also the difficulty of recruiting good teaching and domestic staff, issues of food rationing and all the air raid precautions which had to be taken. When shortage of staff became acute, boys found themselves being served buns in the Grubber by their headmaster. He was also very visible around the School, dressed in his mackintosh and trilby hat and accompanied

by his Irish setter 'Paddy'. 'The Arch', as he was called, could be severe, leaving boys in no doubt that he meant what he said, and uncompromising in his decisions, but he was also a kind man who inspired affection from those boys who came to know him. Patrick Mayhew (Sc 1943), as a novi, observed to Whitworth at one meal that he lacked a bicycle to get home for Sunday lunch. 'Would you like to borrow mine?' replied Whitworth.

By 1940 the geography of the school was very different. A tank trap was built on the Upper Hundred, concrete blocks for the same purpose were placed along the edge of Martins, and poles to prevent gliders landing could be seen in the open fields. The school's iron gates and railings had been taken away to be melted down, while water tanks and sand buckets to counter incendiary bombs were dotted around the school grounds. Old Judde became the ARP HQ for north Tonbridge, and Ferox, when it closed in 1941, became a Kent County Home for the Aged.

Two housemasters retired during the war – Arnold from Manor in 1942 and Page from Parkside in 1944 – but in other respects house life went on more or less as it had before in what was a strongly house-based school. The five boarding housemasters remaining by the end of 1941, including Whitworth, helped by John Knott, in School House, and the two day housemasters, were all senior figures who had been at Tonbridge for at least 20 years. 'Pagga Page was nearing the end of his career when I entered Parkside and was a shrewd manager of boys,' one boy wrote. 'He had a superficially gruff manner and could explode alarmingly when riled, but he and his kindly wife "Ma Pagga" inspired affectionate respect'. Another recalled 'Hoffy' Arnold in Manor as always being accessible in his study to any boy who wanted to talk, but was seldom seen on the boys' side, which he left to the praes, a situation which sometimes but not always resulted in a well-run ship. Ironically, when 'Tin Fin' Morris took over and was constantly wandering around the boys' areas, this was seen by some boys as spying.

For the novi, war brought some unusual challenges. Patrick Mayhew's father was in the Observer Corps and his mother was driving ambulances, so neither was available to take him back for his first day at Tonbridge. He was put on a train at Chislehurst, told to get out at Tonbridge and make his way to the School. On his arrival in the Games Porch he told an older boy 'I'm new here,' and was then passed around like an unwanted parcel among others before Whitworth found him and gave him reassurance.

Generally however, novi remained at the bottom of the heap, their rough edges knocked off and moulded to a uniform style. The 1937 Parkside magazine mused about 'ten little novi in a long line, one forgot to run a bath and then there were nine,' and this terror of getting things wrong could dominate the existence of the more

'The Novi who mistook the Praes' Room for the bootroom', Holly Leaves, *1924.*

timid. Fagging was a fact of life, benevolent in some hands but with plenty of scope for abuse. Housemasters mostly abdicated disciplinary control of the house to their praes, and this system of delegated justice left excessive power in the hands of senior boys. Novi had to learn quickly, not just the rules but house lore, most notably the 'bumph test'. They were instructed in the infinite gradations of seniority – in Parkside run up stairs two at a time and down one step at a time, no hands in pockets and all jacket buttons done up. A third term boy was allowed two buttons undone, a strong step up the pecking order, and, when one cheeky Manor novi asked some third termers how long he would have to wait to leave all his fly-buttons undone, he was stood on the table and told to sing while he ducked a barrage of litter. Novi, their bonding strengthened by common experience and suffering, looked forward to the day when they would be at the top of the hierarchy and calling the shots. But by 1942, boys reaching 18 were immediately being called up, not only depriving them of a last fulfilling term or two, but the School of experienced senior boys. In 1943 there were three different Heads of School.

War brought rationing, problems in acquiring domestic staff and therefore considerable difficulties for the housemasters and their wives or housekeepers in the feeding of their houses. One boy recalls the sterling efforts of Miss Cochrane, Manor housekeeper, to preserve both quality and quantity of food. Others accepted the constraints as part of their wartime duty. Personal butter and sugar rations were put out each mealtime and had to last a week – one jar with an ounce of butter, another with two ounces of margarine, a third with jam. There was plenty of bread and potatoes, sometimes with a meagre cheese topping, and other delicacies included reconstituted dried egg with a few tinned sardines stirred in, and dreadful mince full of tubes (was it horse or hedgehog?). Alan Jones (JH 1942) recalled Somervell getting angry when boys refused to eat boiled fish on both Tuesdays and Fridays, while one School House boy took exception to the cook's regular offering of kippers, which were mostly skin and bone, and pushed his through the Headmaster's letter box. The inventive could supplement their rations. John Powell (MH 1938) enjoyed sitting in the outside toilets eating pork sausages cooked in a biscuit tin 'oven'. Another recalls a novi bicycle outing from School House with Whitworth, picking blackberries together on a hill near

Underriver and losing some of their homesickness, with the fruit duly contributed to the house table.

Supplementing the rations became an integral part of the Tonbridge week. The Shipbourne Road field was given over to the growing of vegetables and in four years produced 62 tons of potatoes and 17 tons of cabbages. House gardens also grew vegetables, and there were allotments on part of Martin's and on the land now covered by the running track, which was tended by people from the town. Lyn Thomas was the member of staff whose untiring supervision made all this agricultural productivity possible. A minute from the Housemasters' Meeting of 22 September 1941 explained that one game would be released each day for work on school vegetable patches. Malcolm MacNicol (PS 1941) remembers 'Pagga' Page handing out spades to some novi and telling them to double-dig the vegetable patch. He left, and the thrill palled to the extent that

Above: *The last potato crop from the Shipbourne Road field, 1946.*

Left: *School House Novi, 1944. Patrick Mayhew second from right.*

Tonbridge Home Guard, led by James Stredder (CR), march down the High Street, 1944.

soon they were throwing clods of earth at each other, which earned them a severe lecture from Page on the seriousness of the national situation. MacNicol also found himself in a group of 20 boys combing through the potato crop to find and eliminate the Colorado beetle. In addition boys were encouraged to live on farms in their summer holidays, picking fruit or helping to bring in the harvest. Barry Pain (SH 1938) had instruction in summer 1941 on how to drive an old Fordson tractor from two very pretty land girls, and worked on a farm that summer taking hops from the fields to the kilns. Another land girl called Brenda looked after the grounds at Hill Side, a pretty redhead who gathered with the boys around the radiogram close to the fire escape as it played the popular tunes of the time.

Sport continued to dominate what was a thin programme of extra-curricular activities, made thinner by wartime austerity and difficulties of travel. Every boy was required to take some form of exercise daily, with team games predominating. One boy who failed to turn up for rugger in November 1940 was reprimanded by the Games Committee, and set to weed The Head every afternoon for the rest of term. This not only helped solve the shortage of labour on the grounds but was replicated by similar punishments across all the house allotments. The Boat Club only functioned with the loan of oars from the evacuated King's Canterbury and by parents lending cars and precious fuel supplies to get boys to regattas. School plays continued and, at the housemasters' meeting on 7 February 1944, the revolutionary possibility of inviting girls to take female parts in plays was discussed. In 1940 the Film Society was started, which proved very popular as Saturday night entertainment. The OTC Sing-Song remained a welcome event, but Whitworth told the organisers in February 1943 that it would be discontinued if 'the standard of quality and taste was not higher than last year'. *The Tonbridgian* found it increasingly hard to obtain paper supplies so that by 1944 it had shrunk to a mere 20 sides of thin, poor quality paper printed in Bible type, and even the exam boards decreed that candidates could write on both sides of the paper.

During the war the OTC was renamed the Junior Training Corps (JTC), with two compulsory parades a week, featuring boys dressed in Great War khaki with puttees and peaked caps. Senior boys also served in the Home Guard. Rodney Windsor (PH 1940) underwent not only conventional weapon training but also learned to make Molotov cocktails and operated a fearsome bomb-throwing weapon called a 'Blacker Bombard', regarded as more dangerous to its operator than the enemy. Edmund Crawford (SH 1940) had the joy of riding a 600cc Sunbeam motorbike up and down the playing fields, practising for his role as a Home Guard dispatch rider, a job also taken on by John Mew (SH 1942) in Tunbridge Wells. Angus Macgregor (JH 1944), in the Signals section, was in the radio room above School House one afternoon when he made contact with an American Flying Fortress bomber returning from a mission. The plane wireless operator asked the boys where they were and then flew over them for several minutes, remaining in voice contact.

In 1941 the JTC was inspected by the recently appointed Area Commander, one Lieutenant General Bernard Montgomery. The contingent was drawn up on parade for his arrival and after his first inspection round he asked that the cadets remove their peaked caps, whereupon he went round again. The reason for this remained a mystery until his memoirs revealed that he had ordered the removal of caps to 'see whether the light of battle was in their eyes'. In summer 1942 Sholto Douglas,

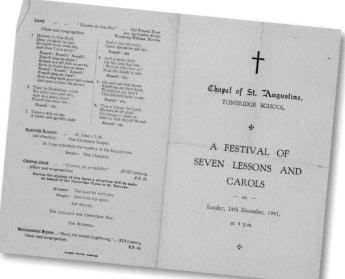

Top: *Carol service, 1941 – the first 'Festival of Seven Lessons and Carols'.*

Above: *Art School, 1943.*

Head of Fighter Command, came down to his old school to inspect the Air Training Corps.

About two-thirds of the 1939 teaching staff had been appointed before or soon after the 1914–18 war, and only one was in his 20s. Whitworth therefore saw it as his task to bring in new people and ideas to challenge the customs and habits of

Above: *Common Room 1945. Front row from left: Bathurst, Morris, Somervell, Watts, Vere Hodge, Whitworth, Herman, Eames, Staveley, Hoole, Knott.*

Below: *Housemasters' Meeting minutes, 5 October 1942. 'Girl friends and other school matters.'*

earlier decades, but it was very difficult in wartime to find suitable young teachers. He quickly identified a weakness in the Music Department, with only 48 boys learning a musical instrument in 1939 and no school orchestra, and appointed Allan Bunney as Director of Music. Bunney, who was on the staff of City of Westminster School evacuated to Judd, quickly established an orchestra and trained the choir to the highest standard, instilling an enduring love of music in many boys and introducing the first Christmas service of seven lessons and carols. He and Hervey Adams, the new Head of Art, did much to revive the cultural life of the School, very important at a time of low wartime morale.

The war meant that older men like H.S. Vere Hodge and K.T. Gemmell were asked to stay on beyond retirement, which had an impact on games coaching and other extra-curricular initiatives. Two of the pre-war younger staff joined up and were killed. Hector Chadwick, who had joined in 1937 as a scientist, was killed at El Alamein in 1942, while Oscar Browning, who taught Maths from 1935–8, was killed in Italy in 1943. For the first time however, ladies were appointed to the staff, and by 1945 there were four in all, Somervell musing on whether a co-educational staff would normally be a good thing for a boys' school. Either way, by 1946 an all-male staff had been restored. One consequence of the war was that science became the most popular subject. Nevertheless John Leahy (Sc/PH 1941), who stuck with classics, was never, to his great regret, introduced to even the most elementary science nor ever set foot in a laboratory, a situation which endured until well after the war.

Looking after the younger boys in class was Philip Bathurst, 'Bathy', OT, form-master of the lowest form and housemaster of Welldon. Every memory speaks well of him: 'Bathy just exuded love – of Tonbridge, his son and schoolboys in general.' He had a pronounced stutter, which disappeared when he sang the Gilbert and Sullivan patter songs. This he had done with two encores for 30 years. His form tended to contain more sportsmen than Oxbridge scholars and he was easily diverted from the business of the day with a question like, 'In your day, sir, is it true they served beer for breakfast?' One day in his class there was loud machine-gun fire overhead. Bathy, a Gallipoli and Western Front veteran, ordered the boys to get under their desks while he went under the table. When they re-surfaced, Bathy said, 'Whoever has written under my table "Bathy is a bloody old fool" is to do a hundred lines'. In break each

member of the form wrote one line: 'Bathy is not a bloody old fool'. 'Everyone spent a long time in Bathy's form,' said one boy, 'because they did not really want to leave.'

The problems exercising School authorities can often be discerned by what housemasters discuss at their meetings and the wartime minutes give a sense of these. The early days of the war are dominated by ARP matters such as a decision to fit the blackout first in the servants' quarters, and discussions about evacuation. In October 1940 the procedure for dealing with incendiary bombs in classrooms was organised, while souvenir-collecting by boys was forbidden. By 1942 more mundane topics were surfacing, with Whitworth telling housemasters he had de-praed a boy (in fact Stuart Hills) for playing bridge during school hours in the Library. Meetings with girlfriends were to be discouraged except at the girl's home and at her parents' invitation, and praes were not allowed to take a girlfriend out to tea at a cafe unless her parents were also present. In October 1944 Whitworth announced that catapults were forbidden and the 'prevalence of practical communism among boys' was to be discouraged; it is not mentioned what form this left-wing idealism took.

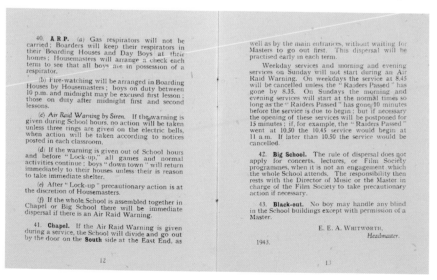

Memoranda 1943.
'ARP rules'.

The greatest danger to life came from bombing in the winter of 1940–1 and then from the flying bombs of 1944. Tonbridge's figures are not known, but in the nearby, much smaller parish of Leigh, more than 150 bombs and over 700 incendiaries fell during the Blitz, and nine planes crashed. The war for the young brought incredible contrasts of excitement and commonplace, of the 'saw Messerschmitt shot down; did difficult Latin prep' variety, but the dangers should not be underestimated, nor should the degree of luck in avoiding serious damage and casualties. The School did what it could to mitigate potential mass disaster by ordering immediate dispersal if a warning went during a Chapel service or Assembly, but a stray bomb could easily have fallen on a boarding house.

The blackout was a major exercise not possible with Chapel, so Sunday evening services had to be held during daylight hours. The only really near miss in the Blitz was the bomb which fell near the Chapel in October 1940, but a burning Blenheim bomber also crashed into Dernier Road with part hitting the Sanatorium, and many German and British planes came down in the fields around Tonbridge. John Brown (FH 1940) remembers being in the San with measles when he suddenly heard very loud machine-gun fire. Running to the window he saw two Hurricanes shooting at a Dornier, which had smoke pouring from one engine. John Powell recalls seeing a Spitfire shot down and the pilot bale out when on his way down to play squash, the incongruity of one person fighting for his life while two schoolboys played squash only striking him later. The Tonbridge Club Hostel in St Pancras was badly damaged by bombs in September 1940.

Senior boys joined staff in fire-watching. Malcolm MacNicol was on fire duty at Parkside one busy night during the Blitz, ready with stirrup pump, sand and water. He and Pagga were out in front of the house when they heard the whistle of a bomb. 'Get down, get down,' Pagga shouted, and they both lay in the gutter as the bomb exploded nearby. In School House junior boys often slept in ground-floor rooms and, if the aerial activity had been particularly heavy, the School porter would be sent round the classrooms to announce that afternoon school would be cancelled and 'the School will sleep'. Some masters suggested that was normal anyway. Night-time fire-watchers were also excused part of morning school, breakfasting, in the Headmaster's words, like 'gentlemen at ten o'clock'.

Despite the rule against collecting souvenirs, the temptation was too great. As the aerial dogfights and the bombing continued, so boys could find plenty of spent bullets and bits of shrapnel around the open spaces of the School, including the Quad, and Donald Birrell's diary makes clear that a sophisticated 'swap scheme' was used. John Mew recalls naively dismantling unexploded cannon shells from aircraft, while bits of metal also had to be cleared from cricket and rugby pitches before games. Some of the souvenir-collecting was of a higher order. One Smythe boy returned with a Messerschmitt machine-gun tied to his bike's crossbar, which he then swapped for a motorbike with someone in the town. John Powell's gruesome memory is of a Sunday expedition with a friend to a plane crash site, picking up part of a handle from some part of the plane and seeing a small piece of flesh attached to it.

In June 1944, just as everyone assumed the war was won, came the V1s or 'doodlebugs' which disturbed the routine more than anything in the Blitz. The sirens were unable to give any adequate warning and consequently, for the last six weeks of that term, morning Chapel was dropped and Skinners' Day cancelled for the first time in history. Impersonal and remorseless, the doodlebugs made people uneasy in the way bombers never had. The throbbing hum of their motors made the radiators in school vibrate as they approached but, the moment you heard the motor cut out, you knew they would come down nearby. Dozens went over every day, about 1,500 in a two-month spell, with many exploding in the area. Boys avidly watched them and the attempts by fighters to bring them down in open fields by 'wingtipping' them. At night anti-aircraft batteries made sleep difficult, and one night an anti-aircraft shell came through the roof of Manor and exploded in a lavatory.

It was on 23 June, however, that the School had its luckiest escape, which was witnessed by many boys. Peter Steer (Sc 1943) was reading a book in the house one evening when he looked out of the window to see a V1 directly above and a fighter pilot trying to flick it over with his wing. At that moment the engine of the doodlebug cut

out. David Kemp (PS 1942) was also watching with others from the top floor of Parkside, and they all raced down the stairs to take cover, landing in a heap at the bottom. How much the pilot's action saved the School is open to conjecture, but it fell and exploded with an almighty bang on a tennis court just to the east of Ferox. Many windows were shattered around the school, and Steer hid in a bathroom cupboard where the ceiling fell in, but not a single boy required hospital treatment. The luckiest escape was Whitworth's, who was playing bridge in his study with his wife and John Knott. The blast brought down the ceiling in the drawing room above and smashed the skylight and other windows in Skinners' Library, but in the study they were protected by a heavy curtain from the

'The RAF saves School House and me.' Peter Steer (Sc 1944) sketch of the doodlebug which nearly hit the School on 23 June 1944.

shattering glass. Whitworth suffered a slight cut but reflected that he could have been killed if they had played bridge elsewhere. In School House, which suffered the worst damage to windows, the beds were covered in shards of glass. One junior boy, not known for his religious fervor, suffered minor injuries to his back, prompting John Knott to ask him why he had been out of bed. The reply was immediate: 'I was saying my prayers, sir.' The next day senior boys, armed with hammers, shovels and buckets were dispatched to knock out broken glass and clean up, which gave the school doctors some work in stitching up cuts.

On another afternoon in early July, David Kemp (PS 1942) and John Wrightson (PS 1942) were batting together on the Head in a house match, when John was caught at cover from a poor stroke. Just at that moment a flying bomb came low over the School and the skies were full of bursting shells. All the players raced to take cover under the trees with bits of shrapnel raining down. As the storm subsided Kemp and Wrightson emerged and stood staring at each other. David looked very serious and John thought him about to comment on the danger just past, but instead he said: 'Wrightson, you really must stop chasing those balls outside off stump'.

Tonbridge School 1944-5

VE Day was the fourth day of the summer term on 8 May. Michael Fisher (MH 1944) was in the nets the previous afternoon when another boy came up with a radio on which he had picked up the news of Germany's surrender. VE Day was a school holiday and a fine sunny morning. In the Thanksgiving Service in Chapel, 'Now Thank We All Our God' was sung as loudly as any hymn has ever been sung and that afternoon many listened to Churchill's broadcast on a radio in Big School. All the timber was taken out of the anti-tank ditch on the Upper Hundred and burned in a huge bonfire round which boys danced and threw in bent and battered 'barges'. A three-day holiday was decreed and Peter Mieville (PH 1945), a Tonbridge boy for just four days, was taken by his mother to London to share in the national rejoicing. He was at Buckingham Palace when the Royal Family and Churchill appeared on the balcony, and that night searchlights lit up the sky and huge crowds danced and sang in a spontaneous outburst of national relief and rejoicing.

In an article written in *The Tonbridgian* in 1943, Peter Marshall (SH 1938) reflected on the war. 'I often look back to my first year here,' he wrote, 'and try to imagine what my schooldays would have been like without the war. Philosophising is a good refuge against the uncertainty of the future.' That of course is the nub, for those at school during the war could not know when it would end, so that the future was on hold and the prospect of death always very close. Boys craning their heads upwards in 1940 could see men dying in burning planes and readily imagine themselves suffering the same fate. Many also had fathers or brothers in the forces, adding to their sense of anxiety. Patrick Mayhew heard within a few weeks of his arrival in 1943 that his brother had

Opposite: Mosquito viewed from School House studies, 1944.

died of wounds. Whitworth's interview with him was kindly but brief and he then went home for two days. 'On my return,' he wrote, 'no one took any notice of me at all, and I would have felt like dying if they had. You got on with it. In Chapel I fought fiercely private battles against tears as the Chaplain prayed the prayer for use in time of war: "Succour the wounded, comfort the dying".'

What the war also gave the School was a stronger sense of community. This was not the jealously guarded self-contained community of the 1930s, but one which looked out more to the needs of the local area and the wider nation. This was shown in the service given in the Home Guard, the farming work done in holidays, the use of school buildings for local organisations, the sense of all being in it together. Peter Marshall wrote in 1943 that 'school life was not a landscape in itself anymore; it was a small scene in the panorama of life'. But school life in wartime was certainly a varied and exciting landscape for schoolboys whose memories of it are still clearly recalled:

Gargling with potassium of permanganate each bedtime to prevent infection; Aplin's tea rooms; the half-holiday for Nicolson's VC; Chapel in the twilight singing 'Bright the Vision that Delighted'; lessons in winter dressed in overcoats, hat and gloves; nights spent in shelters; collecting spent bullets; a Mosquito parked in the Quad; Matron dealing with boils; Sgt Major Sturgess's 'Parade Shun' heard half a mile away; sweet coupons in the Grubber; the taste and texture of 'Spam'; hearing church bells ring in 1942 for the victory at Alamein; taking exams in Big School as the radiators started to vibrate with the approach of a doodlebug; the unbridled joy of VE Day; the galaxy of private cars on Skinners' Day 1945 as petrol became obtainable again.

BERNARD VAN HEEK

The story of Bernard Van Heek (PS 1938) is one of remarkable generosity and fortitude. From Boekelo in Holland, he was sent to Tonbridge on the recommendation of Bernard Ross Collins (HS 1915), a friend and business associate of Bernard's father. It must have been tough for a 13-year-old to be suddenly uprooted from Holland into Tonbridge, but he was helped to learn English quickly by Marjorie Page ('Ma Pagga') and Mrs Birnie, the assistant housekeeper. To his contemporaries he became known as 'Van Tromp'.

The start of the war delayed his return to school in September 1939, his parents agonising about whether to send him at all both then and in January, but he was happy and settled by then at Tonbridge. In view of the international situation, he spent the 1940 Easter holidays with the Ross Collins family in Hertfordshire, but in May 1940 the German army occupied Holland and Bernard was cut off from contact with his family for the foreseeable future.

Bernard Ross Collins stepped forward to take full responsibility as young Bernard had no relatives in England and no means of support. 'You will appreciate that responsibility for Bernard now falls on me until after the war,' he wrote to Reverend Page in July, 'and naturally I would like to carry out the wish of his parents so that he is able to complete his education at Tonbridge.'

The question of the fees was a delicate one, and the subject of long correspondence between Ross Collins, Whitworth and the Governors. The Governors accepted a payment from Ross Collins of £100 per year towards the full school fees of £142, with the proviso that Mr Van Heek make up the difference later. When the war ended Ross Collins travelled to Holland, where sadly Mr Van Heek had died in 1942, and agreed with his widow to settle the full amount himself.

Letter from Bernard's father in occupied Holland to Marjorie Page, September 1940.

Left: *Bernard van Heek training in Canada for the RAF, 1944.*

Below: *Bernard van Heek greeting Queen Beatrix of the Netherlands in Enschede, 1994.*

Thus for the rest of his time at Tonbridge, Bernard was looked after in every sense by Bernard Ross Collins and his family, but repaid this by going on to a successful Tonbridge career, in which he was immensely popular, gained the School Certificate and became a house prae, no mean feat for a boy with Dutch as his first language. He left in 1943 to join the RAFVR.

His story would probably never have come to light had he not kept through his time at Tonbridge a remarkable scrapbook full of Tonbridge wartime memorabilia and original correspondence. It is a remarkable historical document, which he gave to the School archive in 1974. He himself remained a generous supporter of Tonbridge, keeping up with his Parkside friends and going on to a successful business and civic career. Through this scrapbook we can relive the world of a young bewildered Dutch boy cut adrift from his family, about whose fate in occupied Holland he could glean little. Tonbridge gave him a safe haven and an oasis of normality, and he wrote that the 'responsibility of Tonbridge was great in forming my character'. Tonbridge however is in his debt for providing a remarkable insight into the life of the School during the war.

CHAPTER 3:

THE SKIES OVER TONBRIDGE

All through the school holidays in August and September 1940, and mostly in the skies over Kent, the Battle of Britain was fought and won to save this country from invasion. It is a remarkable and proud statistic that 13 Tonbridgians fought in that battle. The youngest was 19, the oldest 32, for fighter pilots needed the sharp eyes and quick reactions of youth. Four of them died, four were killed subsequently in the war, and one of them, Flight Lieutenant James Nicolson, won the only Victoria Cross (VC) to be awarded in the Battle of Britain. It is unlikely that any school can claim a prouder record.

How Tonbridge came to produce so many Battle of Britain pilots is a matter of conjecture. Tonbridge had no separate air section in its OTC until 1939, but all boys had basic military training and there was a steady flow of leavers into the services; twenty-two went to the RAF College Cranwell between 1921 and 1939, compared with 116 in the same period to the military academies at Sandhurst and Woolwich, and 25 into the Royal Navy or Royal Marines. Eight of the pilots were pre-war RAF officers and the other five joined through the Volunteer Reserve, established in 1936 to provide a larger pool of pilots if war was to come, and trained to fly through private flying schools and university air squadrons. Trevor Wade (Sc 1933), for instance, joined the RAFVR in 1938 while studying law at the Law Society, while his contemporary John Bailey (Sc 1933) learned to fly in the Cambridge University Air Squadron. Flying the ever faster planes being produced demanded a particular aptitude and a high level of technical skill, so the RAF selectively recruited from the best-educated section of the population.

The oldest and most senior of the Tonbridge pilots was Squadron Leader H.R.L. 'Dick' Hood (DB 1923). He was a daredevil tree-climber as a boy and a considerable athlete at Tonbridge, rowing in

Battle of Britain pilots on standby.

Squadron Leader Hilary Hood standing beside his Spitfire, 1940.

the 1st IV and winning the Cras before entering Cranwell and then a fighter squadron. From 1936 to early 1940 he was a flying instructor, but in April 1940, at the age of 32, he took command of the Spitfires of 41 Squadron. Through the Dunkirk campaign he led his squadron into battle with a quietly determined but paternally caring style of leadership. One of his pilots described him as 'a lovely chap' who joined in games of cards with his pilots at dispersal, taking their minds off things as they waited for the telephone to call them into action. When the battle started 41 Squadron was at Catterick, but on 3 September they came south to Hornchurch to relieve another exhausted squadron. Hood shot down two enemy aircraft the next day and, on the afternoon of 5 September, he led off his squadron with orders to patrol over Maidstone and intercept a large enemy formation heading towards London. The scramble was a hurried affair, and Hood was still climbing when he encountered the enemy formation, so turned his 12 Spitfires for a desperate head-on attack on the German bombers. They sliced through the middle of them but a fierce dogfight then ensued with the Me109s in which four Spitfires were lost. When the squadron landed, Hood was missing; it is possible that he attempted to bale out of his damaged aircraft, which fell near Nevendon, and became entangled with it, but his body was never recovered. He was however posthumously awarded the Distinguished Flying Cross (DFC) for gallantry on air operations.

Most of the pilots in the Battle were younger than Hood, and there is a timelessness about the nonchalant young men who fought through it. 'It was just beer, women and Spitfires,' wrote one.

Letters to a friend from Katherine Sykes, guardian of Dick Hood, about Hood being missing and the subsequent DFC investiture at Buckingham Place.

'When you are 19, you couldn't give a monkey's.' Pilot Officer Trevor 'Wimpy' Wade was one of those young pilots, just 20 in 1940, a law student who learned to fly at Gatwick Flying School, joining 92 (Spitfire) Squadron in late May 1940. He emerges in the pages of *First Light*, a best-selling book by a fellow pilot in the squadron, Geoffrey Wellum, who tells us that Wade's nickname derived from an accomplished trencherman in an American cartoon. 'Small and rather rotund,' he wrote, 'there is an impishness about Wade which becomes infectious and his eyes twinkle with a mischievous humour'. He was also relaxed, generally asleep in a deck chair as he waited at dispersal, but a fine pilot who enjoyed his luck. During a year of combat he baled out once and crash-landed three times, once trapped upside-down in his cockpit, but shot down eight enemy planes and won the DFC. By the end of 1940 Wade was one of the few survivors of 92 Squadron, his impishness and boyish pranks gone, his face markedly older. Sustaining action for days on end, sometimes five or six times a day, and seeing friends come and go, aged the survivors rapidly. In late 1941 Wade became an instructor and then a test pilot of captured enemy aircraft for which he was

awarded the AFC. After the war he became Chief Test Pilot for Hawkers and was killed in 1951 when an experimental jet aircraft crashed near Lewes.

The main attraction for young pilots was the glamour and sheer excitement of flying the latest fighter aircraft. One described his first flight in a Spitfire as 'a glorious feeling of sheer joy and beauty', but to take it into combat was a very different matter, requiring not just flying skill but the instincts of a hunter and immense courage. The rapid manoeuvres of dog-fighting turned stomachs inside out while necks twisted this way and that to spot the tiny speck in the sky which might mean sudden violent death.

Squadron party, 1940. Trevor Wade front right.

Fear had to be publicly overcome day after day, particularly the fear of fire from sitting behind 85 gallons of high octane fuel, which developed 1,000° temperatures within seconds of being hit. Many pilots recalled the last screams over the intercom of colleagues going down in flames.

No story is more tragic than that of Flying Officer Arthur Rose-Price (JH 1934), killed on 2 September. He was the son of an OT farmer in Chile, and one of three brothers in Judde, who joined the RAF on a short service commission in 1938, aged just 19. After a year as an instructor he joined 501 Squadron, operating Hurricanes from Gravesend. A fellow pilot described what happened to Rose-Price: 'One lunchtime at Gravesend, a chap came in a beautiful Riley car and, as it stopped, we looked in and saw squash rackets, tennis rackets and even golf clubs. The CO told the newcomer, "Grab yourself some food but forget sleeping quarters at the moment. We're on readiness in a quarter of an hour. We lost three blokes today so you're on." "Yes, sir," replied Rose-Price. I will always remember his face. Anyway we took off at about two o'clock and he was dead at a quarter past.' Rose-Price died over Dungeness in what was his first hour of combat. He was not an inexperienced pilot, with his three-year service and time as an instructor, but flying skill alone could not compensate for lack of combat experience.

Pilot Officer John Bailey was also in combat for the first time that day and died four hours later than Rose-Price. The son of a high-ranking

RAF officer and from the same School House entry as Trevor Wade, Bailey had learned to fly at Cambridge University and was called up at the start of the war. After converting to Hurricanes only in June 1940 at a training unit commanded by Wing Commander John Pott DSO (PS 1921), later Station Commander at Biggin Hill, he was posted to 46 Squadron. On 1 September they joined the main battle at Stapleford in Essex, and the next day Bailey flew his first two combat patrols. Just before six o'clock he was taking off on his third patrol, climbing over the Thames Estuary to intercept about 70 enemy aircraft. That last sortie of the day proved fatal even to experienced pilots; emotionally strained and physically tired, the 20-year-old Bailey was shot down by an Me109, crash-landing and dying on the airfield at Detling.

Bevil Mabey (WH 1930) remembered a Tonbridge tutorial with James Nicolson (WH 1930) and two others when they felt the master was not taking sufficient interest in them. Nicolson therefore threw a firework, concealed by paper, into the waste paper bin during the next tutorial, which landed them all in trouble but showed something of his later spirit. Nicolson joined the RAF in 1936 and by May 1940 he was a flight commander in 249 Squadron, based at Church Fenton in Yorkshire, which came south to Boscombe Down with their Hurricanes on 13 August to reinforce an increasingly beleaguered Fighter Command. A friend and fellow pilot describes him at the time as 'a six foot three inch ex-public schoolboy with hair like a black mop and a uniform that looked like it had been slept in. He was an inveterate raconteur who told stories from morning to night and was an expert on

Flight Lieutenant James Nicolson (front second right) at his son's christening, 1941.

War's most amazing air exploit wins V.C.

It was his first air fight

PILOT ABLAZE, FOUGHT ON

Got his man, baled out, then wounded again by Home Guard

Daily Express Staff Reporter

AN R.A.F. officer, wounded by cannon shells, who battled with a Messerschmitt and shot it down from a blazing plane while both machines were diving at 400 miles an hour, has been awarded the first V.C. won by a fighter pilot in this war.

No braver deed has been recorded. From none of the war fronts has come a more astonishing story.

Flight-Lieutenant James Brindley Nicolson is the hero's name. The story tells how—

Cannon shells wounded him in the eye and one foot and exploded his petrol tank;

While his dashboard was melting "like treacle" and his left hand blistering in the flames, he put a hail of bullets into the German;

While he was baling out, with seventy bits of metal inside him, he was wounded again by gunshots from a Home Guard, who, mobbed by an angry crowd, had to be taken away on an ambulance.

FOR WIFE'S SAKE

Flight-Lieutenant Nicolson is now recovering. His wife, who was expecting a baby at the time of his great fight, said last night: "I believe it was his determination to pull through for my sake that has helped him."

His squadron call him "The Professor," because of his shock of wavy brown hair. He wears a permanent smile.

He stands 6ft. 3ins. He is so tall that the seat of his plane had to be adjusted to fit him into it.

This is the official account of his feat:—

"Flight-Lieutenant Nicolson has gained his V.C. for refusing to jump from a blazing Hurricane until he had destroyed his enemy, although it was his first flight and he had been twice wounded. For forty-eight hours he fought for his life.

"Flight-Lieutenant Nicolson, who is twenty-three, was on patrol over the Southampton area with his squadron on the early afternoon of August 16.

→ BACK PAGE. COL. FOUR

FLIGHT - LIEUTENANT J. D. NICOLSON, V.C.
His squadron call him "The ...

Daily Express, 1940.

broadcast by the Ministry of Information, he said in his best public school accent: 'When I saw the Messerschmitt in front of me, I remember shouting out "I'll teach you some manners, you Hun."' Just as he was landing he was unfortunate enough to be shot in the buttocks by a member of the Home Guard with obviously limited eyesight. A nurse who arrived on the scene was horrified to see the extent of his injuries; his trousers were burned to shreds, he had severe burns and he was bleeding from cannon shells and shotgun pellets. In the words of his later citation 'by continuing to engage the enemy after he had been wounded and his aircraft set on fire, he displayed exceptional gallantry and disregard for the safety of his own life.'

Nicolson spent the next six months in hospital recovering from burns to his hands, face, neck and legs, as well as removing bits of cannon shell from his legs and cockpit perspex splinters from his face, one of which had all but severed his left eyelid. While in hospital Nicolson learned that he had been awarded the VC, an award enthusiastically celebrated at his old school. He returned to operational flying in late 1941 and was posted to the Far East. On 2 May 1945 he joined the crew of an RAF *Liberator* as an observer on a bombing raid over Rangoon. Two hours after

an expert on everything including how to intercept the enemy, so it was somewhat ironic that he was shot down on his first sortie.'

That first sortie, however, was to make history. On 16 August Nicolson led off a flight of three Hurricanes to intercept enemy formations over Southampton. While still climbing, they were bounced by enemy fighters and Nicolson's Hurricane was hit by cannon shells, which wounded him severely and set fire to his fuel tank. He was about to bale out when an Me110 came past, so he stayed in his burning cockpit and opened fire from about 200 yards, shooting it down, until fire and his own wounds finally forced him out. When taking part in a later

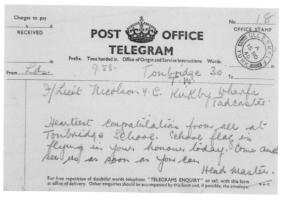

Congratulatory telegram to James Nicolson.

*Wing Commander
Eric Thomas.*

take-off, the plane's starboard engines caught fire and it was forced to ditch in the Bay of Bengal. There were only two survivors from the crew of 11, and Nicolson was not one of them.

The White Hart in Brasted was where the pilots from Biggin Hill came down to drink in the evenings. Laughter and drink edged out thoughts of death. As they came off the day's operations, releasing emotions in the long evenings became essential, also strengthening the bonds of friendship and loyalty within the squadron. When the pubs closed, pilots at the London perimeter bases might pile into cars and head for a West End night club where they could bask in the admiration of beautiful women. Robert Page (MH 1908) ran 'The Old Kimmul Club' in Covent Garden. He had been wounded near Ypres in 1916 before transferring to the RFC balloon section. He wore his RFC tie all the time and his club became a haven for many pilots, not least because Page was also a theatre producer and brought to his club actress friends like Deborah Kerr. Always too there was a pile of

blankets handy so that pilots could snatch a couple of hours sleep before heading back to Hornchurch or Kenley to clear their heads in the fresh morning air and brace themselves for another day which might bring death or serious injury.

A regular visitor to that White Hart at Brasted was Flight Lieutenant Eric 'Tommy' Thomas (SH 1932). Thomas joined the RAF in 1936 and served for two years before the war at Duxford with 19 Squadron, which was the first to be equipped with Spitfires. During early summer 1940 he was training young pilots at Cranwell and itching to return to operations, but came south on 19 August to join the battle with 266 Squadron at Wittering and then 222 Squadron at Hornchurch. His logbook shows that he went on combat patrol two or three times a day during this hectic period, shooting down a bomber on 15 September and then on 9 October an Me109 over the Elham valley, Thomas watching it belly-land in a field where the pilot set it on fire and surrendered to farmhands. Patrolling the Thames Estuary on 20

September he laconically records: 'dogfight with 18 Me109s. Damaged one'.

Thomas was rapidly promoted, commanding 611 Squadron in 1941 and then the American 133 'Eagle' Squadron at Biggin Hill, his Spitfire marked with his initials 'EHT'. He introduced the Americans to English beer at Brasted and they referred to him as 'that quiet reserved Englishman who through sheer quality of leadership made a cohesive unit out of a bunch of individualistic Yanks.' By the end of 1942 he was a Wing Commander leading the Biggin Hill wing on numerous sweeps over enemy territory, including the Dieppe operation in 1942. He shot down at least seven enemy planes and was awarded, between 1940 and the end of his operational career in November 1942, the DSO, DFC and Bar, and the French Croix de Guerre. The citations talk of 'his high qualities of leadership combined with great courage and skill in the face of the enemy'. Thomas was clearly an exceptional pilot

and leader of men, very popular in the squadrons he commanded, with a good sense of humour and always tugging on his horrible, rarely lit pipe. His logbook has many of those modest touches which reflected the RAF ethos against 'shooting a line'. One entry in September 1941 reads: 'Escorted bombers to Lille. Extremely heavy accurate flak. Came out over Gravelines with a number of Me109s who trailed and nibbled at us, waiting for stragglers. A very quiet Sunday afternoon's enjoyment'.

No fighter pilot had a more demanding war than Pilot Officer Peter 'Pip' Lefevre (PH 1931), who joined the RAF in 1938 after learning to fly in the Cambridge University Air Squadron. In May 1940 he embarked with 46 Squadron's Hurricanes on the aircraft carrier HMS *Glorious* to take part in the doomed Norwegian campaign. He stayed behind to destroy stores when the rest of the squadron re-embarked on *Glorious*, which was then sunk by German battle-cruisers with massive

Eric Thomas's log book, September 1940.

loss of life, including most of Lefevre's fellow pilots and a Tonbridgian naval officer, Walter Forbes (PH 1926). Lefevre was therefore one of the few survivors when the squadron re-formed, but he was joined in July by his Tonbridge and Cambridge contemporary, John Bailey. On 3 September, the day after Bailey's death, Lefevre shot down a German bomber but returned to base badly shot up and a fortnight later he survived baling out of his stricken aircraft over Chatham. The margins between life and death were never wide.

The Battle of Britain was but a short period in a long war and in May 1941 Lefevre was sent to Malta where he shot down three enemy bombers and was awarded the DFC. In April 1943, back in England and flying Spitfires on fighter sweeps over France, he was shot down over Brest, found by the Resistance and spent weeks in hiding before the Comet escape line helped him to cross the Pyrenees into Spain and return to England in August. He added more enemy planes to his score but, on 6 February 1944, leading 266 Squadron in a low-level attack in Brittany, his Typhoon was hit by intense anti-aircraft fire. He was seen to bale out as the Typhoon went out of control but too low for his parachute to open and his body was never recovered. Lefevre was a very experienced and skilful pilot but luck could sooner or later run out, even for men like him.

One other Tonbridgian was killed in the battle itself, Pilot Officer David Harrison (Sc 1925). Harrison worked in a bank, only joining the RAFVR in 1939, and must have been one of the older fighter pilots in training. Not until late August 1940 did he fly Hurricanes for the first time, aged 29, but he joined 238 Squadron on 12 September at Middle Wallop. He survived a forced landing on 25 September, his controls badly damaged, and was then shot down by Me109s over the Solent three days later during a large afternoon attack on Portsmouth. Harrison's plane crashed

into the sea and his body, still in its Mae West, washed ashore at Brighton ten days later.

Two who survived the battle were later killed in 1941. Pilot Officer John Rothwell (FH 1934) came straight from Cranwell with a permanent commission to fly Hurricanes in September 1940 and was killed in a crash in February 1941, while Flying Officer Joseph Hobbs (JH 1929) flew with 232 (Hurricane) Squadron and was later shot down in December 1941 over the Western Desert. Flying Officer Derek Hammond (FH 1935), the youngest of the Tonbridge pilots in the battle, did survive the war after joining 54 (Hurricane)

Squadron Leader Ted Wolfe beside his Defiant.

Air Commodore William Elliot, left, commanding Balkan Air Force, 1944.

Squadron on 20 September and then serving in Malta and the Desert Air Force.

It is sometimes thought that the Battle of Britain just involved Hurricanes and Spitfires, but a rather different form of courage was needed by those who flew the slow and obsolete two-engined Blenheims, which suffered large casualties in the Dunkirk campaign and had to be withdrawn from daytime action to be converted to night fighters in June 1940. Flying Officer Paul Tomlinson (Sc 1935), the brother of the actor David Tomlinson (Sc 1931), himself a pilot in the war, flew Blenheim night fighters in 29 Squadron, experimenting with early forms of airborne radar to try, mostly unsuccessfully, to intercept German bombers. Both Paul Tomlinson and another brother (Peter, Sc 1930)

served later in the war as Personal Assistant to Sir Arthur Harris at Bomber Command.

Equally vulnerable was the Boulton Paul Defiant. This two-seater was 50 miles per hour slower than a ME109 and had no forward-firing gun, instead relying on a gunner behind the pilot, more like 1914 than 1939. It had some success in the Dunkirk campaign, but on 19 July the Defiants of 141 Squadron were all but totally destroyed over the Channel by Me109s and what was left of the squadron was pulled out of the battle and sent to Scotland. Ted Wolfe (PH 1924), a Blenheim pilot and flight commander, was given command of 141 Squadron on 13 September to convert them to night fighters. Wolfe, described by a fellow pilot as a 'splendid chap and a fine leader' brought the squadron south that month to undertake night

15 Nov 40

Judde House
Tonbridge

Dear Nicolson

You will be receiving many letters but I feel I that, as your old housemaster I want to send you my congratulations and your marvellously brave and brilliant performance and on the reward it has received. As you can well imagine, at least half the boys now in the school cherish the ambition of being RAF pilots someday, and you may be sure they are one and all intensely pleased and proud that the first V.C. awarded to a fighter pilot should have gone to an old boy of their school.

I very much appreciated your coming to see us at Judde last year with your charming wife — I think you were then newly married. Now I see that you have a child. How proud your wife must be — and glad also I have had you 'safe in hospital' for a bit! I hope you have been making a complete recovery from your injuries. If at any time when you are

'has completed 174 hours of night flying since the outbreak of war and, in command of 141 Squadron, has shown great determination, skill and courage, and his leadership has imbued his pilots with the same characteristics.' In 1994 Wolfe became the last of the 'Tonbridge Few' to take wing on his final flight.

Senior Tonbridge officers, including Sholto Douglas, also played their part in the victory. His Tonbridge contemporary, Wing Commander William Elliot (JH 1910), had won the DFC in 1918, and then a bar in 1919 when, supporting White forces in the Russian Civil War, he was forced down behind Bolshevik lines and only narrowly escaped with his life. Elliot worked in the Air Ministry in the late 1930s, at the heart of policy-making, and in September 1939 became main air adviser to the War Cabinet, in which role he was present at the crucial meeting between Churchill and Dowding on 15 May 1940, when the latter won his argument to keep vital fighter squadrons in England rather than squandering them in France. Elliot described Dowding as 'being white in the face with strain' as he put his arguments to Churchill. Elliot later controlled night fighter operations at Fighter Command under Douglas and in 1944 commanded the successful Balkan Air Force, based in Italy. He retired from the RAF as an Air Chief Marshal in 1954.

patrols during the Blitz. The available technology made the interception of German planes at night almost impossible, but on Wolfe's return to Scotland in 1941 he was awarded the DFC for shooting down a German raider on the night of 6 May 1941 over Ayr. His combat report recorded that he closed to within 20 yards of a Ju88, no mean feat at night, allowing his gunner to fire five bursts. 'This officer,' the citation signed by Sholto Douglas reads,

Each September the few surviving veterans, along with their sons and daughters, grandchildren and great-grandchildren, come to Westminster Abbey to give thanks with the nation. As they file out, heads are craned upwards and ears cocked for that unique pulsing tone of a Spitfire's engine as it flies past, a sound which can still produce shivers of emotion. No one who lived through the Battle of Britain, airman or civilian, was in any doubt that they were in the middle of a struggle which would determine whether Britain would survive as a free country. The values of those who fought were the same as those of the people they were defending, and their battlefield was the England of churches and green fields they could see beneath them. The Battle of Britain is the most iconic event of the war as far as our sense of national consciousness is concerned. It was fought in the skies over Tonbridge and was viewed in brief violent snatches of action by Tonbridgians craning their heads upwards to glimpse the Spitfires and Messerschmitts in their dogfights and death throes, and at that unforgettable moment in time the fate of country and School were as one. When Eric Whitworth gave his report on Skinners' Day 1941, he rightly concluded that 'young Old Tonbridgians have earned their share in the great tribute paid to them by the Prime Minister in speaking of the debt of the many to the few.'

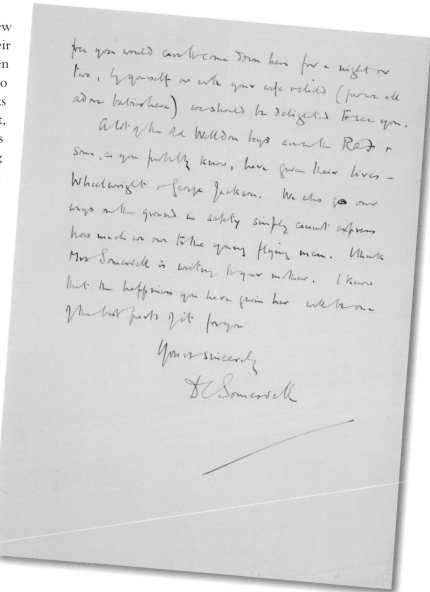

David Somervell writes to James Nicolson to congratulate him on his VC.

MARSHAL OF THE RAF LORD DOUGLAS OF KIRTLESIDE (1893–1969)

Sholto Douglas (DB 1908) became one of the most senior RAF commanders in the war. He was brought up in straitened circumstances by his mother, his parents having divorced. After a distinguished school career as a school prae, 1st XV and Chapel chorister, he won a Classical Scholarship to Oxford in 1913. His memoirs recorded that he was happy at Tonbridge, which he also described as 'quite a civilised place'. He particularly remembered OTC Camp at Farnborough in 1912, when he spent much of his spare time watching aeroplanes for the first time. His Oxford career lasted one year before he was commissioned into the Royal Field Artillery in 1914, transferring into the fledgling Royal Flying Corps the next year, in which he had a very distinguished war. He ended it as a Lieutenant-Colonel, having commanded two squadrons in almost continuous action and won an MC, DFC and Croix de Guerre. His younger brother Archie (DB 1910) was killed in 1916 while on aerial reconnaissance.

After deciding not to return to Oxford and flirting for a short time with a job in civilian flying, he rejoined the RAF in 1920 and was one of the first to attend the new Staff College in 1922, putting him on the fast track to promotion. His career prospered in the inter-war years and in 1938 he became Assistant Chief of the Air Staff (mainly concerned with weapons and equipment), where he was involved in encouraging the development of radar as well as the coming on stream of new fighter aircraft and a well-planned command and control system. In April 1940 he was promoted to Deputy Chief of the Air Staff, involved in operational policy at the highest level during that epic summer.

During the Battle of Britain he disagreed with Dowding, C-in-C Fighter Command, over the tactics to be used, believing that larger formations of fighters would have shot down more enemy planes. He also believed that it was immaterial in the achievement of air superiority if the enemy was shot down before or after they reached their target, while Dowding argued the need to protect airfields and London from being attacked. When Dowding resigned in October 1940, Douglas succeeded him as C-in-C Fighter Command. Here he initiated an aggressive policy of regular fighter sweeps over occupied Europe, which cost relatively high casualties, but fulfilled the wider strategic purpose of keeping Luftwaffe units in France when they were needed on the Russian front.

Sholto Douglas, portrait by Sir Herbert Gunn, 1940.

Sholto Douglas signing autographs for airmen.

In December 1942 Douglas, now promoted Air Chief Marshal, moved to become C-in-C Middle East, where he stayed until January 1944, presiding over British advances and victories from El Alamein to Tunis, and then the invasions of Sicily and Italy, and reorganising the vast Mediterranean air command. In January 1944 he came back to England to head Coastal Command, where he remained until the end of the war, achieving final victory over U-Boats.

In 1945 he succeeded Montgomery as senior British member of the four-power Allied Control Commission in Berlin. This position involved difficult negotiations with the Russians and responsibility for confirming the death sentences of the Nuremberg War Crimes Tribunal, one of which was on Goering, whom Douglas had fought over the Western Front as a young man. In January 1946 he was promoted Marshal of the RAF and retired from the service the following year. Douglas and Sir Arthur Harris of Bomber Command are the only men to have reached this highest rank in the RAF without being Chief of the Air Staff. In 1948 he became Baron Douglas of Kirtleside, sitting on the Labour benches (he was a member of the Fabian Society in his year at Oxford), and from 1949–64 he was Chairman of the newly created state-controlled British European Airways, presiding over a period of huge expansion in air travel.

Douglas, with Ironside, is the most senior military figure to have been educated at Tonbridge, both of them reaching the highest rank attainable in their service. Douglas was regarded as one of the ablest senior officers of his generation, quick to assimilate arguments and decisive in his actions, a big man in every sense, with a powerful personality and driving ambition. As with all senior commanders, some of his actions have been criticised by historians, but Douglas had responsibility for the direction of a successful war strategy at the highest level and contributed much to ultimate victory.

CHAPTER 4:

BOMB DISPOSAL

'There has been an awful lot of bad news on this bomb disposal training course, sir. Do you have anything good to tell us?' asked the new recruit. 'Yes,' the training officer replied, 'I do as it happens. The medical boffins have discovered that when a bomb goes off, it explodes faster than the human nervous system can react. In short you won't feel a thing.'

Before the war very little thought had been given to the problem of bomb disposal. Then in May 1940 a decision was reached to split work between the RAF, responsible for bombs that fell on airfields, the Navy for those on ships and dockyards as well as for mines, and the Army for all others. Very few unexploded bombs (UXBs) had to be dealt with until the start of the Blitz in September 1940, but then it became a big issue; by the end of September nearly 4,000 UXBs were waiting to be dealt with in London alone.

One young officer suggested that the main qualities required were to be 'unmarried and a good sprinter', but the majority were older men considered fit only for home defence duties, with the officers often having some kind of engineering or scientific background, subjects incidentally in which Tonbridge was strong. The haphazard recruitment process became increasingly urgent as the Blitz began, but recruits needed to be temperamentally suited to the job.

Fear of bombs or any tendency to take short-cuts was likely to be fatal, for each procedure had to be gone through in a methodical, measured way. Luck and experience helped, but even the most experienced died, and it could be a very lonely task. As one officer later wrote: 'It's very difficult to understand what it's like to be down a deep hole on your own with a cold sinister steel bomb. One minute you are there and the next oblivion.'

Bombs often had to be dealt with in awkward, inaccessible places. The usual procedure was for the men to dig the shaft and clear the space around the bomb, while the officer removed the fuse, in the early days with just a hammer and chisel, and sometimes lying on his stomach in muddy water at the bottom of an unstable shaft. At any point in this process the bomb could go off. Removal of the fuse was the crucial task and survival depended on staying one step ahead of German time-fuse technology. 1940 was the heroic age of bomb disposal, when urgency and a lack of knowledge and suitable equipment led to the taking of fantastic risks, miraculous escapes and the deaths of over 120 bomb disposal personnel.

Eyre Ievers (DB 1917) joined the RAFVR on the outbreak of war and, with some scientific background from his family engineering business, volunteered in 1940 for bomb disposal. By April 1942 he was Flying Officer in charge of a Bomb Disposal Squad at RAF Church Fenton in Yorkshire. On 29 April 1942, York was bombed by about 50 German aircraft, and two UXBs were discovered in a built-up area near Clifton airfield. Ievers was summoned to deal with them and decided to conduct a reconnaissance to determine the difficulty of the task, accompanied by a sergeant and two corporals. They found two German 250kg UXBs, and were just examining the size of the holes of entry when both bombs exploded one after the other. Ievers had massive injuries to both legs and died on the way to

hospital. The corporals had broken legs and the sergeant, amazingly, not a scratch on him.

Malta provided some of the greatest UXB challenges. The island was of great strategic significance and a vital Royal Naval base but, lying only 58 miles from Sicily, it was desperately vulnerable to air attack. Throughout 1941 and 1942 it was relentlessly bombed by German and Italian planes, sometimes as many as eight attacks in a day. All of this ordnance raining down on Malta created multiple headaches for bomb disposal teams. Bombs rarely penetrated the rocky ground, but the numerous UXBs were often covered with rock and debris from damaged buildings, and there were many delayed action bombs.

The RAF squads had the important priority of keeping bomb-damaged airfields operational, and one of their officers was Henry Dickinson (PH 1902), who had served in both the Indian Army and the RFC in the Great War before becoming a fruit-farmer. He was 52 years old by 1939 and an ARP warden, but volunteered for the RAFVR and, remarkably for a person of his age, was accepted for bomb disposal work and sent out to Malta in 1941. Stationed at Luqa airfield as Flight Lieutenant in charge of a squad, he defused over 100 bombs between 1941 and 1943.

Dickinson was a good example of the complete amateur becoming the consummate professional. He had little training and, before coming to Malta, had never seen the inside of a bomb. But he quickly had to learn and, working an average of 16 hours a day, he had so much practice that he became the acknowledged expert. The sight of him unscrewing the fuse of a bomb used to frighten his superior officer to death but, by a mixture of judgement and luck, he survived and rendered enormously courageous service. He was awarded the George Medal on 10 July 1942, the citation reading: 'Flight Lieutenant Dickinson has displayed outstanding courage and devotion to duty. When intense and almost continuous air attacks were commenced against Malta, he volunteered for special duties and performed dangerous work while the attacks were in progress. He displayed remarkable powers of leadership and indomitable courage.'

Another George Medal was won by a much younger Tonbridgian serving in the Mediterranean with the Royal Navy. Anthony Firminger (MH 1933) was one of two brothers in Manor; his elder brother Lisle (MH 1930) served as a navigator in Bomber Command, but was shot down into the North Sea in July 1942. Anthony trained as an accountant but by 1941 was a commissioned officer in the RNVR. He does not seem to have had any significant science aptitude at Tonbridge but volunteered for naval mine disposal and by the summer of 1943 was based at HMS *Cannae*, a shore establishment at Bone in Algeria.

Here he developed considerable experience in dealing with mines, and it was for this work that he was awarded the George Medal. Between February and July 1943 he made safe 17 bombs, five mines and an Italian circling torpedo. On two occasions he towed mines ashore, once swimming beside one, holding on to the horns while securing a line to the lifting gear and then rendering it safe on the beach to see if the enemy was using any new fuse device.

In July 1943 the Allies invaded Sicily, and by late August the island had been cleared. The use of the harbour of Messina was crucial to the imminent invasion of Italy, but the Germans had laid more than 200 depth charges, mines and booby-traps to deny its use. Firminger led a reconnaissance party to Messina, where he found a daunting task, especially from groups of depth charges lashed together and scattered about the harbour, some of them underwater with a new type of anti-handling mechanism. For two days he methodically worked his way through the

problems and successfully dismantled some of the charges. Then on 23 August he attempted to lift a lashed group of depth charges lying in the water at the end of the main jetty. He went into the water to secure a lifting rope to them from a pulley attached to a vehicle. As the vehicle slowly drove away, the depth charges were lifted clear of the water but swung against the underside of the jetty. There was a massive explosion which destroyed the jetty, killing Firminger and four other men supervising the operation. His courage at Messina was recognised only by a posthumous mention in dispatches, to go with his earlier George Medal, but many thought he deserved more.

German sea mines dropped on land by parachute during the Blitz became a major threat. They weighed a massive 1,000kg, had a fuse and a clock designed to explode the mine within 17 seconds of landing, and caused enormous blast damage to houses over several hundred square metres. Because these were mines, responsibility for them lay with the Royal Navy RMS (Rendering Mines Safe) Squads operating from their base, HMS *Vernon* in Portsmouth. In September 1940 there were not enough men to cope with this new menace, so volunteers were called for from the RNVR. One of these was Harold Newgass (HS/DB 1913), and his story is perhaps the most remarkable of all the Tonbridge wartime exploits.

Newgass was brought up on the family estate at Shernfold Park near Frant. He enjoyed Tonbridge but wrote later that there was little to record about his schooldays except almost universally bad reports. He left school in time to join the tail-end of the Great War in the Royal Field Artillery. The family was well off and Newgass both worked in the family business and involved himself in voluntary work at a club in London for problem boys. Married in 1931 but divorced in 1937, with two daughters, he lived at Clapton Manor near Kettering, where he

Harold Newgass GC.

served on local councils and was Secretary of the Fitzwilliam Hunt. He is described in a local paper as the 'Lord of the Manor in Clapton', a patron of the church, promoter of a horticultural show and local scoutmaster. His main interests were hunting and sailing, winning cups in the Santander and Fastnet ocean races, but in 1938 he suffered head injuries falling from a horse, affecting his eyesight.

When war broke out, Harold was 40 years old and keen to do his bit, but his age and poor eyesight were against him. He applied to the RNVR in April 1940 and was turned down. He then tried to become a Third Officer on a Shell oil tanker but was told he did not have the qualifications. In July 1940 he finally obtained an interview from the Admiralty, but in a subsequent letter was told that they were unable to place his name even on a waiting list because of 'physical unfitness'. The letter did however add that 'there

are occasional vacancies for service ashore in the Special Branch'.

Finally, with the war situation becoming more critical, the Admiralty offered him a temporary commission in the RNVR subject to medical fitness. On Friday 13 September he was medically examined, found fit and reported for duty to HMS *King Alfred* at Hove. While he was there undergoing preliminary training, volunteers were requested for 'special duties' and he was one of 12 selected in late September for an intensive course on rendering safe mines and bombs. His qualifications and skills for this dangerous work are not immediately apparent. He was 40 years old, small in build and wearing an eyeglass for his poor eyesight, but he must have been physically and mentally strong, perhaps from his sailing and horsemanship.

When the course finished Newgass was posted to London in the second half of October 1940 to join an RMS squad. His first job was a parachute mine in London and he gradually increased his experience on a dozen others. In all nearly 200 unexploded mines had been dealt with by early November in London and, of these, nine had exploded while being made safe, killing the officers. An immunising device had been invented to deal with the mines but it was in short supply and, as a temporary measure, squads were issued with a length of string with which the fuse could be pulled out from a moderate distance. This added only slightly to the safety margin of 17 seconds warning if the officer was lucky enough to hear the clock on the fuse start to tick. Many men were to die trying to sprint far enough away to avoid the explosion, and Newgass was not by this time a sprinter.

On the night of 28/29 November 1940 the Germans launched a massive raid on Liverpool. Thirty mines fell on the city and one which fell on the Garston Gas Works ruptured a large gasometer, containing 2,000,000 cubic feet of gas, but failed to explode. Its presence paralysed industry over a large area of Liverpool. Six thousand people were evacuated, while three docks and the upper reaches of the Mersey, along with a large railway marshalling yard, had to be closed, and the whole gas supply to east and south Liverpool was threatened.

The mine had pierced the top of the gasometer, continuing downwards until stopped by the parachute rigging catching on the jagged entry hole at the top. This hole allowed gas to escape, so that the top of the gasometer sank until the mine rested on the floor at about 80 degrees to the horizontal, leaning against one of the internal pillars. It was also completely covered by about seven feet of foul-smelling oily water and sludge at the bottom of the gasometer. It was to this unpromising situation that Newgass and his team of three were summoned from London.

When he arrived, he ordered that the water covering the mine should be pumped out by the local fire brigade, an operation which took 30 hours. His feelings of anticipation during this period of waiting can be imagined. When all the water was out, sludge, polluted by poisonous gas, was left to a depth of about six inches, and the gasometer was then tested to see what gas remained. A large hole was cut in the top to allow ease of entry and electric lights to be rigged.

While all this was going on, Newgass was in phone conversation with his superior, Captain Curry, who gave him authority to deal with the mine as he saw fit. Once the water was out he identified it as probably non-magnetic, although his very limited training and experience had hardly made him an expert on these matters. The time was now 11.00am on Tuesday 3 December, about six days since the mine had fallen, and the paralysis in the surrounding area continued. Newgass realised he must deal with it as soon as possible, for the parachute cords might break at any time, causing the bomb to fall over and explode, and there was

the added danger of another bomb falling nearby. The atmosphere in the gasometer was sufficiently harmful to necessitate wearing an oxygen breathing apparatus which he borrowed from the local fire brigade. He then climbed inside, where the conditions were hellish, the atmosphere a highly inflammable and possibly explosive mixture of gas and air. The oxygen cylinders would only last 30 minutes so he would have to come in and out of the gasometer several times to replenish them and finish his task. It was also very dark inside the forbidding steel tank, and he had to stand in the poisonous sludge. In one's worst dreams a more frightening 'no escape' situation would be difficult to imagine.

On this first visit Newgass carried out a thorough inspection and made a plan. On his second he took down his tools, a flameproof lantern and a short ladder to enable him to reach the top of the mine and to get in and out more easily. On his third he stabilised the mine by building sandbags round its nose and lashing its other end to the pillar against which it rested. All of this was a hugely demanding physical effort for a 41-year-old with poor eyesight.

When he went in for the fourth time, it was to work on the fuse. Unhelpfully this was facing the pillar against which the mine was leaning so he had to bring in a special hoisting lug to turn the mine round, again very difficult physically and an extremely hazardous operation. The keep ring of the fuse was very stiff, making it impracticable for him to pull it out from a safe distance with a piece of string. On his fifth visit, not knowing if the removal of the fuse might have started the clock ticking, he removed the magnetic primer and undid the clock ring, but again he needed to renew his oxygen. Finally he went in for a sixth time to remove the clock. He did later say that he thought once he heard the clock was ticking and moved away until realising this would be fruitless. Although the detonator was still in the mine, it could now be considered reasonably safe. The now exhausted Newgass allowed his team to remove it and then hoist the mine out of the gasometer to be taken away.

It is hard to exaggerate Newgass's achievement and courage on what was only his 13th assignment. Among his peers his task was recognised as probably the most difficult and dangerous assignment mine-disposal men ever handled. The official report noted that 'this officer was altogether some three hours at work in an oxygen apparatus and had to return from time to time during the operation to rest and refill his oxygen. The extreme coolness, courage and ability of this officer's work cannot be overestimated.'

He was awarded the George Cross, the highest award for gallantry not in the direct face of the enemy. It was officially gazetted on 4 March 1941, although, for security reasons, the full circumstances and detail were not released until after the war. The 1941 citation read: 'The King has been graciously pleased to approve the award of the George Cross, for great gallantry and undaunted devotion to duty, to Temporary Lieutenant Harold Reginald Newgass RNVR.' The recommendation had come from his commanding officer at HMS *Vernon* but was supported by a huge number of letters from Liverpudlians, including the Chief Constable. Apart from the GC, he was very touched to receive a gold cigarette case from the Garston Gas Company and a set of gold cuff links from their employees. Many of the 6,000 who had to evacuate their homes while the bomb was defused also sent him letters of thanks and small gifts.

Newgass, left front with eyeglass, with other RN officers, London.

He received many letters of congratulation. The Vicar of Clapton wrote on 5 March 1941: 'Your parson and his wife are most terribly proud of their patron. Well done, sir and well done again.' A senior colleague in the RMS section, Captain John Miller, wrote that 'yours is the greatest of the actions which have brought George Crosses and George Medals to us all. We are more proud of the Garston show, and the man who did that job, than of any other. Courage is a matter of psychology and it is just because you were willing to face that strain of being shut up in a gas-holder and to do that job under those conditions that we honour you.'

Newgass returned to his duties although his celebrity status meant these now involved more than rendering mines safe. He toured ARP centres, spent some time in Greenock on welfare work and was finally discharged from the RNVR on health grounds in June 1944. After the war he married again, was active in Dorset local government and politics, and died aged 85 on 17 November 1984 at his home in Dorchester. In a moving funeral address Canon Eric Staples reflected on his calmness under

pressure. He remembered a dinner conversation when the subject of courage came up. 'Harold,' he said, 'was not listening but we turned to him as one who would know, and asked about his thoughts that day in Liverpool as, with supreme courage he dismantled the mine. "I don't really know," he said, "I was too interested in what I was doing."'

The cold-blooded nature of the courage required to return time after time to devices which might at any moment blow you to bits makes bomb disposal work a source of both admiration and fascination to the present day. In Michael Ondaatje's novel *The English Patient* there is a character called Kip, a Sikh bomb disposal officer. Playing around with bombs had given him a sense of calm and, despite bombs being inherently unpredictable, a certainty and confidence about his place in the world. Those qualities of calmness and certainty can certainly be found in Henry Dickinson and Harold Newgass, who survived their encounters with bombs and mines, but also in Eyre Ievers and Anthony Firminger, who were equally brave but less lucky.

Swordfish attack on Taranto, November 1940.

TONBRIDGE AND THE ROYAL NAVY

HM Submarine Seraph *before Operation Mincemeat. 1943. David Scott standing centre foreground.*

The most famous Tonbridge sailor is Admiral Sir Sidney Smith, who was a captain in Nelson's navy and defended Acre against the forces of Napoleon in 1799, but it is not a school with a strong naval tradition. Nevertheless, many Tonbridgians served in the Navy during the war; 25 of them died and there are some remarkable stories.

One of the earliest war casualties was Ronald Burch (DB 1920), who in April 1940 commanded the submarine HMS *Narwhal*, and was awarded one of the earliest DSOs of the war for laying minefields off Norway. On a similar mission in July, *Narwhal* was caught on the surface by a German bomber and sunk with all hands. Another submariner was John Haward (FH 1933), who won the DSC as First Lieutenant of HMS *Unison*, which carried out 14 war patrols in 1942–3, sinking more than 6,000 tons of enemy shipping. In July 1943 *Unison* left Bizerta to join a Malta convoy, but in the dark the nearest merchantman mistook her for a U-Boat and put two

shells into her, killing one man and badly wounding others including the captain. Haward, in the control room below the bridge, saw blood dripping down the conning tower, but took over command to sail the submarine safely back to Bizerta.

On Tower Hill stands Lutyens's impressive memorial to the Merchant Navy dead of two world wars who 'have no grave but the sea'. They are the forgotten heroes of the war, braving the merciless waters of the Atlantic to keep Britain fed, and one name on the memorial is a Tonbridgian. Tom Johnson (HS 1936) left school at the age of 16 to become an officer apprentice with the Elder and Fyffe Line, carrying fruit across the Atlantic. On 19 October 1940, aged just 19, he was serving on SS *Sulaco*, part of Convoy OB229, when U-124 fired one torpedo at about two o'clock in the morning, hitting Sulaco amidships and breaking her back. The terror on board the rapidly sinking ship on a stormy Atlantic night can only be imagined as the crew raced to free life-rafts or threw themselves to the mercy of the sea, and there was just one survivor out of 63.

David Scott (PH 1934) took part in an exchange visit from Tonbridge in 1936 to a German Napola, established by the Nazis to train future leaders, which were apparently, and alarmingly, based on British public schools. In 1938 Scott joined the Royal Navy, volunteering in 1942 for submarines, and in April 1943 he joined HMS *Seraph*, a submarine used for carrying out difficult special operations. His widowed mother took him out to lunch just before he sailed for the Mediterranean and had tears in her eyes when they parted, making Scott realise that she thought this might be their last meeting, a realistic possibility with 50 per cent of Mediterranean submarines being sunk.

Scott's first operation was the celebrated and fascinating 'Operation Mincemeat', when *Seraph* embarked a special canister in its torpedo tube for a highly secret operation. In this canister was a corpse disguised as a drowned Royal Marines officer, Major Martin, carrying secret papers to mislead the Germans about where the Allies would land in southern Europe. The task of *Seraph* was to ensure that he was washed up on the beach at Huelva in southern Spain, apparently the victim of an air crash, where German intelligence would soon get to hear of him. Only the four most senior officers on *Seraph* were allowed on deck on 30 April as the submarine came as close to shore as it dared and the body of Major Martin was released from the canister and prodded towards the beach, Scott's final role being to fire a revolver into the empty canister to sink it. The deception was to prove very successful. A month later, with the Germans expecting an invasion of Greece, Scott and *Seraph* helped guide the invasion forces onto the beaches of Sicily..

One of the most daring operations of the war involved Bobby Going (DB 1926), scrum half in the 1930 1st XV and a regular naval officer in the Fleet Air Arm. By early 1940 he was an observer in 819 Squadron, based on the aircraft carrier HMS *Illustrious* and flying the Fairey Swordfish torpedo bomber. The 'Stringbag', as it became affectionately called, was a relic from an earlier age. It had two open and very cold cockpits for pilot and observer/air gunner, carried one torpedo or 1,500lbs of bombs and had an alarmingly slow maximum speed of 150mph. Nevertheless it inspired tremendous affection among its crews.

The Navy was concerned about the potential threat from the Italian fleet in the Mediterranean and planned an attack on their main base at Taranto. The best means seemed to be a night torpedo attack by carrier-based Swordfish aircraft and a task force headed by HMS *Illustrious* was in place about 170 miles from Taranto on the night of 11 November 1940. In the outer and inner harbours of Taranto were moored six battleships and several cruisers and destroyers. Between them and shore-based anti-aircraft guns they possessed formidable firepower against aircraft attack.

The first wave of 12 Swordfish left *Illustrious* at about 21.00hrs, followed by a second wave about an hour and a half later. Bobby Going was in the second wave, flying as observer to Lieutenant Clifford, but their participation was nearly scuppered by a taxiing collision on the deck which damaged the wing fabric. Determined not to be left behind, Going and Clifford pleaded with the Captain to be allowed to go, and they took off 30 minutes behind the others. The flight there on their own left plenty of time for thinking about what lay ahead. The cold was intense. The first wave scored some hits with torpedoes and bombs, losing one plane and lighting up the harbour with flares and explosions. The second wave therefore arrived to a sky lit up by flames, searchlights and a huge firework display of anti-aircraft fire. Going wrote: 'I gazed down on a twinkling mass of orange-red lights which I knew was a solid curtain of bursting shells through which we had to fly. It looked absolutely terrifying.' The torpedo bombers did their work at a height of 30 feet before Going and Clifford arrived to finish off the night's events by dive bombing cruisers in the inner harbour. They screamed down on their targets, scoring hits on a heavy cruiser, before soaring away through the flak to return to *Illustrious* as the last plane.

The attack was spectacularly successful, the Italian fleet losing half its strength in one night and forcing the abandonment of Taranto as an anchorage, while only two Swordfish were lost. It pushed the balance of naval power in the Mediterranean firmly towards the Royal Navy (and also incidentally gave the Japanese a blueprint for Pearl Harbour). Going and Clifford were both awarded the DSO, rare for junior officers but Going's luck did not last. In January 1941 he had a leg blown off, when *Illustrious* suffered severe damage in a German bombing raid, but remained in the Navy for the rest of the war.

In that same Mediterranean theatre John Blackie (PS 1936) joined the destroyer HMS *Kashmir* just in time to take part in the fierce battle for Crete in May 1941. As the Royal Navy evacuated troops from Crete, its ships came under sustained and brutal air attack and *Kashmir* sank in a few minutes after being blown in half by a Stuka dive-bomber. Blackie was in the water for several hours, surviving machine-gun attacks, and just found the strength to swim to a rescue ship, HMS *Kipling*, which had bravely returned to look for them. For years afterwards he re-lived in his nightmares that moment of terror as he scrambled aboard *Kipling*, which then sailed slowly back to Egypt, with the wounded packed below, and miraculously dodging over 80 further bombs. As they limped into Alexandria, their gallant efforts were saluted by the entire fleet. Blackie was to survive many other actions, including being sunk again off the D-Day beaches, his experiences exemplifying many other Tonbridge naval men who did hard and largely unsung work in seas around the world.

Lt Bobby Going DSO.

CHAPTER 5:

PLAYING THE GAME

Most of the games played at Tonbridge originated in the 19th-century public schools and were then carried by their alumni to every corner of the Empire. Schoolmasters of that century, many of them clergymen, believed that games, and team games in particular, encouraged not just health and fitness but strong moral values such as teamwork, loyalty and courage. To a large extent that belief has endured. 'Vitae Lampada', Sir Henry Newbolt's famous poem about cricket on the Close at Clifton School, illustrates the noble motives cricket is supposed to inspire, and goes on to suggest that war should be fought in the same spirit:

Tonbridge v Sherborne on the Fifty, 1934.

But the voice of the schoolboy rallies the ranks:
'Play up! Play up! and play the game.'

For the 1914 generation, sportsmanship was the best guarantee of success in the 'great game' of war, and 'playing the game' meant not letting down your friends or your school or your country. A Liverpool paper wrote with endearing pathos of Percy Kendall (Sc 1890), an England rugby international killed in France in January 1915: 'Well we knew dear old Toggie Kendall would face death like a hero and take it like a man. His record on the rugby field does not tell you the half of what he was. The thing was that he played the game.'

Games dominated school life. *The Tonbridgian* of July 1939 devoted two thirds of its content to sport, with four pages to the OTC and just two to anything resembling cultural pursuits. The levelling of The Head in 1838, with earth brought from the railway line then being constructed through Tonbridge, had put cricket right at the centre of the school on one of the finest grounds in the country, as Tattershall Dodd's famous print of 1851 reminds us. Nowadays we would hopefully not ascribe any more value to the best batsman in the 1st XI than to the leader of the orchestra or the main role in a school play, but that is not how things were judged in the 1930s. A debating motion in November 1939 to give colours to the

An early sketch of the C.T. Dodd print of The Head, 1840s.

school orchestra as well as the 1st XV was soundly defeated, the chief objection seeming to be the lack of athleticism in the orchestra!

The stories of fated young men who delight with their talents have a concentrated significance in their beginnings, and a natural poignancy in their premature ends. Sport is a young man's game, as largely is war. Binyon's famous words 'they shall grow not old' have a particular resonance as schoolboy prodigies are remembered in their youthful fearlessness. The most famous Tonbridge cricketer to die in the Great War was Kenneth Hutchings (MH 1897), who scored a hundred against Australia in Melbourne in 1908, but retired from the game years before his death on the Somme. Rex Sherwell (PS 1912), on the other hand, with a cricket record of equal promise, might have emulated Hutchings, but was only 18 when his plane was shot down in 1916, a few months after leading Tonbridge out at Lord's.

To look now at photographs of school and house teams from the 1920s and especially the 1930s is a moving experience. Their young and eager faces, proud with their status and achievement, will soon become the grim and drawn infantry subalterns or bomber pilots. In the 1st XI cricket photo of 1934 John 'Gertie' Graham and David Day stand proudly side by side. They joined School House together, batted four and five in the 1st XI, were the Fives Pair of 1934 and died fighting the Japanese in Malaya and Burma. 1930s schoolboys had to grow quickly into men, and particularly poignant are the team photos of 1938 to 1942, those who left school just as the storm clouds broke over their lives, many of them experiencing nothing of life beyond school and war. Over 90 died from those who were at Tonbridge in those four years, with many more having their lives permanently scarred.

On 30 July 1940, Tom Wood played what is regarded by common consent as one of the finest schoolboy innings at Lord's against Stowe, replacing for one year the traditional opponents, Clifton. Stowe set Tonbridge 193 to win in about two hours in their second innings, a stiff task for schoolboys on a ground as big and daunting as Lord's. 'Wood and Leahy', *The Times* reported, 'made it plain which way things were going to go. Wood has strength and strokes, and he made immediate use of both. 111 runs were scored in an hour, and, although Leahy was then lbw, Wood went from strength to strength, cut, pulled and drove his team to victory.' He finished his school career in a blaze of glory with 126 not out as Tonbridge cruised to a decisive nine-wicket victory. It was the last important innings Tom Wood would play.

This card does not necessarily include the fall of the last wicket

2d. Lord's Ground

TONBRIDGE v. STOWE

MONDAY, & TUESDAY, JULY 29, 30, 1940   (Two-day Match)

[Scorecard details — handwritten scores alongside printed names for STOWE and TONBRIDGE innings, bowling analyses, and fall of the wickets.]

STOWE WON THE TOSS

---

wistful longing for days of security not long past. Within little more than a year of this letter being published all those mentioned in it were dead.

Tom Wood (Sc 1935) was brought up in British Guiana and had a good enough brain to be an Oxford candidate, but it was as a games player that he made his mark, playing in all three major teams and the rackets pair. He would undoubtedly have won a cricket blue and quite possibly gone further. Immediately after leaving school he joined the RAFVR, and, after pilot training, was posted to 115 Squadron of Bomber Command. In November 1941 he injured his shoulder when forced to bale out over England, but he earned a DFC for gallantry over the next six months of operations. On 3 June 1942 he took off on a raid to

Above: *Roly Leahy in RAF uniform, 1942.*

Top left: *Scorecard of Tonbridge v Stowe at Lord's, 1940.*

Roly Leahy (PH 1936), opening batsman that day, volunteered with Wood for the RAFVR after the match. In late 1940 he wrote a letter to *The Tonbridgian* giving news of contemporaries: 'There are about a dozen pilots under training whose names may be remembered by those at School. P. Wood, of cricketing fame, has got his wings and is a Pilot Officer, just about to complete his advanced training, G. Mieville is in the final stages of flying training, and Leahy and T. Wood are doing their elementary flying course. It may interest the science and maths masters that no Tonbridgian has yet failed in the passing out exam. We send our best wishes to our friends at Tonbridge, wishing everyone the best of luck and in particular next term's cricket XI'. There is a youthful bravado about the letter but also a

Bremen. As with so many others, the precise details of whatever terrifying end cut short his young life are not known, but his Wellington crashed in the sea which eventually gave up his body.

Peter Wood (PS 1934) was no relation of Tom but just as outstanding a cricketer. The son of a senior official in the Indian Civil Service, he captained the 1939 XI but was prevented by illness from playing at Lord's or as Captain of the Public Schools XI against the Army. That 1939 Tonbridge XI has some claim to be the best ever. They won virtually all their matches and ended with a crushing win over Clifton at Lord's by 213 runs, mainly thanks to the devastating slow left arm bowling of Patrick Rose-Price, who took a still-unsurpassed 78 wickets in the season. Wood was also a Cambridge exhibitioner in the Classical Upper VI, with a richly fulfilling life ahead, and in better days he and Tom would have been in opposition in the University Match. Peter also volunteered for the RAFVR, flying operationally from April 1941 with 207 Squadron; in May his aircraft was damaged by a fighter and limped home. On his 16th operation on 31 August 1941, he died when his Manchester bomber was shot down by flak over Cologne. His elder brother Eric (PS 1933), in all three major teams in 1936–7, was killed seven months later over Essen, a grievous double blow for the family. Geoffrey Mieville (HS 1934), a 2nd XI cricketer in such a strong year but scrum-half in the last pre-war rugby XV, was killed in July 1941 in a training accident, one of many similar casualties.

The author of the letter, Roly Leahy, was the last to perish. He was second of four brothers in Park House, the youngest of whom, John, went on to a distinguished career in the Diplomatic Service. Roly was in both the 1939 and 1940 successful cricket XIs. A chunky and gritty left-hand opening bat, he was a good foil for the more extrovert stroke players around him, made plenty of runs in both years and kept wicket in 1940.

Tonbridge taking the field v Clifton at Lord's, 1939. John Dew captain/ wicket-keeper.

On his return from pilot training in Rhodesia, he joined 235 Squadron of Coastal Command in May 1942, flying Beaufighters from Chivenor in Devon on coastal reconnaissance and convoy protection. He was clearly a very good pilot, just as determined and quick to react as in his batting. On 1 November he brought down two German planes at very low level over the Bay of Biscay, closing on one of them to a distance of 150 yards to deliver a lethal burst of cannon fire. Three weeks later he brought down a German seaplane, but the strain of constant operations over the grey and inhospitable winter ocean must have been beginning to tell on a

20-year-old not long out of school. His letters to his mother became shorter, less chatty and talked of the killed and injured and his need for sleep.

On 1 December 1942, a day bad enough for Bomber Command to cancel all operations, Leahy was on patrol again with two other 'Beaus' over the Bay of Biscay in search of U-Boats at a crucial time in the Battle of the Atlantic. Flying in formation at only 100 feet over the waves, they were jumped from above by nine enemy planes, which gave them little time to react. One Beaufighter managed to escape but Leahy was never seen again and must have been shot down into the winter Atlantic from a height and in sea conditions that left no possibility of survival. The

Eric Whitworth's letter to Mrs Leahy.

telegram, announcing that he was missing, arrived at his mother's house in Worthing the next day. 'Missing' could mean so many things for loved ones, always keeping open a small sliver of hope. Not until July 1943 did the Air Ministry finally close its file on Roly by regretfully concluding that he had lost his life. He was commemorated on the Runnymede memorial, but the absence of any body or grave was very hard for families. By a tragic irony the Stowe opening bowler, George Marshall, hit round Lord's by Leahy and Wood, died over Germany with Bomber Command in the same year. Eric Whitworth's beautifully worded letter of condolence to Mrs Leahy was one of many he must have written.

Four others also died from those cricket XIs of 1939 and 1940, including Michael Lloyd (PH 1935), the Head of School. Whitworth paid an enormous tribute to him on Skinners' Day 1940 as

'a boy who has had more at heart the best interests of the School than any I have known'. Lloyd was intending to become a doctor but put this on hold for the war's duration to join Bomber Command. He died aged just 21 on the night of 22 September 1943 over Cassel, the Lancaster crashing near Bielefeld; it was his second operation, the average age of his crew just 20, truly lambs to the slaughter. Lloyd lies now in Rheinberg, a few rows along from Peter Wood, his former captain.

Reymie Bousfield (WH 1935) played in both 1939 and 1940 as an off-spinner and elegant batsman, and went on to serve in the Royal Navy on Atlantic and Arctic convoys. He recalls the fun of away matches as, encouraged by John Knott, they usually called in at a pub or two on the way back, where he was introduced to beer. The match against Sherborne in 1940 was a two-day away game and must have been quite a journey by train in the

Sandy Smith batting at Lord's, 1939.

Pegasus Bridge, 1944. Sandy Smith's glider in the background.

chaos of June 1940. Four Tonbridgians, including Bousfield and Sandy Smith (FH 1936), were put up by the Sherborne headmaster. After dinner on the first evening one of the Sherborne boys easily lured the Tonbridge four into the local pub. At closing time, well entertained, they reckoned that the Headmaster would be watching out for them, so they climbed in over the garden wall. Sandy Smith became stuck on the wall, being violently sick, but managed to scramble in after the others. A door then suddenly opened and a voice boomed out, 'Tonbridge, is that you?' Amid stifled giggles, an apology for the noise was somehow stammered out and they escaped retribution, but there were stern looks from the Headmaster at breakfast. In the morning Sandy Smith belied his alcoholic intake to make a fine century, but the game was drawn.

Sandy Smith was an outstanding rugby player at fly-half for three years in the 1st XV (and a wartime blue at Cambridge), as well as a successful fast bowler and hard-hitting bat. The son of the last British Director of Indian Intelligence and three times married, he had the adventurous, devil-may-care character which moved easily from the school games field to the excitement of war, and he was a born leader of men. Joining the Ox and Bucks Light Infantry, he volunteered for one of the most hazardous D-Day missions: to seize the bridge over the Orne Canal (now known as Pegasus Bridge) to protect the eastern flank of the invasion. After several months of intensive training, the main force was sealed in its base for security reasons, but typically Smith managed to break out of camp on 31 May to have dinner with his girlfriend.

His platoon embarked on its Horsa glider, the last of three to land near Pegasus Bridge just after midnight on 6 June. Climbing into a glider to be towed at night across the Channel and then land as close as possible to strongly defended enemy positions has several obvious points of extreme hazard. Although the glider pilots were feted for the finest feat of flying in the war, Smith's glider had a particularly rough landing, and he was catapulted through the cockpit windscreen, momentarily knocking him out. 'I went shooting straight past those pilots like a bullet,' he recalled, 'and landed in front of the glider. I was covered in mud and had lost my Sten gun and I didn't really know what I was bloody doing. Corporal Madge, one of my section commanders, brought me to my senses. "Well sir," he said, "what are you waiting for?"'

Smith collected his men and moved across the bridge to clear enemy positions which he recalled had to be done ruthlessly: 'We were not taking any prisoners or messing around, so just threw phosphorus grenades into the dugouts and shot anything that moved.' On the other side of the bridge he came face to face with a German soldier about to throw a grenade. Smith shot him but the grenade exploded, wounding Smith in the wrist. He had also hurt his knee in the landing, so was forced to hobble around, but continued to co-ordinate the defence of the bridge until relieved and was awarded the MC. After recovering from his wound, he returned to duty with his regiment in time to take part in the Rhine crossing in March 1945. This time his glider was shot down by heavy flak and, as one of only two survivors, he had to hide in a cellar until Allied troops caught up with him. These two experiences were such that many years later Smith would still say that he never felt real fear again.

Tonbridge football was first bruisingly played on the gravel behind the school until the introduction of formal rules by the Rugby Football Union in the 1870s. School matches were then held on the Fifty in Elm Lane, as good a pitch for rugby as The Head has been for cricket. The Pillman family is one of Tonbridge's great rugby dynasties. Charles Henry Pillman (Sc 1904) played 18 times for England between 1910 and 1914 as a big strong wing forward. A contemporary described his 'superb skill, his long black hair all over his forehead as he smashed up the opposing backs'. He served throughout the Great War, winning the MC at Cambrai, and all three of his sons duly followed him into School House, including Charles Pillman (Sc 1934), the eldest, who was also a fine rugby player, captaining the 1939 XV. Charles and his brother Bobby (Sc 1937) both then joined the same armoured regiment, the 4/7 Royal Dragoon Guards, and were training together for D-Day.

In April 1944 the brothers took time off to play golf near the Dorset coast. Bobby sliced his drive into the rough and, while looking for his ball, stepped on a forgotten British landmine placed there during the 1940 invasion scare. Charles was a few yards away and rushed over, but his brother was beyond help. His feelings can be imagined as he first had to break the news to his parents and then return without his brother to his regiment, where he commanded a troop of Sherman tanks. On 6 June he landed on Gold

TONBRIDGE SCHOOL v. TONBRIDGE R.F.C.
CHARITY MATCH. Oct. 1st, 1938.

A. Dodds W. Brooke D. Roberts
Dr. H. J. Brewer P. A. O. Graham P. Maggs A. F. N. Ladefoged D. Owen C. L. Welford J. Lawrence G. N. C. Miéville F. J. Inglis J. L. Rampton K. E. Seel D. N. Scott B. H. Elkington W. W. Wakefield, M.P.
Referee.
L. M. Taylor J. M. Pothecary L. N. Reynolds M. J. Ephraums J. B. W. Delvigne J. A. Dew P. K. Rooke C. H. Pillman A. Parkin
Capt. *Capt.*
B. W. Burnett R. D. Vasey L. C. Greenhalgh C. R. Kirkpatrick J. F. Stutchbury C. M. S. Turner D. Lloyd-Morgan

Charles Pillman with Sugar, 1944.

Captain Michael Ephraums MC, Royal Marines.

Beach and led his troop a couple of miles inland to Creully. Held up there by German anti-tank guns, Pillman dismounted from his tank to consult with his commanding officer when there sounded the roar of incoming shells. He sprinted towards the cover of his tank but never made it, bowled over and instantly killed by a shell which tragically came from a British cruiser, HMS *Orion*, directed in error on what were thought to be German tanks. His Tonbridge contemporary, Keith Osborne (JH 1935) remembered passing his temporary grave when he started the breakout from Caen with his armoured car squadron of 11th Hussars. Losing two sons within two months was a tragedy from which the Pillman parents never properly recovered.

The outstanding player of the 1938 XV was Michael Ephraums (Sc 1934), who played three years in the 1st XV and shot at Bisley in only his second year. He was clearly a natural leader, a strong back row forward 'whose excellence becomes almost monotonous' in the words of *The Tonbridgian*. He joined the Royal Marines in 1939 and volunteered for the new Commando force. In August 1942 he took part in the raid on Dieppe with 40 Commando and then fought through the campaign in Sicily, where he was awarded the MC. In the darkness of 3 October 1943 he landed with 40 Commando behind German lines at Termoli on the Adriatic coast of Italy in an attempt to block the coast road to the retreating enemy. The town was seized and held amid savage close-quarter fighting with German paratroopers, which led to heavy casualties. Ephraums was killed by a sniper during this fighting and lies in the Sangro River War Cemetery; on his headstone is carved the crest of the

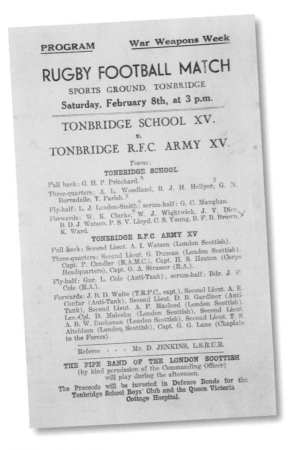

PROGRAM   War Weapons Week

RUGBY FOOTBALL MATCH
SPORTS GROUND, TONBRIDGE
Saturday, February 8th, at 3 p.m.

TONBRIDGE SCHOOL XV.
v.
TONBRIDGE R.F.C. ARMY XV.
Teams:
TONBRIDGE SCHOOL
Full back: G. H. P. Pritchard.
Three-quarters: A. L. Woodland, B. J. H. Hellyer, G. N. Borradaile, T. Parish.
Fly-half: L. J. Lendon-Smith; scrum-half: G. C. Maughan.
Forwards: W. K. Clarke, W. J. Wightwick, J. V. Dier, B. D. J. Watson, P. S. V. Lloyd, C. S. Young, B. F. B. Brown, K. Ward.

TONBRIDGE R.F.C. ARMY XV
Full back: Second Lieut. A. I. Watson (London Scottish).
Three-quarters: Second Lieut. G. Duncan (London Scottish). Capt. P. Candler (R.A.M.C.), Capt. H. S. Heaton (Corps Headquarters), Capt. G. A. Strasser (R.A.).
Fly-half: Gnr. L. Cole (Anti-Tank); scrum-half: Bdr. J. F. Cole (R.A.).
Forwards: J. B. D. Waite (T.R.F.C., capt.), Second Lieut. A. R. Confar (Anti-Tank), Second Lieut. D. B. Gardiner (Anti-Tank), Second Lieut. A. F. Macleod (London Scottish). Lec.-Cpl. D. Malcolm (London Scottish), Second Lieut. A. B. W. Buchanan (London Scottish), Second Lieut. T. S. Aitchison (London Scottish), Capt. G. G. Lane (Chaplain to the Forces).

Referee - - - Mr. D. JENKINS, L.S.R.U.R.

THE PIPE BAND OF THE LONDON SCOTTISH
(by kind permission of the Commanding Officer) will play during the afternoon.
The Proceeds will be invested in Defence Bonds for the Tonbridge School Boys' Club and the Queen Victoria Cottage Hospital.

Wartime Rugby, February 1941.

Royal Marines together with the words: 'Happy in life, glorious in death, thy will be done.' His troop corporal later wrote to Michael's mother: 'Where he led, the boys followed without question and he died as he lived – a leader. He was out on a forward reconnaissance and a hidden sniper ended the life of one of the greatest men I have known.' In that same cemetery lies a young Tonbridge member of staff who might have taught Michael Ephraums, Major Oscar Browning, killed on 2 November 1943. 'For teacher and taught touch hands and part, but the School, the School remaineth.'

From September 1939 fixture lists were becoming truncated, but Tonbridge beat all five schools played, including Dulwich and Haileybury. The war had no impact on enthusiasm for sport, except for the limitation on fixtures, but inevitably

some experience was lost as boys left school younger. One was Kenneth Ward (WH 1936), who rowed two years in the 1st IV, played for the 1st XV in 1940 and had colours in athletics, swimming and gymnastics. He stands out clearly in the last peacetime Welldon photograph, proudly wearing his rowing blazer and tie. Rowing on the Medway had a long and honourable tradition at Tonbridge for about 100 years, and the older generation can still remember Messrs Bathurst, Morris and Staveley racing along the towpath on their battered old bikes, shouting advice and occasionally riding headlong into the river in their excitement. Ward left in 1941 and joined 158 Squadron of Bomber Command. On 31 August 1943, aged just 20, he was the pilot of a Halifax bomber, one of 600 aircraft raiding Berlin. The German capital on a summer night was a target dreaded by pilots, the length of the trip in the moonlight and the obviousness of the goal a magnet for German night fighters. Forty-seven aircraft were lost that night, an unsustainably high rate, and Kenneth Ward's plane was one of them. His port engine was set on fire by a night fighter but, as the flames engulfed the plane, he sacrificed his own life to hold it steady for a few vital seconds, allowing half his crew to escape before it exploded.

One final little sporting tragedy waited until very near the end of the war to be played out. Stuart Hills (JH 1938) and Denis Elmore (SH 1937) were great friends at school. Denis was both a scholar and a fine cricketer, Stuart a tough games player and convivial companion. They found themselves in plenty of scrapes, once being beaten by the praes for leaving out games equipment and failing to conceal their disdain for the supposed triviality of the offence. Hills had played as a youngster in that 1939 House Rugby Final for Judde, and made the 1st XI Cricket in 1941. Elmore joined him in the team in 1942, their friendship strengthened by the support Elmore gave when Hills's parents were interned by the Japanese in Hong Kong.

At Lord's in 1942 they opened the batting together in what was not a vintage Tonbridge XI, which lost to Clifton, but Elmore top-scored with 78 in the first innings and Hills took six wickets in the match. The day after Lord's they joined the Army together in Maidstone and managed to be posted in 1943 to the same armoured regiment, the Sherwood Rangers. Hills, the more natural soldier, enjoyed his last school report from Whitworth: 'If I was back in the Army as a company commander, as in the last war, I should like Hills with me as a platoon commander, especially in a tight corner'.

On D-Day both commanded a troop of DD Sherman tanks in the vanguard of the assault on Gold Beach, tanks designed to swim in from a thousand yards or more to support the infantry on the beaches. Hills's tank was sunk offshore by a shell and he was picked up to land a day later, but Elmore came ashore successfully. They were then both in the thick of vicious fighting in the Normandy bocage, where Elmore was seriously wounded. He did not return to the regiment until January 1945, but Hills went through the whole campaign unscathed and won an MC for gallantry in July 1944. They crossed the Rhine together, Hills commanding the recce troop, while Elmore had a rest from action as liaison officer.

On 19 April 1945, near the German port of Bremen, Hills was anxious as Elmore had wangled a return to a fighting troop to see some action before the war ended. He saw Elmore go past, leading his troop up a road to consolidate a position taken earlier in the day, but a few minutes later heard that a German 88 gun had put an armour-piercing shell right through Elmore's tank turret, killing him instantly. Elmore is now buried in Becklingen, close to his batting hero Tom Wood.

Hills found himself numb with pain and shock, and on VE Day, less than three weeks later, described his feelings in his diary: 'The real sense of aching was for Denis, who had shared so much of my life at Tonbridge and in the war over the last eight years. It was just so unfair that he was not here to enjoy this moment of victory, which he had done as much as anyone to deserve, but instead lay in the cold earth a few miles back down the road we had just liberated.'

Denis Elmore was the last of 300 Tonbridgians to die in the Second World War. Not all of them were games players but most had participated willingly or unwillingly in some sporting activity or other at school or house level. Many had shared and enjoyed the bond that sport can bring at any level, whether on the Head or the Fifty or running the Cras just as their successors do 70 years later. Many of them too were inspiring leaders on both games field and battlefield, but the fate of their generation was to 'play the game' with their friends amid the dust and smoke of the battlefield.

Stuart Hills and Denis Elmore opening the batting at Lord's, 1942.

SIR LESLIE ROWAN

Leslie Rowan (DB 1920) spent a major part of the war as private secretary to Winston Churchill. He came to Tonbridge as a scholar and not many have been blessed with so many all-round talents. He became Captain of the School in 1925–6 and was in all the top teams for cricket, rugby and hockey before winning a Cambridge scholarship. He graduated with a first in languages and captained the hockey team for two years against Oxford, going on to win several international caps and to captain his country in 1937–8 and remarkably again in 1947;

1st XI Hockey 1925. Leslie Rowan back row second from right. Ronald Burch, killed while commanding HM submarine Narwhal 1940, end right.

by that time he had become a very senior civil servant. Rowan served primarily in the Treasury where he became assistant private secretary to Neville Chamberlain, Chancellor of the Exchequer. He moved from the Treasury in 1941 to become private secretary to Winston Churchill, rising in early 1945 to principal private secretary. He worked in shifts with the other secretaries through the day and much of the night, ensuring that the prime minister's regime was remarkably disciplined in dealing with all the urgent matters which came to him for decision. Minutes were circulated within an hour or two of meetings taking place, even after midnight.

Sir John Colville in his diary account of his own days at Number 10 describes Rowan as 'one of the ablest and most endearing men I have known. Outgoing and outgiving, he had a first class memory for detail and the pleasantest of social graces. Churchill delighted in his company.' Rowan himself recalls accompanying Churchill to Yalta, where the Russians were impressed by the 'daily service of official papers received from London'. For four years Rowan was therefore at the heart of the British war effort, serving the greatest prime minister of modern times, at a time of growing political sensitivity in dealings with both the Russians and Americans. He went with Churchill to all the important Allied conferences and his intelligence, diligence and humanity earned him the lasting affection and respect of the prime minister. At the Potsdam Conference, when news came that Churchill was defeated in the 1945 General Election, he told Rowan to give Clement Attlee the same loyalty and support, whereupon the loyal Rowan apparently broke down and cried at the voters' ingratitude and his master's gracious acceptance of it.

Rowan then worked for Attlee until he returned to the Treasury in 1947. He is remembered as a civil servant of immense authority and integrity, with a gift for fluent, forceful expression, firmness of conviction and deep loyalty to the people and institutions he served.

CHAPTER 6:

IMPERIAL TONBRIDGIANS

The Edwardian Chapel contained many individual memorials now sadly destroyed by the 1988 fire. One commemorated Percy Vaux (DB 1884), a Police Superintendent in the Andaman Islands who 'died from an encounter with natives in the forest of Wibtang 24 February 1902'. Percy Vaux may have met an unusual end but his chosen career path was typical of his generation. The public schools prepared their pupils for what became for many a lifetime of service to an empire at the heart of what it meant to be British. This preparation emphasised self-reliance, team spirit and Christian duty, and in return the Empire offered adventure, responsibility at an early age and a belief in a civilising mission. Tonbridge played its part in all this; from the 1895 entry, for instance, one third made their lives in the Empire.

Britain ended the Great War with a larger empire than in 1914, but it was a watershed. Imperial enthusiasm had waned and the principle of national self-determination, on which the Versailles Treaty was supposedly based, was incompatible ultimately with the Empire's survival. Nevertheless the opportunities to carve out an imperial life were still plenteous. The OT Society Blue Book of 1939 records the names of 125 OTs with addresses in India, 96 in other countries of Asia and 140 in Africa. They included the Archbishop of Ottawa, the Governor-General of the Sudan, and the Director of Intelligence for India, as well as businessmen, government officials, missionaries, soldiers, engineers and policemen.

Malaya and Hong Kong contributed extensively to imperial prosperity and were important strategic bases. Malaya was the biggest exporter of rubber in the world, most of which came through Singapore. Yet just 31,000 Europeans politically and commercially dominated a polyglot community of about five and a half million Chinese, Malays and Tamils. Hong Kong was as commercial as Singapore and also socially isolated from the local Chinese community, but the British way of life in both was agreeable, revolving around their clubs and sport. Those Tonbridge boys whose parents lived overseas had to endure long periods of separation. Stuart Hills was brought up on The Peak in Hong Kong, his house full of servants and reached only by tram and rickshaw. From this idyllic world he was first sent to school in England at the age of seven and saw his parents only four more times in the next eight years.

The outbreak of war in Europe did not change much in the way of life. Britain needed all the financial and material resources it could gather, so imperial trade and investments became increasingly important. What did change things was the military catastrophe in France in 1940,

Hong Kong harbour, 1941.

the French surrender and the effective isolation of Britain. This meant that the Far East went even further down the scale of already low defence priorities, while Japan occupied French Indo-China, bringing it that much closer to Malaya and the oilfields of the Dutch East Indies.

The forces assigned to the defence of Hong Kong could only be described as token, for the British chiefs of staff had effectively decided that nothing could prevent the Japanese from taking the colony in the event of war. The Japanese invasion of China had brought them to the borders of Hong Kong, which had just six infantry battalions, supplemented by locals in the Hong Kong Volunteer Defence Corps (HKVDC), together with some naval patrol craft and five obsolete aircraft. On 7 December 1941, all British units were put on a war footing as news came of Pearl Harbour and the massing of 60,000 Japanese

troops just across the border from the colony. The campaign in Hong Kong was gallant but brief. Within a few days the defenders had been driven back onto Hong Kong Island, where Japanese forces landed on 18 December to begin a week of fierce fighting which ended on Christmas Day when the Governor, advised by the military and his Attorney-General, Sir Chaloner Alabaster (Sc 1893), surrendered the colony.

Private Geoffrey Kerbey (DB 1916), a senior businessman, was in No. 2 (Scottish) Company of the HKVDC. Nothing he learned in the Tonbridge OTC would have prepared him for what he now faced, as the battle resolved itself into furious struggles by isolated British detachments to prevent the Japanese advance. Kerbey's was one such detachment, fewer than 100 civilians, commanded by a chartered accountant with Great War experience and with their own piper.

Above: *Sub Lt David Legge.*

Right: *The sinking of the Lisbon Maru.*

but was knocked down, his mutilated body found some hours later. The Japanese troops then began a frenzied attack, bayoneting the wounded, and raping and murdering the nurses.

Harold Eales (PS 1907) and Herbert Hills (JH 1901) were veterans of the Great War and businessmen in rival merchant houses. Harold volunteered for ARP work and was killed on Christmas Day. Herbert, an engineer, served in the signals section of the HKVDC and survived, together with his wife Edith, who had nursed at Gallipoli and now again in a hospital for battle

For two days in bitter hand-to-hand fighting they courageously resisted the Japanese infantry and tanks around Stanley Village but accountant, piper and Kerbey all died together.

On Stanley Point St Stephen's College had been made into a makeshift hospital, the classroom desks pushed back to accommodate the wounded. One of the two doctors was Captain Peter Witney (HS 1926), who had joined the RAMC on the outbreak of war and had worked throughout the battle trying to save lives. Early on Christmas morning, while fighting continued nearby, about 200 Japanese broke into the hospital. Both doctors tried to prevent them from entering the wards and indicated their wish to surrender but Colonel Black, the senior doctor, was bayoneted. Witney moved forward to help him casualties. They endured years of hunger and ill treatment at Japanese hands in Stanley Camp, supplemented only by what extras they could acquire on the black market. Edith had hidden some rings in her hair and exchanged these with a senior Jardine Matheson manager for an IOU to buy additional food for all the internees. To their credit Jardine's redeemed this IOU when the war ended. When Herbert was freed in 1945 he resembled a skeleton, suffering from tuberculosis and beri-beri, so that he only survived a short time, but Edith lived to the age of 91.

Some internees were transported to work elsewhere. Stanley Maughan (SH 1929), a chartered accountant who served as a gunner in the HKVDC, was shipped to Japan to work in mines and factories as a slave labourer. Here he was severely malnourished, causing partial blindness, but survived. Another was John Jupp (PH 1916), who worked for the Hong Kong Bank and served as a Naval Warrant Officer. On 27 September 1942 he boarded the Lisbon Maru, together with nearly 2,000 other prisoners, but the ship was tragically torpedoed by an American

陳中委策將軍率領香港陸海空軍官兵由港突圍抵達惠川留影 民三十年十二月廿九日 29TH DEC. 1941
ADMIRAL CHEN CHAK WITH BRITISH OFFICERS AND MEN WHOM HIS EXCELLENCY LED THROUGH THE JAPANESE LINES AFTER THE FALL OF HONG KONG AND ARRIVED SAFELY AT WAICHOW

Hong Kong escape group at Waichow, 31 December 1941. David Legge seated on ground second from right, John Yorath seated fifth from right in row behind him.

submarine. The Japanese abandoned ship and left the prisoners battened down in the hold to die, but Jupp and about 800 others managed to escape as the ship sank and were picked up. He was, however, in such a poor physical state, worsened by long exposure in the sea, that he died soon afterwards in Japan. Ralph King (PS 1924), a subaltern in the Middlesex Regiment, survived the sinking of the Lisbon Maru and worked in Japanese mines.

A remarkable escape was shared by John Yorath (HS 1913) and David Legge (SH 1931). Yorath was a retired naval officer working in Hong Kong. Through the fighting he was attached to the main naval headquarters, which retained control of a small flotilla of motor torpedo boats (MTBs),

on one of which Legge was serving as an RNVR officer. Despite heavy bombing Legge's MTB miraculously remained in action right through the siege, including a high-speed attack on Japanese landing craft. On Christmas Day the MTBs were standing by in Telegraph Bay, waiting to make their escape as best they could, when Yorath rowed out in a skiff and ordered them to take out of Hong Kong some senior British and Chinese officers whose contribution to the future war effort would be valuable. Yorath himself joined the escape party and was responsible for rescuing from the shore Admiral Chan Chak, the senior Chinese officer. The escape party beached their MTBs the next day and after several days of arduous climbing and walking in freezing mountainous conditions, with help from Chinese guerillas, Yorath and Legge eventually reached safety in Free China.

While no one believed that Hong Kong was defensible, Malaya was a different matter. Considerably greater forces had been deployed and most of the residents believed in the invulnerability of 'Fortress Singapore'. By late 1941 nearly 40 OTs were based there, 16 of whom were rubber planters up country, but there were also soldiers, businessmen and government officials like Maurice Cobb (FH 1907), Chief Engineer of Malayan Railways, and Ronald Marsh (JH 1929), School Captain 1933–4, a colonial administrator. Virtually all of the civilian residents had been mobilised into the Volunteer forces or had joined service units.

Early in the morning of 7 December a RAF Catalina flying boat left Singapore on a reconnaissance mission about 15 hours before the Japanese attack on Pearl Harbour began. The Catalina was piloted by Flying Officer Patrick Bedell (PS 1924), who had worked in pre-war Singapore as a flying instructor. The Catalina spotted the Japanese invasion fleet but was shot down before it could send off a radio message, exploding in the air with no survivors. Bedell therefore has the unenviable distinction of being the first casualty of the Pacific War.

The Japanese landed in Malaya about midnight on 7 December, just as their planes were attacking the American fleet at Pearl Harbour. A few days later they sank the battleships *Repulse*

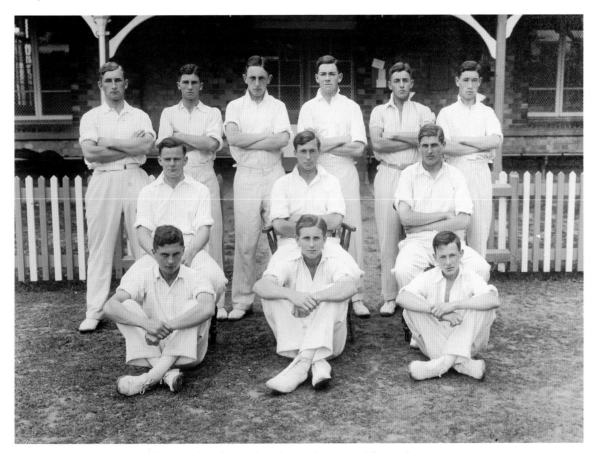

1st XI, 1934. Back row David Day is third from right, John Graham second from right.

and *Prince of Wales* off the coast of Malaya with Eric Peal (HS 1928), a naval officer, surviving the disaster to become a prisoner. The military campaign was one long British retreat down Malaya without any defensive air cover. On 31 January 1942 the last forces crossed the causeway on to Singapore Island, which finally surrendered on Sunday 15 February.

One gallant action involved John Graham (Sc 1929), who had played for first teams in cricket, rugby and hockey at Tonbridge before joining the 1/8th Punjab Regiment, Indian Army. On 3 January, having already fought the Japanese from the initial landing, the Punjabs were ordered to counter-attack to dislodge the enemy from high ground at Kampar. Graham, the battalion's second-in-command, knowing the extreme danger involved, chose to lead the attack himself. One of his sepoys recorded: 'I was Graham Sahib's runner during the attack. The position on which the attack was launched was a very strong one. Before the attack the Sahib addressed the company and told them at all costs the attack had to succeed. The honour of the regiment depended on it.' About 60 men charged suicidally with Graham across open ground towards the first enemy position and they took it at the point of the bayonet through a hail of fire. Graham then went round each platoon, still under heavy fire, to order the attack on the second enemy line. Only 30 of the original 60 were left but they took the second position. Just as they reached the enemy trench, however, a mortar blew off both Graham's legs below the knee. Kneeling on his shattered stumps he yelled his men on and continued to throw grenades. 'Was the attack successful?' he asked, and then died. He was mentioned in dispatches but many thought him unlucky not to have been awarded a posthumous Victoria Cross, perhaps because gallantry is recognised less generously in defeat than in victory.

John Graham's grave, Taiping War Cemetery Malaya. 'At the going down of the sun.'

In the Malayan campaign, as in Hong Kong, elderly civilians joined the Volunteer forces and found themselves involved in heavy fighting. One was Edward Pennefather (DB 1909), a school prae in 1913, who had served throughout the Great War before becoming a rubber planter in Johore and now was Company Sergeant-Major of the Johore Volunteer Engineers. He survived to become a prisoner, as did Cyril Morgan (MH 1918), another planter, who was wounded serving with the 4th (Pahang) Battalion of the Volunteers, and Michael Tweedie (PH 1921), curator of the Raffles Museum. Frederick Meyrick (JH 1897), a rubber planter near Penang since 1912, managed to escape Singapore just before the surrender on HMS *Giang Bee*, a coastal steamer which was sunk in the Banka Strait

Tonbridge group on bank of Lower Hundred, c.1935. James McNeill seated centre, Dennis Williams second to his right.

by Japanese planes. Meyrick therefore became the oldest OT to be killed in the war.

Those who went into captivity entered a long dark tunnel of suffering and privation for three-and-a-half years, and bore the mental and physical scars for the rest of their days. Conditions were bad in Singapore, but nothing compared with what some endured on the Burma–Siam Railway, or in smaller camps in Borneo and elsewhere, or on hellish transport ships.

One of the prisoners was Dennis Williams (FH 1933), a territorial gunner in the HAC. In November 1941, just 21, he sailed for Singapore as an officer in the 80th Anti-Tank Regiment, armed only with captured Italian guns, such was the shortage at home of British guns. On arrival he

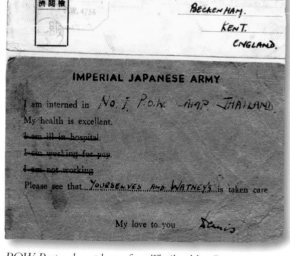

POW Postcard sent home from Thailand by Captain Dennis Williams.

Alistair Hay's grave, Kanchanaburi War Cemetery on the Burma-Siam Railway.

took a large convoy 500 miles north to the Siam border where defensive positions were hastily constructed, only to be abruptly abandoned as the Japanese landings forced the 11th Indian Division, untrained in jungle warfare, to retreat. For the next nine weeks Williams was constantly in action before his guns were one of the last units to cross the causeway into Singapore. A fortnight later Williams became a prisoner, one of at least 40 Tonbridgians, civilians as well as soldiers, to endure this ordeal at the hands of the Japanese. He spent his first night of imprisonment in the unlikely environment of a Japanese brothel, about the only kindness he was to be shown for the next three-and-a-half years, before he joined other British troops in Changi Jail.

In June 1942 he volunteered to join one of the first work parties to travel north to Thailand to build a strategic railway into Burma. They moved up the railway as each stage was completed, hacking new camps out of the jungle as they went, incredibly arduous work even for fit men. Williams helped to build the original wooden railway bridge over the Kwai river and then moved further up to Three Pagoda Pass on the Burmese border. All this time the prisoners suffered from lack of food, overwork and brutality from the guards, and inevitably many fell ill, Williams himself suffering from festering tropical ulcers and dysentery. He then caught cholera from the polluted water supply and was put into an isolation hut with about 40 others. Most of these died in the next three weeks and Williams's weight fell from his normal 12 to seven stone, but he survived and was still in Thailand when Japan surrendered. By the time he went home by ship just four of the eight officers with whom he had started out were left and his only piece of original equipment was a torn and sweat-stained officer's cap which he took off and threw into the Suez Canal, determined to start his life afresh.

Less lucky was Alistair Hay (PH 1912), who had a distinguished academic career at Tonbridge and Oxford, and served with the Royal Engineers on the Western Front. Appointed to the Malayan Civil Service in 1922, he was by 1939 a senior official in the Chinese section. In mid-1940 he sent his wife and children off to safety in Australia and then joined the Singapore Volunteers. He was captured and spent several months in Changi before being transported to the Railway in 1943. He was neither young nor particularly fit but was forced into heavy manual work on meagre rations. In his already weakened state he fell ill and died on 21 October 1944. His family had some communication with him in the camps through pre-printed cards but these took months to arrive and they did not hear news of his death until September 1945.

Peter Salmon (PH 1934), an Indian Army artillery officer who had been in the last peacetime Tonbridge hockey XI, was another victim of Japanese brutality. Captured at Singapore, he left there in October 1942 with 6,000 other POWs on a transport ship. The destination was meant to be New Guinea, and British officers in Changi were led to believe that the ship was torpedoed and all on board lost. Not until after the war was the truth discovered, when a large mass grave was found on Ballale Island near Rabaul in New Guinea by an Australian war graves unit. The Japanese had used the men as slave labourers to construct an airfield under appalling conditions and, when the job was finished, those left alive were massacred.

Two other Tonbridgians who died in captivity in Borneo in 1945 had played rackets for the School at Queen's. Norman Brown (Sc 1928), a Singapore businessman, and Edric Selous (JH 1923), Secretary for Chinese Affairs in Sarawak, were imprisoned in the camp at Kuching. This tested the human struggle for survival to the limits, with over two-thirds of the prisoners dying, the daily food ration four ounces of rice and strong men of 14 stone reduced to skeletons of less than eight. Selous died on 2 March 1945, one report saying he took his own life to avoid giving away information to the Japanese secret police about contact with Chinese outside the camp, and Brown on 19 June, only two months before the end of the war.

Meanwhile, three future Tonbridgians were enduring some remarkable experiences of their own. David Farrow (PS 1951) was five years old in January 1942, living in Java where his father was director of a company growing rubber and cocoa. The family lived in some style with Javanese servants, a Humber Super Snipe and an English Norland nanny. On 28 February 1942 Japanese forces landed on Java and the Farrow family left that day on the last train for the port of Tjilatap 300 miles away, the army destroying the railway lines behind them. David was sitting on a prickly bamboo case in the last carriage with a good view of the bridges being blown.

An air raid was in progress when they arrived on 1 March, but they boarded SS *Zaandam*, a Dutch cargo ship with room supposedly for only 15 passengers, and left that night. The ship was desperately overcrowded, with more than 1,000 finally aboard. Japanese warships had already sunk 30 out of 38 ships trying to escape the previous week, but that day they had been diverted to deal with three Allied cruisers, all of which they sank in the Sunda Straits. The destroyer escort was also sunk, but the *Zaandam* had enough speed to out-run the Japanese ships as they re-grouped, the strong head of steam blowing out sparks from the funnel which burned Mrs Farrow's hair. They stopped to pick up some survivors from other ships and finally made Fremantle six days later. Revisiting the experience in later life made David all too well aware of just how lucky they had been.

Indian 1914–18 Memorial, Neuve Chapelle, designed by Sir Herbert Baker.

Further north in the Philippines and less fortunate, Guy and Philip Meredith (PH 1950 and 1952) were in the lounge of a golf clubhouse when a Japanese fighter strafed the building. Together with their mother they had been evacuated from Hong Kong, where their father was a banker, on the false premise that the Japanese were unlikely to attack an American protectorate. The Japanese invasion of the Philippines in December 1941 saw them interned in San Tomas Camp, which became their home for three-and-a-half years, together with 6,500 others. J.G. Ballard's autobiographical *Empire of the Sun* described the experiences of a boy interned in Shanghai, and his preoccupation with securing enough food was shared by the Merediths. Guy grew a small banana tree and remembers the horror of dropping a small jar of rice. He wrote out his own recipe book on the inside of unused cigarette wrapper paper, with two loops of string to hold it together, which he still has. By 1945 starvation was becoming an increasing threat, as the weaker ones began to die, but they were rescued from this by the American invasion under Macarthur. In due course Philip and Guy stood with their mother at Waterloo Station watching a crowd of freed Hong Kong internees come towards them, trying to guess which was their father.

Japanese strategy included the capture of Burma and a possible invasion of India. At the start they swept weak British forces aside, including a battalion of the Duke of Wellington's Regiment in which William Coningham (PH 1930) was a company commander. He was killed in March 1942 when his company was overrun, acting as the final British rearguard on the retreat, while Cecil Dickson (WH 1934), one of the earliest air cadets, died on a remote jungle airstrip when the bomb his Lysander was carrying fell off and exploded on take-off. By 1944 the British had built up a substantial army under General Slim and overcome some of their logistical problems of mountainous jungle and just one narrow road linking India to the main British base at Imphal. Wingate's Chindit expeditions had also disrupted Japanese communications and given the British a new confidence in jungle fighting. George Astell (HS 1924) knew Burma well from working there before the war. He volunteered for the second Chindit expedition in February 1944 behind Japanese lines and won the Military Cross for his leadership in arduous conditions against much larger Japanese forces.

The Japanese then forestalled a planned British advance into Burma by launching their own offensive in early 1944, which forced Slim into a largely defensive battle around Imphal and Kohima. Twelve Tonbridgians died in this fierce phase of fighting, the largest number of any single military campaign of the war, but this was the turning-point. By August 1944 the Japanese had broken off the attack and were retreating back to the River Chindwin. One casualty was Major James Heywood (HS 1924), fighting with his African soldiers of the Gold Coast Regiment, who was killed in March 1944. His CO wrote to Heywood's mother to tell her that his company was overrun and he was last seen by one of his NCOs lying unconscious; on such letters rested many straws of hope, but his body was never found.

Burma was also the final campaign of the old Indian Army, ironically fighting for the return of that assured imperial world which had provided so many Tonbridgians with employment and adventure. At Neuve Chapelle on the Western Front stands Sir Herbert Baker's (JH 1875) stirring memorial to the Indian Army of the Great War. Now in the next war it was fighting again alongside its British comrades in Malaya and North Africa, Italy and Burma. One of its British officers was Major David Higgins (MH 1925), a company commander in the 4/5th Mahrattas: small, tough, disciplined soldiers. His battalion was ordered to delay the Japanese advance on Kohima by creating a blocking position at Sangshak. For four days totally surrounded in a small, congested perimeter, under relentless Japanese artillery fire and short of food and water, they resisted 30,000 Japanese only for Higgins to fall on the final day of what became a bloodbath. Another Indian Army officer was Major 'Pat' Patterson (WH 1931), a pre-war Gurkha from that world so wonderfully described by John Masters in *Bugles and a Tiger*. By 1945 he was a company commander in 1/6 Gurkhas and won the MC in the crossing of the Irrawaddy. Patterson, a tough and inspirational leader, went on after the war to become Major-General, Brigade of Gurkhas, for whose welfare he fought hard in Whitehall. His 1996 obituary records that his life was one of outstanding service to his beloved Gurkha soldiers.

Lieutenant Colonel Laurence Kelly (PH 1925), a doctor of the Indian Medical Service, served as a surgeon at a Casualty Clearing Station in Burma, later commanding a general hospital. He saw the full horror of what jungle warfare can do to Indians, British and Japanese alike, was twice mentioned in dispatches, and was awarded the MBE. He once had to treat his younger brother Major Hugh Kelly (PH 1931), who won an MC in the Arakan in February 1944, when he was wounded in a counter-attack. He had to be left temporarily behind and remained hidden among searching Japanese until his men came back to collect him, an experience which left him with post-war nightmares.

One Tonbridgian with a rather different background in the Far East war was Lieutenant Colonel Richard Marson (MH 1916), who came to Tonbridge from Australia in the same year remarkably as his OT father arrived with Anzac forces

Major General A.G. Patterson.

in France. He became a school prae and Bisley marksman before returning to Queensland to his family sheep farm and territorial soldiering. In 1941 he was involved in the defence of Tobruk before being transferred to New Guinea in command of 2/25th AIF. He commanded this Queensland battalion for the rest of the war through the vicious fighting back and forth along the Kokoda Trail, combining jungle and mountain warfare in its most gruelling form. Marson, a tough and highly respected Anzac, was wounded in October 1942 and won the DSO in 1943 for his gallantry and leadership, as well as being mentioned in dispatches three times.

The war in the Far East would also have been harder to win without one of Tonbridge's greatest scholars, Maurice Wiles (WH 1936). Head of School in 1941, Wiles was in Cambridge successfully taking a Classics scholarship in December 1941 when he read at breakfast of the Japanese attack on Pearl Harbour. This found Britain with few proficient Japanese linguists, and Oxbridge Classics tutors were asked to suggest people with the necessary linguistic aptitude. The tutor at Christ's put forward Wiles's brother Christopher (WH 1933), who had won the prestigious Porson Greek Verse prize at Cambridge, and then added Maurice's name as an afterthought, even though

Richard Marson (right) with James Barr, 1922.

sent to Bletchley Park to work on deciphering Japanese military codes. Later they were joined by Maurice Burnett (WH 1936), who had sat next to Wiles in class and now worked on naval codes. Maurice Wiles moved on to deciphering the Japanese Army Air Force code, which was of vital importance to the Burma campaign and the wider Pacific war. He later became a leading theologian and Professor of Divinity at Oxford.

In September 1945, a month after VJ-Day, Leslie Wright (JH 1938), nearly the victim of the 1940 Chapel bomb and later Head of School, was in Java, where nationalists were resisting the return of the Dutch colonial power. Under the command of Brigadier Richard Bethell (FH 1920), his artillery battery had the task of disarming the Japanese, when they found themselves attacked by Indonesian nationalists and heavily outnumbered. Bethell therefore asked the Japanese to fight with the British, a request they counted 'a great honour'. Wright thus found himself in command of a company of Japanese soldiers, and together they fought their way back to safety.

Tonbridgians played an important role in the Empire's acquisition, maintenance and defence, and many of them lie in still-beautifully maintained cemeteries across its breadth. The British returned to Rangoon and Singapore, yet the Empire could never be the same again. The war was a last glimpse of greatness but, in destroying German and Japanese aggression, they were also calling time on their own imperial heritage. Paul Scott in his great novel *Staying On* characterised the British relationship with India as an enduring love affair finally brought to an end in 1947. Tonbridgians, however, still sing in Chapel that great Victorian evening hymn whose words anticipated the end of empire and testified to its sense of Christian mission: 'So be it Lord: thy throne shall never, like earth's proud empires pass away. Thy kingdom stands, and grows forever, till all thy creatures hold thy sway.'

he was still at school and he had only met him once. A brief interview followed in London, probing Maurice's interest in chess and crosswords and then in February 1942, as the School Letter recorded, 'the country demanded the services of our Head Boy for a job of national importance'.

Wiles found himself on a six-month course learning Japanese, along with his brother and Bobby Robins (PS 1935), before they were

PETER DORESA AND THE SIEGE OF KOHIMA

Peter Doresa (Sc 1938) is one of the last survivors of Kohima, perhaps the most fiercely fought battle of the war. He enjoyed his time at Tonbridge, although something of a rebel. Frustrated at not being promoted to The Head in 1940, he gave up cricket and became the best shot in the school, which would stand him in good stead in the jungle. This decision was not universally popular, and a Games Committee meeting minute states that 'Doresa was reprimanded for cutting cricket to shoot for the 1st VIII'.

He was commissioned in India in January 1944 into the 4th Royal West Kents, joining them in the Arakan for his first action, before the battalion was transferred to Kohima in March. The Japanese had launched an offensive towards Kohima, a small administrative station and supply depot at the top of a pass astride the main road from Dimapur to Imphal. If it could be seized, not only would the British IV Corps be cut off in the main British base at Imphal, but Kohima itself could be turned into a virtually impregnable fortress, able to resist not only Allied relief attacks along the road to Imphal but also any subsequent advance into Burma.

Peter Doresa, 1945.

The task of 4 RWK, assisted by some Indian Army units, was therefore to deny Kohima to the Japanese – a scratch garrison of only 1,500 properly battle-hardened troops facing 15,000 Japanese attackers. On arrival they raced to construct a defensive line of trenches and bunkers round a series of hills leading up to the battalion command post on Garrison Hill.

On 6 April the Japanese attacks began. Peter was now in continuous action for 14 days until his battalion was relieved, with fighting of the most dramatic intensity as the perimeter contracted under the pressure of relentless assaults. In the early stages he used his marksmanship skills to pick off the enemy at longer range, but, as they came

closer, the fighting became more savage. With the front lines in places only yards apart, such as across the District Commissioner's tennis court, a state of immediate alert had to be maintained to break up screaming Japanese charges, using grenades, bayonets or whatever came to hand. Artillery fire from mortars and heavier pieces pounded the British positions, while snipers were a constant menace. Shortage of food and particularly water made the plight of the defenders more desperate. By 18 April the battalion had lost a third of its strength and the perimeter had shrunk to a 350-yard square round Garrison Hill. The Japanese were only 100 yards from the command post and the Advanced Dressing Station, where the

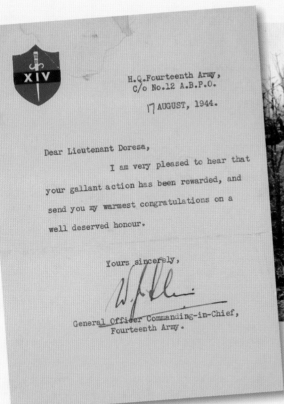

Above: *Garrison Hill, Kohima, after the battle.*

Left: *Letter from General Slim to Peter Doresa, August, 1944.*

wounded lay without shelter. The trees had been stripped of their foliage by thousands of mortars, shells and grenades. It was a scene of utmost horror, but relieving British forces managed to smash their way through Japanese roadblocks on the road from Dimapur. A witness described the survivors as 'sleepwalkers, filthy, bearded, their faces caked with dried blood, some palpably crazed with fatigue'.

Peter's platoon corporal, John Harman, won the VC for a suicidal lone attack on a Japanese machine-gun position, and then died beside Peter saying, 'It was worth it, sir. I got the lot.' Peter's position was overrun and he was wounded by a bullet through the leg, which probably saved his life, as only three from his platoon survived the battle. Nearly a fifth of the battalion was killed and more than half the rest wounded, but it was one of the war's foremost feats of arms which did much to turn the tide in Burma.

Peter was awarded an immediate battlefield MC. The citation records that he 'personally bombed enemy positions, driving the occupants into the open where they were shot by the remainder of the Company. The ammunition dump was on fire and shells, mortar bombs and small arms ammunition were exploding in all directions. In spite of this Doresa carried on with his counter-attack and throughout the engagement showed a high standard of courage and devotion to duty which was an inspiration to all those around him.' It was quite an accolade for a 19-year-old.

He returned to action in 1945 and was wounded again. His part in what has become a historic battle is clearly a source of enormous pride to him and also of anguish. He has never been back, needing to remember Kohima as it was. If he had, he would be moved like countless others by the cemetery on Garrison Hill and the inscribed Kohima epitaph: 'When you go home tell them of us and say, for your tomorrow we gave our today.'

CHAPTER 7:
VOICE OF WAR

War Poet

I am the man who looked for peace and found
My own eyes barbed.
I am the man who groped for words and
    found
An arrow in my hand.
I am the builder whose firm walls surround
A slipping land.
When I grow sick or mad
Mock me not nor chain me;
When I reach for the wind
Cast me not down:
Though my face is a burnt book
And a wasted town.

                March 1942

Sidney Keyes (HS 1935) was one of the finest poets of the Second World War, a group generally less well known than those of 1914–18. They could not repeat the impact their predecessors had in evoking the horrors of the Western Front, partly because the war itself and the range of experience were more diverse and partly because by 1939 the horrors of war were well known and the capacity to shock were therefore more limited. However there is a very strong body of poetry which emerges from 1939–45, and Keyes can stand comparison with the best, who include Keith Douglas and Alun Lewis, both also killed in action.

Sidney Keyes (left) with Geoffrey Oswald at Whitby.

Keyes was born at Dartford on 27 May 1922, his mother dying of peritonitis soon after his birth. Entrusted to the care of his grandparents by his soldier father and often left to his own devices, Keyes did not go to school until he was nine, and subsequently took the Common Entrance for Tonbridge in 1935. He entered Hill Side the same term as Geoffrey Oswald and Peter Stainforth in an intake of eight boys fated to leave as war broke out. Keyes had no Latin and was suffering from flu when he was taking Common Entrance, so that he was put initially into the bottom form, but by September 1938 he was in the Modern Upper VI. Oswald recalls Keyes' voracious reading, his interest in the supernatural and his imaginative invention and narration of ghost stories. They shared a study and stayed with each other's families in the holidays. During their first year Keyes used to gather the novi in the lower study and hold them spellbound with his stories, and he invented a jingle to describe HS food which went: 'Ashes to ashes, and mud to mud, died of eating bread and spud.' 'Mud' was the generic term given to the eight novi at the bottom of the pecking order.

Keyes loathed the OTC, describing those who participated in it as 'brick-red faces', and he was no games player either. James McNeill, however, remembered asking his scholarship set whether they thought they should have the privilege of not playing compulsory games and Keyes, the most incompetent athlete McNeill ever met, replied: 'Certainly not! If a boy is stupid and lazy we agree he should be made to work. Why shouldn't I be compelled to play games?' Once he was apparently chosen to run in the Cras and came in last. When asked the

reason, he explained he had resolved to ease the pain and pass the time by reciting Milton's *Paradise Lost* but was distressed to find he had forgotten a line, so stopped for several minutes until the missing words came back.

Intellectually he flourished at Tonbridge and came under the particular wing of Tom Staveley, his form-master in the Upper VI and a poet himself. Keyes had talents all across the humanities, in his final year winning the Floyd Reading, the English Essay, the Welldon Divinity and the Goggs' History Prizes, as well as a History scholarship to Queen's, Oxford. The exam report on his HSC English in July 1939 said that 'Keyes wrote an essay of very great distinction, which would have graced a Final Honours School of English.' McNeill recalls an arrangement Keyes had with Tom Staveley that if, as frequently happened, some moment of inspiration occurred in the middle of a history lesson, he could give a signal to Staveley and cease attending while he tried out his idea. He was also lucky in that his year contained some deeply intellectual boys, including John Fage, Maurice Wiles and Bobby Robins, all of whom went on to great distinction in university posts.

On the whole he found Tonbridge a civilised and tolerant school and ended his school career successfully as a School Prae and Editor of *The Tonbridgian*. He also edited a literary magazine which appeared in June 1940 called *The New Phoenix*

Welldon House 1939. Seated – Housemaster Philip Bathurst, Charles Turner third from right, Reymie Bousfield second from right. Standing in row behind – Kenneth Ward fifth from left, Maurice Wiles sixth from right.

in which he persuaded the First World War poet, Edmund Blunden, to contribute a poem. He played Prospero in *The Tempest* of 1938 and Polonius in *Hamlet* of December 1939. He was also secretary of the Natural History Society, a flourishing little group and, in the 1938 Skinners' Day exhibition, he and Geoffrey Oswald jointly exhibited tropical fish. He debated regularly and in one 'Parliamentary' debate in November 1939 on Britain's war aims he emphasised the need for Britain to prove by example our worthiness to lead the forces of democracy in the war, something we had singularly failed to do in India. A contemporary described Keyes as 'timorous-eyed', but he gained the respect and even the

admiration of his fellows and he stands out in the list of School Praes of Summer 1940 as one of the very few who were not first team games players. There is no doubt that those who came to know him best at Tonbridge, especially his year in Hill Side, loved him for what he was.

Tom Staveley was the master who encouraged him most in his writing. Not only was he his form-master but Keyes frequently visited his home and they went walking together, discussing poetry and music. Staveley described him as 'a very normal schoolboy – sociable, well-dressed and tidy. He was good-looking, with a slightly olive complexion and dark, curly hair. His rather unhappy face was perhaps the only sign that he was in any way different from other boys. He started writing poetry and short stories when he was about 15 and I knew at once that his was the work of genius.'

Keyes went to Oxford in October 1940 to read History and spent 18 months there. Oxford in wartime was self-absorbed and 'noisy with trivialities' but in the background was that drumbeat of war which Keyes knew he must in time follow. He threw himself into his studies and especially his own writing, producing three or four poems a month as well as his weekly history essay and a number of short stories; by the end of 1941 he had written enough poems to form a small volume, *The Iron Laurel*. The poet Herbert Read visited him at Oxford after Keyes had sent him some of his poems and realised that they were exceptional.

He was called up into the Army for initial training in Northern Ireland in April 1942 and was commissioned into the Royal West Kent (RWK) Regiment that September, later training in Scotland for overseas service. Those who knew him well, including Oswald and Staveley, feared for him in the army. He must have visited Tonbridge at this time, as Alan Jones (JH 1942) remembers a Saturday afternoon tutorial with Tom Staveley when a uniformed Keyes was present and they played 'Consequences'. His Commanding Officer in the 1st RWK was Lieutenant Colonel John Haycraft (DB 1912), and other Tonbridgians in the battalion were Holger Hansen Raae (PH 1929), a company commander who was to win the MC in Tunisia and was then killed at Cassino; Charles Turner (WH 1934), Keyes's contemporary, Oxford Classical scholar and 1st XV full back, who was the Intelligence Officer; and a young platoon commander James Lendon-Smith (PS 1936), who had played a leading role in winning the Lord's match in 1941.

The battalion left the Clyde by ship for Algiers on 10 March 1943, moving up by sea to Bone. The

majority of soldiers in the battalion were regulars, many of them Cockneys. They had therefore seen not only plenty of action but also many officers come and go. They summed Keyes up as 'dead cush', not a disciplinarian and someone prone to sartorial eccentricity; on one occasion as Orderly Officer he caused amusement by wearing his web anklets upside down. On the troop ship going out Keyes gave lectures on a variety of subjects – poetry, Gibraltar, politics – and on arrival in Algeria he took men on trips to Roman ruins, demonstrated his knowledge of ornithology and impressed them with his fluent French.

They arrived at Bone in an air raid which Keyes took coolly in his stride. He then departed on a mine course to identify the various types before rejoining the battalion along the crest of the Oued Zarga hills in mid-April. Oued Zarga was a quiet sector at this time but some bodies were lying about from previous actions and one night an Argyll piper played a lament for the fallen. Keyes enjoyed neatness and had the habit of lining his slit trench with a blanket, fixing it with metal tent pegs or meat skewers, so that no pieces of loose soil fell on him while he sat or slept in it. He wrote some poetry and was fascinated by the different types of beetle infesting the body of a nearby dead dog, but sterner things were at hand.

The final Allied assault on the Tunis bridgehead began on 23 April. 1 RWK was now in the centre of the line, almost directly opposite Tunis itself and overlooking a crossroads known as Peter's Corner in the area of Longstop Hill, where the Germans were well dug in. Keyes undertook a night patrol behind enemy lines on 25 April, passing a dead German whom he berated in his own language for sleeping on duty.

On 28 April the battalion launched a two-company attack on ground to the north of Peter's Corner along the road leading directly to Tunis. The start line was crossed at 7.30pm under a heavy

Right: *Longstop Hill, Tunisia, April 1943.*

Below: *Sidney Keyes in army uniform, 1942.*

barrage. Keyes and his runner, James Lucas, walked together through the twilight and the smoke and dust of explosions, narrowly avoiding a German minefield where Keyes, in a conversational tone, described to his runner what would happen if either of them stepped on a mine. They came to a German position which they took and Keyes arranged for the prisoners to be taken back. Then, halting momentarily at the bottom of a short slope covered with wheat, they fixed bayonets and continued the advance to the top.

Orders were given to consolidate the position, known as Point 133, and to prepare for a German counter-attack. It was difficult to dig trenches, for they reached rock at about two feet, so they scraped what cover they could with their entrenching tools. At about two in the morning, Keyes was ordered to take nine men out on patrol forward of their position to try to ascertain the

enemy's intentions. The rest of the company lay in the wet wheat awaiting the inevitable counter-attack, aware that their position was thinly spread. Just after first light, crack German parachute troops attacked and overran the company's position, almost every man becoming a casualty or taken prisoner. Keyes and his patrol were isolated out front and must have been attacked as the enemy began their wider assault. He was last seen standing shoulder-to-shoulder with another man firing his tommy gun at the advancing Germans. The rest of his patrol he had ordered to get back into the Company square.

Keyes was certainly killed at this moment in the early morning of 29 April, covering his patrol's retreat, for his body was later found well forward of Point 133. James Lucas described him as the best type of platoon commander: quiet, determined and non-blustering, with impeccable manners and no trace of condescension to his intellectual inferiors. His Tonbridge contemporaries believed him to be as unmilitary as he could possibly have been, but, although he was clearly not a natural soldier, neither was he an unhappy one, and he performed his military duties as bravely and competently as anyone has a right to expect. Lucas regarded the manner of his death as that of 'a gallant Christian gentleman who sacrificed himself for the men under his command'.

Keyes was buried in the war cemetery at Massicault, just a little closer to Tunis than the place of his death. Charles Turner was killed the next day and is also buried at Massicault, while James Lendon-Smith died of wounds and is buried near the field hospital at Oued Zarga. In all the battalion had casualties of 16 officers and over 300 other ranks. It was a heavy price to pay for the final victory in Africa which followed a week later.

Shortly after his death a second volume of poems was published, *The Cruel Solstice*, and Keyes was awarded the 1943 Hawthornden Prize for Poetry. An obituary appeared in *The Tonbridgian* of April 1944, presumably written by Tom Staveley, describing the boy who was 'widely loving, the most wholly generous friend imaginable'. On his simple headstone in Massicault are inscribed the words: 'A poet of great promise. Won Hawthornden Prize in 1943.'

In his last letter (to Renee-Jane Scott, a girlfriend), on the day before his death, Keyes wrote: 'I shall have a lot more to say about this when the time for speaking returns. I cannot think that this campaign can last much longer; but after that, who knows?' He was not yet 21 when he died, but he must not be thought of as an adolescent prodigy. What he achieved is remarkable, not because of his youth or even the wartime circumstances in which he wrote it, but for its intrinsic worth. His voice endures across the generations but 'the red rock wilderness' remains his dwelling-place.

Massicault War Cemetery, Tunisia.

Talking to History

Peter Carpenter, poet and former Head of English, Tonbridge School

In his introduction to his first collection of poems, *The North Ship*, Philip Larkin famously describes bumping into Sidney Keyes when they were both up at Oxford: 'He could talk to history as some people talk to porters, and the mention of names like Schiller and Rilke and Gilles de Retz made me wish I were reading something more demanding than English Language and Literature. He had most remarkable brown and piercing eyes: I met him one day in Turl Street, when there was snow on the ground, and he was wearing a Russian-style fur hat. He stopped, so I suppose we must have known each other to talk to – that is, if we had anything to say. As far as I remember, we hadn't.'

Aside from Larkin's self-deprecatory humour, there is much here to inform an understanding of Keyes' distinctive powers both as a poet and as a man: the enviable, easy and deep erudition; a memorable flamboyance and nobility of bearing, early markings of the incipient hero and leader of men; and most important, the way in which Keyes connected with the voices from the past, with history, with the rhythms and language of the dead, as easily as he did with the living.

The power of Keyes' imaginative life underpinned and allowed the behaviour of the efficient, generous, inspiring and suave player in the 'real world'. Keyes' stoicism is heralded from the start in his poetry by a highly developed awareness and acceptance of death. His major themes, love and suffering, the possibilities for oneness with the natural world ('the continual fusion of finite and infinite, spiritual and physical' as he put it in *Artist and Society*), are all bounded by this. Tom Staveley puts it thus in an article in *The Listener* in 1947: 'his attitude towards the craft of poetry was one of furious urgency and energy.' Like all metaphysical poets, he felt

death everywhere around him. When in one of his letters he stresses Rilke's conception of death as 'A creature that we bear within us, like a child waiting for birth', he recognised a spiritual posture familiar to him from childhood, thus his identification with those close to death or recently dead and the protean quality of his imagination. Also, Staveley's words on Keyes' craft are significant: the act of creating, the 'furious urgency' of process, was part of an attempt to counter death, an act of preservation. There are

Sidney Keyes's grave, Massicault. 'A poet of great promise.'

many other accounts of how rapidly Keyes wrote after the incubatory period: he is with Blake in knowing that 'Energy is Delight' and that poetry is an act of resistance against mutability and, like Blake, he too has the poetic ear and eye to produce imagery at once memorable and resonant.

His poetry is less well known than the other great poet of the war, Keith Douglas, perhaps because of Keyes' modernist leanings: he, along with T.S. Eliot, 'does' his greatest work via 'different voices', a tendency felt in his early fascination with ghost stories. His creed became part of his poetic matter as in the opening line to 'Glaucus': 'The various voices are his poem now.' His poetic is steered towards impersonality: in a letter to Milein Cosmann from May 1942 he declares: 'I am a not a man, but a voice.' Within a year he would be dead: his poetic manifesto and output both prefigure acts of sacrifice, the self making way for others.

Due to his learning and imaginative power his poems endure beyond the historical moment, but are likely to puzzle readers looking for some easy equation with biographical detail. They are not part of a late romantic expressionist movement, whatever Keyes' special affinities with writers of that period (Rilke, Schiller and Wordsworth, for example). His work is often garnished with obliquities, deeply embroiled allusions informing the textures of his best work. Readers of Keith Douglas, Alun Lewis or Bernard Spencer, three of the war's greatest poets, are able to trace a course; the particular theatre of war is evoked or described in navigable ways. With Keyes, this is not the case, and has therefore limited his acclaim and audience; his poems from the African front were lost with him, thus we have no 'direct' poems of combat.

He is a master craftsman, at home with blank verse and inherited metrical and rhyming schemes, but perhaps some of his greater poems (encompassing 'War Poet') come in a phase from March to July 1942, when he favours a shorter line. There are great moments in his longer poems, although the dramatic qualities in his writing are not as well developed as the lyric, and his last poem, 'The Wilderness', is best read next to Eliot's *Four Quartets* (the influence of the recently published 'The Dry Salvages' fresh in Keyes' memory).

His critical reputation is now secure, whatever the problems for a wider readership; a recent essay by Tim Kendall cites Keyes as 'the poet of apprehension'. Kendall takes 'The Foreign Gate' as Keyes' 'masterpiece' and outlines the indebtedness of many of our greatest living writers, in particular, Geoffrey Hill, to Keyes' example here. It is unwise to speculate what Keyes might have written had he survived the war, along with contemporaries such as Larkin. What we have from him, all managed against the enemies of the 'swift departing years' ('Elegy'), is significant enough to allow his reputation to endure. Perhaps the best starting place for a reader new to his work is one of his last poems, 'The Wilderness', where the imagery of the desert becomes part of a prophetic self-elegy. In revision we find Keyes changing the poems from second to the first person, all the more poignant in retrospect:

The red rock wilderness
Shall be my dwelling-place.
Where the wind saws at the bluffs
And the pebble falls like thunder
I shall watch the clawed sun
Tear the rocks asunder.
The seven-branched cactus
Will never sweat wine:
My own bleeding feet
Shall furnish the sign.
The rock says 'Endure.'
The wind says 'Pursue.'
The sun says 'I will suck your bones
And afterwards bury you.'

COASTAL COMMAND

Sholto Douglas, C-in-C Coastal Command, with Dwight Eisenhower, 1944.

Coastal Command had a vital role in winning the Battle of the Atlantic, and 19 Tonbridgians were killed in action serving with it between 1940 and 1944. The life of a Coastal Command crew member was just as arduous in its own way as that of Bomber Command. Operational flights could last as long as 14 hours in all weathers and over unfriendly seas where any engine malfunction or operational damage would mean ditching and almost certain death, while shorter-range shipping strikes were usually conducted at low level through curtains of anti-aircraft fire. Coastal sank over 200 U-Boats and nearly 400 German surface ships, but lost nearly 6,000 men of their own in action, protecting convoys and the seas round Britain.

Many Tonbridgians became senior officers in Coastal, which in 1944–5 was commanded by Sholto Douglas. Wing Commander Peter

Canney (HS 1928) was killed in action leading his squadron on an anti-shipping strike off Norway in February 1942. Another Wing Commander was Rowland Musson (MH 1925), who had been School Captain in 1929 and captained the RAF cricket team. His father and four brothers had all been at Tonbridge, and one brother George (MH 1921) had been lost in 1942 in the Atlantic when an engine caught fire in the flying boat 'Clare' that he was piloting from West Africa to Britain. Rowland in 1938 navigated a Vickers Wellesley on a flight from Egypt to Australia which broke the previous record for a non-stop flight, and then commanded a squadron tasked with finding and attacking U-Boats off the southwest coast. These operations were often carried out at night, using radar and searchlights to find the U-Boats, but on the night of 24 August 1943, his aircraft crashed near Clovelly and all the crew were killed.

Wing Commander Roderick McConnell (JH 1930) was a prize cadet at RAF Cranwell, where he gained his colours for athletics and rugby, as he had done at Tonbridge. He was awarded the DFC in November 1940 when, after his Anson was attacked by four German fighters over Calais, he managed to escape and land safely despite being wounded in the face. In July 1943 he took command of 235 Beaufighter Squadron, becoming one of the RAF's most successful anti-shipping pilots in torpedo, rocket and cannon attacks off Norway, before moving to Cornwall to operate over the Bay of Biscay. The citation for his DSO awarded in July 1944 highlighted his 'outstanding courage and leadership'. He survived the war but was killed in 1950 when his Vampire jet spun into the North Sea.

Wing Commander Peter Hutchings (MH 1929) was the nephew of the England cricketer Kenneth Hutchings. In November 1941 he took command of 608 Squadron, flying Hudson anti-submarine operations over the North Sea, and then went to Gibraltar in support of Operation Torch, sinking a U-Boat and damaging two others in early 1943, for which he was awarded the DSO. Another successful U-Boat hunter was Flight Lieutenant Tom Griffith (Sc 1935), from the 1939 1st XV, who won the DFC in 1944 for damaging a surfaced submarine.

The most remarkable story of all is that of Flying Officer David Johnstone (DB 1924). A scientist at school, he became an expert in wireless telegraphy with the Baird television company, joining the RAFVR in 1940 to specialise in radar technology. In September 1943 he was in Gibraltar investigating signals from German aircraft and submarines when he hitched a ride back to England with a Coastal Command Liberator from 224 Squadron on which he wanted to see a new radar operating.

The Liberator left on 2 September, carrying out an anti-submarine sweep over the Bay of Biscay on the way to England. Suddenly, at about 5,000 feet, it was attacked by four German fighters, one of which fired a deadly burst killing the pilot. The second pilot Ron Foss took over, helped by Johnstone, who had to pull the dead pilot from his seat and then help Foss to evade the German fighters as best they could. For about 20 minutes they weaved in and out of cloud, subjected to relentless attacks, which hit the Liberator repeatedly, killing the rear gunner, wounding all the other crew, setting one engine on fire and damaging the others, so that Foss had to ditch. With Johnstone's help he put the plane down on the Atlantic, where it broke in two with the impact and sank. Johnstone was submerged in the cockpit, but managed to free himself, assisting others to get clear by stepping on his shoulders to squeeze through a hole in the sinking aircraft.

The seven survivors scrambled into a dinghy designed for only five men, equipped with paddles, pump, two tins of water and five tins of emergency rations. Johnstone had shrapnel wounds in his hands and feet, the others similar wounds or worse, but there was nothing with which to dress any of the wounds except handkerchieves. For nine days they were adrift – the two most badly wounded died on the fifth day and were tipped over the side. Finally they were sighted by an aircraft which guided a naval ship to them. The ship found them huddled together, very wet with their feet immersed in water, and extremely cold. Two of the survivors died a few hours after rescue, but the remaining three recovered and were all decorated. Johnstone was given the DSO, rare for a junior officer, an award also possibly unique in its context to a ground-based specialist. His citation spoke of his exemplary conduct both in his response to the attack on the aircraft, without any previous flying training or experience, and for his leadership while adrift in the Atlantic in such unendurable circumstances. Johnstone's story exemplifies perfectly the considerable dangers faced by all Coastal Command crews, from both the enemy and the sea.

Rowland Musson (left) with crew of Wellesley bomber before record-breaking non-stop flight from Egypt to Australia, 1938.

CHAPTER 8:

ESPRIT DE CORPS

In the middle of the Ruhr battle of mid-1943, Sir Arthur Harris, C-in-C Bomber Command, visited one of the many airfields scattered across the eastern counties of England. He told the assembled crews that he knew it was rough, and added that it was going to get rougher. 'I want you to look at the man on either side of you,' he said. 'In six months' time only one in three will be left, but if you are the lucky one I promise that you will be two ranks higher.' As he left the room, the men rose to cheer. Harris half-turned in the doorway and started to speak, but was so choked with emotion that no words came out. Instead he brought himself to attention and smartly saluted them.

120,000 men served in Bomber Command, of whom 56,000 perished, 8,000 were wounded and 10,000 became prisoners, a casualty rate of over 60 per cent. The only service to suffer higher

Inspection of OTC, 1938. RSM Sturgess left.

Westland Wapiti being examined by the ATS, 1939.

casualties in the European theatre was German U-Boat crews. It is therefore not altogether surprising that there were more Tonbridgians killed in Bomber Command than in any other service, 60 in action and another 25 in training accidents, many of them in their early 20s. The youngest, Sergeant Guy Muffett (SH 1939), an air gunner, was just 18 and should have been still at school, when he died over Mannheim in 1943. Wartime bomber crew were all volunteers, many of them from an educated public or grammar school background who in kinder times would have been going to university, although the RAF was adept in its recruiting by often sending volunteers on short university courses. Educated specialists were needed, especially those with some background in science or engineering, and in Bomber Command Tonbridgians served not just as pilots, but wireless operators, bomb aimers, navigators and air gunners.

The Officers Training Corps (OTC) at Tonbridge had given initial training to all of them. Founded in 1860 as one of the original volunteer corps, it became a compulsory school activity, with its own fife and drum band and a military proficiency exam, known as 'Certificate A', which was a passport to a commission. The seriousness with which the OTC was taken is shown by the very senior soldiers who came down to inspect it, including Field Marshal Lord French in 1917,

OTC Parade on Quad, 1938.

OTC Camp, 1933. George Jackson (with leopard skin) standing behind James Nicolson.

General Montgomery in 1941 and General Ironside on three occasions. By 1939 even the less military-minded boys realised that the OTC had become all too relevant to their lives. There were two parades a week and annual camp at places like Tidworth Pennings, where Tonbridge joined in manoeuvres with other public schools. Tom Staveley and Gilbert Hoole, Western Front veterans, both commanded the OTC in the inter-war years, while RSM Sturgess, a Coldstream Guardsman and 'Old Contemptible' of 1914, ruled the parade ground with his stentorian words of command, a terrifying figure to small boys. The OTC Sing-Song was an annual institution, as each house put on a musical act and regular songs like 'In Camp' were belted out by all present, accompanied by the Band under Bandmaster Fitzgerald:

> Then shout hurrah for the gallant lads in red,
> Who serve their King at Aldershot as well as
> on The Head.

Jimmy Watts, an RFC veteran and maths teacher, volunteered to set up an Air Training Section for senior boys within the OTC in September 1938. Somewhat deaf as a legacy from his flying days, white-haired and with a rather squeaky voice easily mimicked, he was nevertheless full of knowledge and enthusiasm about flying, which boys much valued. This was shown in 1941 when he was presented with a book by six of his pupils with a dedication inside which read: 'J. W. Watts – hoping that this will remind you of many happy hours spent with us who are deeply grateful.' Two of those pupils were later killed, and Watts's sense of guilt at the loss of so many he had encouraged to fly led to his retirement from teaching in 1944.

The Air Ministry provided training officers and gave the School an old Westland Wapiti two-seater bi-plane, which was housed in a purpose-built shed behind the cricket pavilion. The section had about 15 senior boys who spent parades listening to lectures and exploring with Watts the Pegasus engine and airframe of the Wapiti. In August 1939 seven of them, including Bill Brown, attended a camp with other public schools at Norton Priory, near RAF Tangmere. They camped in tents, were taken by plane to visit RAF front-line stations and treated to flying displays by Spitfires. *The Times'* correspondent enthused about the programme but was somewhat critical of the cadets' demeanour, suggesting that 'obvious enthusiasm is considered bad form in the public schoolboy'.

The early days of the bomber war were small-scale and amateurish compared with the mass onslaught that was to follow from 1942 onwards. Bomber Command possessed neither the quantity nor quality of aircraft to mount a successful strategic offensive, and too many experienced crews were lost in suicidal daylight raids or in bombing targets by night which their equipment gave them little chance of hitting. Nevertheless, after Dunkirk only Bomber Command was in a position to carry the war to Germany, and there were many Tonbridgians from the pre-war RAF who now found themselves in the front line.

George Jackson (WH 1929), son of a distinguished local OT, Sir Robert Jackson, was one of them. George was Head of Welldon in 1934, a big 1st XV forward in what was described as a 'pack good enough to master any they met', and a genial easy-going personality. He left Tonbridge from the same Army Class as James Nicolson to spend three years in the City, before joining the RAF in 1938. He returned to England from Egypt in June 1940 as losses in the bomber force began to mount, and joined 37 Squadron in Norfolk, taking part in night raids on Germany and the Channel ports as the threat of invasion reached its climax. The bomber offensive in that summer of 1940 in fact cost more lives than the more celebrated Battle of Britain, and eight of them were Tonbridgians.

On 1 September 1940 death found George Jackson. He was second pilot of a Wellington which successfully bombed Hanover and then for some reason flew into the North Sea on the return leg. The pilot was the only survivor after two days adrift in a dinghy and admitted that he might have fallen asleep, but faulty instruments and inexperienced navigation often caused problems to tired crews. Jackson's body was washed up on the Dutch coast and buried at Bergen-op-Zoom, surrounded by many who shared his end in different planes, on different raids and along different stretches of beach. A month later his father died suddenly, perhaps a victim of grief, his funeral attended by Whitworth and many Tonbridge staff.

For much of 1941, Bomber Command was ordered to divert from the offensive against German cities to counter the U-Boat threat; the French port of Brest, with its important U-Boat base, came in for particular attention. Sidney Misselbrook (Sc 1928) was just the kind of tough professional airman in increasingly short supply as casualties mounted, and in March 1941, now a Wing Commander with nine years RAF experience, he was given command of 44 (Rhodesia) Squadron with its motto 'Fulmina Regis Justa' (the King's Thunderbolts are Righteous). In July his singular leadership was acknowledged by the award of the DSO for sustained gallantry, and on 13 December 1941 the squadron was ordered to drop mines in daylight at the entrance to Brest harbour. After disastrous losses during previous daylight attacks

AIRMAN KILLED IN ACTION
Pilot-Officer G. Jackson

WE regret to announce that Pilot Officer George Jackson, R.A.F., who was reported missing in September while returning from night operations over North Western Germany, is now reported killed in action.

He was the second son of Mr Robert and Lady Jackson, of Meadow side, Tonbridge, and was born in Montevideo, Uruguay, on Feb. 22, 1916. He was educated at Tonbridge School during 1929–34, and won house prize in 1933 and a school prize in 1934. Also in 1934 he became head of Welldon House and played for the School Rugby team. In the same year he was made captain of boats and was in the rowing four.

After three years in the City he entered the R.A.F. and was drafted to Iraq, where he carried out many important flying operations. At this station he was held in high esteem by officers and men alike.

In June, 1940, he returned to England and was attached to a bomber squadron.

His genial personality made him popular wherever he went, and his death will be mourned by a great number of friends, who realize, as we all do, that he died while fighting with a Service to which we all owe so much.

Pilot Officer George Jackson.

over this heavily defended target, Misselbrook protested strongly to higher command, knowing that such operations produced heavy casualties for little or no gain. When his protest had no effect, he insisted on leading the raid of three aircraft himself and chose to drop his mine third, knowing that the enemy defences would be at their most alert. He pressed home his low-level attack in the face of intensive flak but was hit and lost without trace in the winter sea. His loss was felt well beyond his squadron and his Station Commander commented that 'the failure of this very fine and gallant officer to return from operations is a loss that this country can ill afford.'

The German battleship *Tirpitz*, anchored in Trondheim Fiord, ready to break out into the Atlantic to attack convoys, was another naval threat the Admiralty was keen to eliminate. On 27 April 1942 the heavily defended ship was attacked by Lancasters from 97 Squadron, in one of which Pilot Officer Thomas Tree (HS 1927) was navigator. His was an experienced crew with 16 operations under their belt, including a daylight attack on the German battleships *Scharnhorst* and *Gneisenau* in Brest in December 1941, for which their pilot won the DFC. Tree had been a publisher and was a gentle, erudite man well suited to the key role that the navigator had in charting a course to the target and back. On their bomb run the plane was hit by flak from *Tirpitz*, setting the aircraft on fire and sending it, engulfed in flames, spiralling into the mountainside. Tree, cocooned in his small windowless navigator's compartment

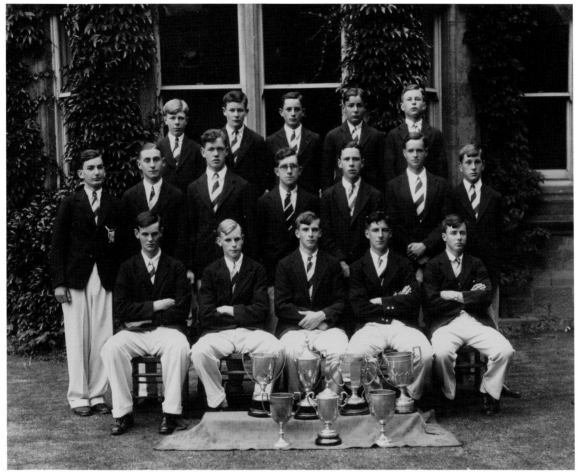

Welldon House Athletics team, 1937. Sitting Gray Healey centre, Brian Burnett extreme left. Middle row John Healey third from right, Maurice Burnett second from right. Back row Reymie Bousfield centre.

inside the plane, would have been aware only of the shrieking terror in his headphones as the fire took hold and the Lancaster spun out of control.

By mid-1942 Bomber Command had a new chief (Sir Arthur Harris), a new aircraft (the Lancaster, coming off the production line in large numbers) and a new policy of area bombing German cities. On 30 May Harris launched the first 1,000 bomber raid against Cologne. This great demonstration of air power lifted the nation's morale, paved the way for the systematic destruction of German cities and created an insatiable demand for manpower. By late 1941

most of the pre-war generation of aircrew had been killed, made prisoner or promoted to non-operational posts. Now the first volunteers of 1939 were filling the squadrons, including many Tonbridgians – pilots, navigators, gunners, bomb aimers and wireless operators, mostly trained in the clear skies of the USA or Southern Africa. At the Operational Training Units (OTUs) they were brought together and formed into operational crews. The accident rate at OTUs was appalling, some courses losing as many as 25 per cent of their intake, and too many Tonbridgians died at this stage. At completion of training the fresh-faced crews were posted to their squadrons, hoping against hope that they could beat the odds. 'I shouldn't bother to unpack,' one young gunner was told as he arrived at his new squadron, 'you won't be here long.'

One of this new wave of volunteers was Gray Healey (WH 1933), twice winner of the Athletics Cup, who was born a fortnight before the end of the Great War and reached his 21st birthday in October 1939. On coming down from Cambridge he trained as a navigator and flew 11 operations in 1941 in this role, but in September that year heard the tragic news that his younger brother John (WH 1936), just 19, had been one of those killed in a pilot training accident. Gray now decided to train as a pilot himself, returning to 106 Squadron as a Sergeant Pilot to complete his first tour of operations. He was awarded the DFM, before being commissioned and volunteering for a second tour in 1942. 106 Squadron had converted to Lancasters and was commanded by the legendary Guy Gibson, who was to win the VC leading the Dams Raid. On 14 October 1942 the squadron took part in a daring low-level daylight raid against the Schneider armament factory at Le Creusot on the Franco-Swiss border, the Lancasters coming across France at less than 500 feet in a considerable feat of flying. Night attacks on the Ruhr followed, for which Healey was awarded the DFC to add to his DFM. Off duty, he relaxed with other officers in the Black Boy hotel in Nottingham near their base at Syerston, letting their hair down over drinks, chatting up barmaids as young men flirting with death will do, and not thinking too much about the morrow, for it was not difficult to calculate the chances of their mortality.

Healey was by now a 24-year-old veteran and one of the most decorated pilots in 5 Group, but on the night of 13 January 1943 his luck ran out. The target was the industrial city of Essen,

Lancaster being prepared for a night raid.

for the seventh time that month, but Healey's Lancaster was caught by a night-fighter which flew underneath into his blind spot and raked the wings and fuselage with an upward firing cannon, setting two engines ablaze. Even such an experienced pilot had little or no chance of keeping a stricken burning aircraft in the air long enough for the crew to escape, and they all died together, to be buried in Apeldoorn, Holland, where every year local children lay flowers on each grave.

Between mid-1942 and the end of 1944, when the German defences had become overwhelmed by the weight of firepower being sent against them, 32 Tonbridgians died in Bomber Command. The youngest was 18, the oldest no more than 30. Others managed to survive the nightly torments as they set out from safe billets on their airfields to try their luck in the skies over Berlin or the Ruhr. The terror of having to fly straight through the flak box barrage to drop their bombs was matched by the lurking and unpredictable threat of night fighters latching on to the usually visible bomber stream on its way to or from Germany. Many bombers were downed on their return journey just as the crew was congratulating itself on another operation completed. If the plane suffered catastrophic damage, the crew had to get out of the small corners in which they were wedged, find and clip on their parachutes and try to reach the few exits – difficult enough if the plane was flying level, but virtually impossible if it was falling out of control and they were pinned to the sides by G-forces.

Airmen say that you start with a full pot of luck and an empty one of experience, and hope that the latter fills up before the former has run out. The cold reality was that less than half of all bomber crews would survive their first tour of 30 operations, but there were some who beat the odds, like Squadron Leader George Hay (PS 1934), who survived more than two full tours between 1941 and 1944, winning the DFC and Bar. It was not just the likelihood of death which kept young aircrew awake in their billets, but the method of it. Death could come very suddenly out of the darkness or keep you lingering for a little longer. If you did not perish instantaneously from fighter bullet or searing explosion, you might be consumed by fire or fall without parachutes from suddenly disintegrating aircraft or drown in the cold waters of the North Sea. Some made it back over the English coast only to die while desperately trying to crash-land a damaged plane. The line between the living and the dead was very thin and fatalism was widespread. 'If you live on the brink of death yourself,' wrote one pilot, 'it is as if those who have gone before have merely caught an earlier train to the same destination.' Men who lived to tell tales of miraculous escape did so because they threw themselves out of their aircraft within seconds of it being set ablaze, and many pilots bravely sacrificed themselves trying to hold steady their stricken planes to allow their crew time to escape.

One of these was Flying Officer Harold Coates (HS 1931), who came back from Peru to join the RAFVR and was posted to 49 Squadron in July 1943, flying Lancasters from Fiskerton near Lincoln. On the night of 3 September he was detailed to attack Berlin, his 12th operation and a dangerous target in those long moonlit summer months. He bombed successfully but his plane was hit by flak as he climbed away, damaging the controls. On the four-hour return journey, which must have seemed endless, Coates fought valiantly to keep his badly shot-up Lancaster in the air, but mist over Fiskerton meant a diversion to a base further north, the last thing he needed when low on fuel and damaged. He did not quite make it as, 15 miles off Tynemouth in heavy early morning mist, he was forced to ditch in the North Sea. It is difficult to imagine the terror he must have felt at that moment as the plane hit the rolling waves nose on and broke up on impact. The bomb aimer and one of the gunners made it into the rescue dinghy to tell the tale of Coates trapped in the cockpit as it sank beneath the waves.

In November 1943 Harris launched the 'Battle of Berlin'. In a minute to Churchill dated 3 November 1943 he said: 'We can wreck Berlin from end to end. It will cost between four and five hundred aircraft. It will cost Germany the war'. This sustained assault saw 16 major attacks on Berlin in the next four months which cost double his estimate. It was a nightmare for the crews involved, the eight-hour round trip in winter rain and snow stretching the planes to their limit while the flak and night fighter force took a terrible toll. One pilot described the Berlin experience as 'like being in a pyrotechnic arena with the glow of the fires below on the wings of the bombers, coloured target indicators going down, searchlights and the tracer of combat. Through this you held your plane steady for two minutes before powering out into the darkness and the dangers of the 600-mile journey home'. Sergeant Richard Cantin (WH 1937), a 20-year-old bomb-aimer in 61 Squadron, endured this terrible journey to Berlin four times in one week. The fourth of these was on 26 November, when over 400 Lancasters attacked and many of the bombs fell on Berlin Zoo, killing many animals and causing escaped leopards to be hunted and shot in the streets. On the return leg it was Cantin's plane which was to be hunted down by a night fighter.

The rear gunner on such trips faced the loneliest night of all, wedged into his compartment behind his guns, separated from the rest of the crew, scanning the intensely cold night sky for hours on end to spot the fighter which was no more than a smear at the corner of a man's eye before it

fired. Long hours staring into the darkness meant it was easy to lose concentration for that vital moment of danger, and the rear turret was first in the line of fire for the fighter's cannon shells. One Lancaster came home to its base with so little left of the rear gunner that ground crew could only hose out the remains. Sergeant Gavin Borradaile (SH 1936) was a rear gunner and a considerable schoolboy athlete – first teams in rugby, rowing, boxing and gymnastics. 'Borradaile tackled very vigorously and not once missed his man,' read one match report. He joined 463 Squadron, full of tough Australians, as rear gunner in the crew of Pilot Officer Messenger and they became an experienced team, with 23 operations under their belt. 'Fighter port, corkscrew' Borradaile would shout as he spotted danger lurking, the signal for Messenger to throw the plane about the sky in a gut-wrenching routine which might just shake off the fighter and bring survival.

They entered the Berlin cauldron first on 18 November 1943, went back three times in a week in late December and five more times in January, when eight 463 Squadron crews were lost out of an average of 14 taking part each time. The state of mind of Borradaile's crew can only be surmised, as the casualties among their mates

Lancaster rear-gunner.

1st XV 1940. Kenneth Ward standing extreme left, Gavin Borradaile standing third from left.

Lancaster crew of Pilot Officer Harold Mitchell (centre). Navigator John Maddex left.

mounted and the sheer physical and mental effort of the dreaded journey to Berlin took its toll. Fear of 'the chop' loomed over everyone, even veterans feeling its shadow. Some had premonitions of its coming, their nervous behaviour before an operation betraying their awareness of death being close. Only the tight comradeship of a crew could counter this, all of them working together to beat the odds they knew to be stacked against them and reach the end of their operational tour together and alive. 'Look at that lovely sunset,' said one pilot as he boarded his plane. 'Sod the sunset,' said his colleague, 'all I want to see is the sunrise.'

On the night of 30 January 1944 Berlin was again the target. Fourteen 463 Squadron aircraft joined over 500 others, and Borradaile's Lancaster was airborne from Waddington at five o'clock. Diversionary tactics fooled no-one and fighters were seen to be gathering over the target four long hours later. 'Too much moonlight', wrote one flight engineer on the raid, 'and too many fighter flares to make one feel happy. We watched seven planes going down in flames as we went in to bomb'. One

of that seven must have been Borradaile's, shot down from 21,000 feet by a fighter and crashing near Wittstock. The bomb aimer and navigator survived when they were blown free by the plane exploding and watched Borradaile and the rest of the crew engulfed by fire.

When airmen of 'different trades' arrived at their OTUs and formed up into their operational crews, there was a mysterious chemistry which brought them together. That which brought together Harold Mitchell (Sc 1937), pilot, and John Maddex (MH 1936), navigator, in the same crew must have been brewed in the labs at Tonbridge. Mitchell learned to fly in the USA after leaving Tonbridge in 1940. He returned to England as an above-average pilot to assemble his crew at OTU and convert to Lancasters, involving just 40 hours of flying in a month, before the crew was posted to 166 Squadron in early October 1943. Mitchell flew his first operation as second pilot to his flight commander, a seven-hour trip to Stuttgart, and then as a crew they completed three operations in four days.

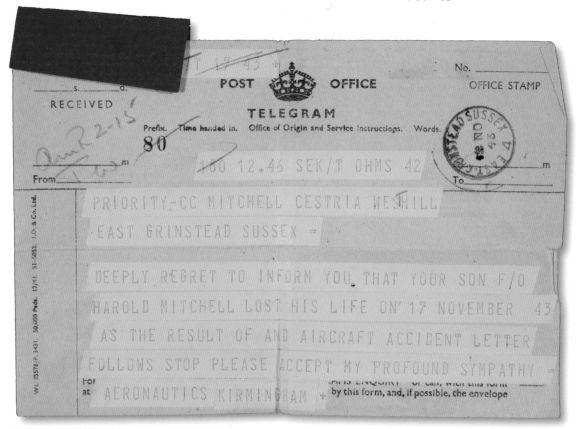

Telegram to Harold Mitchell's father.

On Sunday 14 November Mitchell wrote home to his mother, saying that it had not been a good week. Their Lancaster had been borrowed for an operation by another crew and had been so badly shot up that it was no longer fit for flying, while two of his crew had been off sick, preventing any of them from operational flying. He and John Maddex had been to Scunthorpe to see a film and then 'went to a sergeants' mess dance and had a real wonderful time with a Wren. It's grand to get dancing again. Oh gee what a night!' It was to be his last dance. Three days later, on 17 November, he was doing a night flying test on their replacement Lancaster when it crashed into trees near the base while practising landings, killing himself, Maddex and all but one of the crew. Mitchell was just 20 years old, Maddex 21, the flight engineer only 19. The priority telegram about his only son reached Mitchell's father the next day.

Derek Law (JH 1935) and Richard Stainbank (WH 1937) were two more Tonbridgians who, in 1944, came together in the same crew of 90 Squadron as pilot and navigator, both of them Tonbridge squash players. Law had trained in Rhodesia and tried to foster togetherness in what was again a very young crew by trips to the cinema and to London. On the night of 12 September 1944 they attacked Frankfurt. The Lancaster suffered flak damage to both its starboard engines, making it impossible to reach home, so Law chose to put the aircraft down in France. The local villagers heard the plane circling for some time before Law managed a belly landing in a forest clearing near Vitry-les-Nogent in the Haute-Marne. Unfortunately some ordnance still on board exploded, which the villagers heard, broke the German curfew to climb up to the wreck and found all the crew dead. They brought them back to the village, laid them out in the school house, intact and incredibly young-looking, before burying them side-by-side in their churchyard, the only British graves in this lovely place. Each year a commemoration is held for their young British guests and because German forces left the area on the night of the crash, bringing them liberation.

The fast and versatile Mosquitoes greatly enhanced the capability of Bomber Command; they were used to mark targets, to bomb and as night fighters. Flight Lieutenant Paddy Engelbach (MH 1936) spent two years at Oxford reading languages before training as a night fighter pilot and flying Mosquitoes on operations from the middle of 1943 with 141 Squadron. On the night of 27 June 1944 he was protecting an operation against flying bomb sites when his Mosquito

was attacked over Holland by a German fighter. Engelbach was at 20,000 feet when suddenly his navigator ordered 'hard over on to the reciprocal'. As he threw the aircraft over there was a series of judders as the tail was shot off and the plane went into a spin. At about 2,500 feet it disintegrated, killing the navigator, but Engelbach was blown out through the canopy, only managing to open his parachute just before hitting the ground. The circumstances of his survival were nothing short of miraculous, a fact he acknowledged in a poem he wrote as a prisoner in Stalag Luft III about his near-death experience which ends,

> But this I know, that as you go to meet your Lord
> A strange warm comfort calms you with its kiss.

Vitry les Nogent – graves of Derek Law and Richard Stainbank.

Belying the statistics of Bomber Command stood those with a richer combination of skill and luck. One was Wing Commander Arthur Ingham (MH 1925), School Prae, Engineering Scholar, Shooting VIII for two years and the best middle-distance runner in the School. He worked for the family wool-merchant business in Manchester before joining the RAFVR in 1935. He completed his first tour of operations during the Ruhr battle of mid-1943 and was awarded the DFC. After a spell as an instructor, for which he was awarded the AFC, he joined 97 Squadron in the elite Lancaster Pathfinder force as a flight commander in May 1944. Tall and balding, older than most and not given to talking much about his experiences, Ingham was regarded as a superbly calm operational captain. He needed this on 18 August 1944, when the squadron was ordered to attack U-Boat pens and oil storage tanks at Bordeaux. It was thought to be an easy target, but as they turned in towards it, they met a terrifying wall of flak. Ingham in the leading aircraft flew unswervingly at the target, calling furiously for support on the radio-telephone. They were bracketed by flak as they came in to bomb, the searing metal tearing through wings and fuselage, wrecking the electrics and flaps, holing tanks and wounding two crew members. Somehow Ingham got them home with two engines gone and crash-landed just over the coast at Tangmere.

A week later Ingham was given his own command, 83 Squadron, another crack Pathfinder unit. He took on the role of master bomber, orbiting the target for long periods under fire while giving instructions to the main force to drop their bombs on the coloured markers. He led the devastating raid on Darmstadt on 11 September which destroyed 70 per cent of the city, and then on 18 December against German naval units in the port of Gdynia in Poland, one of the longest bombing raids of the war, for which he was awarded the DSO. His citation referred to 'this brave pilot executing his attack with the greatest coolness and skill in spite of fierce fire'. He ended the war as a Group Captain and one of the most respected and decorated officers in

Logbook of F/L Paddy Engelbach June, 1944. 'Failed to return… but I did a year later!!'

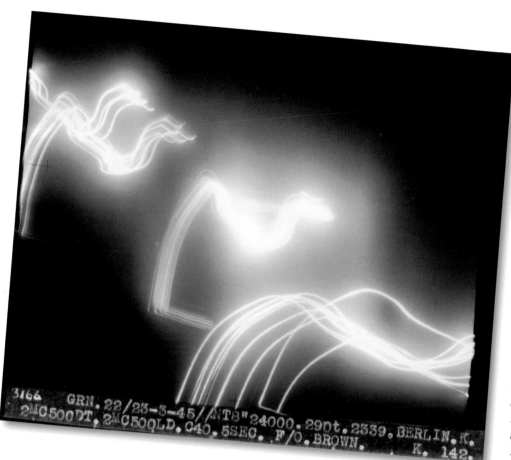

Searchlights over Berlin – the pilot's view at 24,000 feet March, 1945.

Bomber Command, surviving three tours of operations before returning to his family business.

Along the path the bombers took into Germany lie two huge cemeteries, Reichswald Forest near Kleve and Rheinberg near Wesel. Nearly 7,000 Commonwealth airmen lie here, most brought after the war from isolated graves where their plane crashed, perhaps beside a river or on the edge of a forest. The brotherhood of death here is a reminder of what we owe to so many young men of Bomber Command whose sacrifice has been marred by controversy over the area bombing policy and who were shamefully denied the full honour due to them at the end of the war. In the safety of peace, civilians and politicians tried to forget the role and sacrifice of Bomber Command. 'I don't like what I have

to do,' wrote one pilot in a letter to his mother just before he was killed, 'but I know I must carry on and do what my pals who have not returned would have done. I shall try to forget the horrors we are committing.' In cemeteries across Germany, France and Holland, you will find other young Tonbridge airmen, the promise of their lives cut short by unimaginably violent death. At Tuddenham parish church in Suffolk, near the airfield from where Derek Law and Richard Stainbank flew their last operation, a plaque commemorates crews who died. The inscription serves for Law and Stainbank and for all Tonbridgians of Bomber Command:

Went the day well? We died and never knew.
But well or ill, Freedom, we died for you.

BILL BROWN

Bill Brown was at School House from 1934 to 1939, winning a place at Cambridge to read Engineering. He was a founder member of the Air Training Section under Jimmy Watts, about which he still enthuses. He much enjoyed Tonbridge, making plenty of good friends, but remembers it as a tougher place than the school he visits now, the living conditions in School House spartan and the food 'unspeakable'.

He tried to enlist in the RAFVR in 1939 but there were too many applicants for aircrew at that time and he was sent away to complete his degree before being called up in 1941. For pilot training he was sent to California and, after getting his wings, he was posted, somewhat to his surprise, to a Flying Training School as an instructor. In 1944 he volunteered for an operational tour on Mosquitos and on 30 November 1944 joined 142

Squadron at Gransden Lodge near Cambridge, together with his Canadian navigator, Pilot Officer Mitchell. Instructors were often recruited into Pathfinder Force Mosquitos because they were skilled in instrument flying.

The Mosquito Mark XXV used for bombing was the fastest piston-engined aircraft of the war. It could carry a 4,000lb bomb load but was otherwise unarmed to give it greater speed. 142 Squadron's Mosquitoes could fly in any weather and high enough, about 30,000 feet, to elude the German defences more easily than a Lancaster.

Losses in the Mosquito squadrons were lower than in the main bomber force. Bill believes that for a Mosquito pilot the risk of getting 'the chop' was almost solely a matter of flying skill, whereas for a Lancaster pilot luck played a bigger part. Lancasters had to fly at only 18,000 feet making them more exposed to flak, while their comparative lack of speed made them more vulnerable to night fighters on both legs of the operation. Nevertheless a Mosquito was not easy to fly – 'like a Formula One racing car, one just had control of its instability' – and many aircraft were lost in accidents or through momentary and fatal loss of concentration on the part of the pilot.

Bill Brown completed his first operation on 1 December 1944, bombing Karlsruhe successfully despite a faulty navigation system. He recalled: 'I flew on ops on my second day with the Squadron. It didn't do to keep people waiting around because they got nervous. It was an awe-inspiring feeling, one's first trip on ops. You taxi out, then down the flarepath and into the blackness. You know that there is nothing except your own flying skill to get you back. Very few people carry the ultimate responsibility in life, that unless you do things right, you are dead. It is a very good teacher, you learn quickly.'

Bill Brown's logbook.

Group of all Public School Air Squads at Camp, RAF Tangmere, July 1939.

On the night of 13 March 1945 in K-King he took off for Berlin with four 500lb bombs, dropped them successfully through some radar-predicted flak, which burst accurately among the bombing Mosquitos at about 25,000 feet, and then turned for home. The return leg was quicker, the aircraft more responsive with no bomb load, and the height was held at about 25,000 feet to make fighter interception difficult. Back at base, however, fog had reduced visibility to 200 yards and landing required immense concentration on instruments. This time the aircraft ahead had not confirmed it was clear of the runway and the Control Tower did not respond to Bill's request to land, so he had to take a sudden decision to open up the throttle and go round again, 'not a pleasant experience at 200 feet, on instruments and in the foggy dark after a tiring operation', and potentially fatal if he had allowed the speed to drop – but he landed safely.

Bill Brown completed 45 operations in all, including 21 to Berlin. He was promoted Flight Lieutenant and awarded the DFC before the end of the war brought a return to Cambridge and his engineering career. In his sunset years he has been a regular and welcome visitor to his old school, teaching the young about the role of the bomber offensive and the joys and sorrows it brought. 'For me,' he wrote, 'the School and the RAF were golden days – *gaudeamus igitur juvenes summus'*.

CHAPTER 9:

SPECIAL OPERATIONS

The Special Operations Executive (SOE) was set up in July 1940 to conduct subversive warfare. Churchill, looking for a way to carry the fight to the enemy at the nadir of Britain's fortunes, issued an order to 'set Europe ablaze' by organising and arming national resistance to Nazi rule. Operations were controlled by sections, each assigned to a single country. European sections were controlled from London or Cairo, while in the Far East the SOE base was in Ceylon, all of them operating under conditions of extreme difficulty. The dangers of working in enemy territory were compounded by rivalries between different political groups both inside and outside the countries concerned. Agents could be under no illusions about the fate that awaited them if they were captured by either the Germans or the Japanese, whose secret police operations were both effective and brutal.

Recruitment of agents was so largely a matter of accident that there was nothing which deserved the name of a system. In practice, SOE recruited a wide variety of characters and skills, although a level head and a steady nerve were important, as was fluency in the language of the country. The ruthless types who made good saboteurs were seldom patient enough to undertake the relentless and often tedious task of building and training a resistance circuit, and were not suited at all to the

dull and dangerous work of a wireless operator in enemy territory, but all three were needed. Courage was certainly vital, the kind which allowed you to operate often alone in hostile territory, knowing that one mistake or just sheer bad luck could mean capture by an enemy who would show no mercy.

Five Tonbridgians are known to have worked for SOE, all coincidentally entering Tonbridge as boarders within a year or so of each other, in the 1920s. They operated in totally different but equally dangerous environments – in France, Yugoslavia, Malaya and Norway – and only four of them survived. All of them were wartime volunteers without any previous military or intelligence experience, but there does not seem to be much by way of a common thread in their school backgrounds or later. Something they all had, however, was courage and resourcefulness and a real love of the peoples and countries in which they operated. Their stories are each in their own ways remarkable testimonies to human courage and endurance.

Jasper Rootham (MH 1924) was a golden schoolboy: top academic, actor, musician, and school prae, and a double first in Classics at Cambridge. In 1933 he joined the Treasury, but was seconded in 1938 to the Prime Minister's office, as one of Chamberlain's secretaries, in which role he was the conduit for dialogue between the Foreign Office and Downing Street in the lead-up to Munich. He wanted to join the Army in 1939 but was frustrated by Civil Service rules requiring him to stay in post.

John Colville, who succeeded him as Private Secretary to Chamberlain, describes in his diary this frustration: 'I lunched with Jasper Rootham at White's. He has resigned from the Treasury and will join up next month. He complains that the Government makes provision for conscientious objectors, but none for those who are forbidden to fight and conscientiously object to not doing so.'

He succeeded and was recruited into SOE in Cairo. His fluency in Russian and Serbo-Croat made him a valuable asset in SOE's Balkan operations, and in May 1943 he was dropped by parachute into northern Serbia as part of a British mission to General Mihailovic, leader of the resistance movement loyal to King Peter of Yugoslavia. Yugoslav resistance to the Germans was

unique not only because it was fought as a more overt military campaign, but also because it was accompanied by a brutal civil war between the two principal resistance factions, the royalist Chetniks and Tito's Communist partisans, for whom the war created the opportunity for revolution.

Rootham spent a year from 1943–4 with Mihailovic, liaising between him and Cairo and providing military assistance. He was involved in Chetnik military operations, including the destruction of a bridge at Visegrad in 1943, and lived with the fear and consequences of savage German reprisals. His main problem however was political, as he strove to win British Government support for Mihailovic at the same time as others were persuading it to switch to Tito. While Churchill's support initially and sentimentally gravitated to the royalists, growing evidence suggested that Tito's partisans were offering more effective resistance and would be the likely winners in the civil war, while there was also the Russian factor to consider as the Red Army advanced on the Balkans.

Editors of The Phoenix. *Jasper Rootham is centre right.*

Rootham therefore found himself on a mission doomed to end tragically. The rival forces were by now fighting each other, as Tito tried to invade Mihailovic's Serbian strongholds and accused him of collaborating with the Italians and Germans to forestall him. These accusations were not without foundation, but Mihailovic was adept at facing both ways, his main aim being to restore by any means the Yugoslav monarchy he served. Rootham fell ill with malaria in May 1944 and was flown out of Yugoslavia to the SOE base in southern Italy, from where he was not allowed to return. He left a vivid diary of his mission, which became the basis for a book, *Miss-Fire*, published in 1946 and described in a review by Evelyn Waugh as 'irresistibly readable'. In it he recalls his sad final days with the Chetniks as they waited for the British liberation of their country which never came.

At the end of the war Mihailovic was put on trial and executed by Tito's new government and Rootham was refused permission by the Foreign Office to testify on his behalf. The only saving grace of this murky period of history was that Britain retained a generally good relationship with Tito in the Cold War. Rootham however remained loyal to the memory of Mihailovic, believing for the rest of his life that his government had made a tragic error.

David Howarth (JH 1926) became famous as the author of *The Shetland Bus*, a wartime operation which he organised. He worked pre-war as a BBC radio reporter, forming a close friendship with Richard Dimbleby, with whom he recorded Chamberlain's 'peace in our time' speech on the tarmac of Heston airport. After serving as a war correspondent in France and at Dunkirk, Howarth joined the RNVR and moved in 1941 to the Shetlands where, under the aegis of SOE, he was the controller of 'The Shetland Bus'. This used Norwegian fishing boats and their crews to take agents, arms and wireless transmitters into occupied Norway, and to bring out Norwegian volunteers and information. 'To

Jasper Rootham (centre in uniform) with Chetnik guerillas, Yugoslavia, 1943.

Judde House, 1927. David Howarth in row behind housemaster, seventh from right. John Crofton in row behind him, second from left. Walter Mason back row second from right, Edric Selous to his right.

take the Shetland Bus' became synonymous in Norway for escape to freedom.

At first they had 14 fishing boats available, their crews 'men of the coast' who had come across the North Sea in their own boats and had detailed local knowledge. The most famous was Leif Larsen, who made over 50 journeys to and from Norway. The difficulties of operating in wild North Sea conditions, without lights and under constant threat of German attack, can scarcely be imagined. By the end of the war these boats, in 1943 replaced by faster submarine chasers, had made nearly 200 journeys, inserting over 200 agents and bringing out more than 400 people. Nearly 40 crewmen were lost to German attacks or to the sea. Larsen himself had his boat sunk by German aircraft in 1943 and had to row for several days to make the Norwegian coast.

For Norwegians the Shetland Bus was of enormous practical and psychological importance, proving that life and hope outside occupied Norway existed. It also kept a large German garrison in the country, which might have been deployed elsewhere, and there was a tragic cost in terms of civilian reprisals. Howarth was knighted by the Norwegian government, and became a well-known popular historian, including the best-sellers *The Shetland Bus* and *We Die Alone* about his wartime work.

John Davis (Sc 1925) sought a life of adventure in the Empire by joining the Malayan Police in 1930. His Tonbridge background as Captain of boxing, two years in the 1st XV as a prop forward, and winner of the Swimming Cup, as well as a School Prae, was a very suitable preparation for this career, which gave wide-ranging responsibility to him at an early age.

He commanded various police districts and became fluent in both Malay and Cantonese, which made him important enough to the security of Malaya to be denied permission to

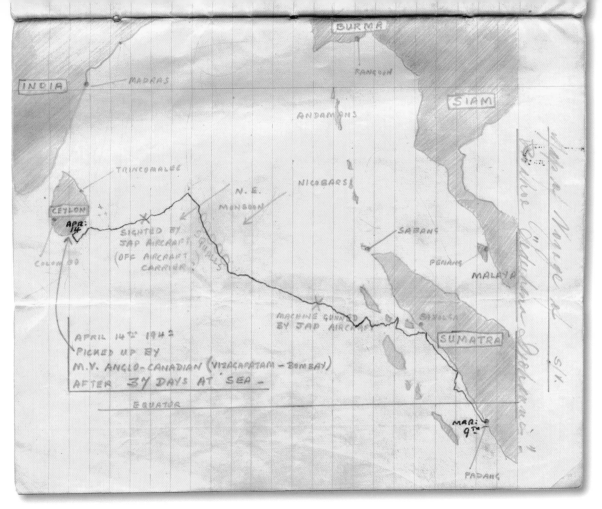

Map of the voyage of the Sederhana Djohanis, *February, 1942.*

join the army in 1939. Instead he was transferred to the Special Branch in Singapore with responsibility for intelligence on the Malayan Communist Party (MCP). As the Japanese threat increased, his command of languages, intimate knowledge of the countryside and its various peoples from his police work, and his powers of leadership brought him to the attention of SOE and a key role with them in planning and executing future resistance.

By January 1942 it was clear that Singapore was doomed, and SOE's plan was to infiltrate 'stay-behind parties' into Malaya to co-ordinate local resistance, provide intelligence about the Japanese and carry out sabotage operations. The cooperation of Chinese communists was essential to the success of this plan, and Davis's knowledge of them made him invaluable. He established supply dumps in the Malayan jungle and took Chinese volunteers up country by car and boat to insert them behind Japanese lines.

In early February, as Singapore was besieged, Davis crossed to Sumatra to establish an SOE base for future operations. Events were however moving too fast, and on 8 March all the Dutch East Indies surrendered to the Japanese. It was now desperately important to keep vital SOE personnel out of Japanese hands, so a small Malay sailing boat was found, the *Sederhana Djohanis*, and 16 European SOE officers were ordered to sail it to Ceylon. By an extraordinary coincidence the SOE naval officer responsible for finding the boat was another Tonbridgian, **Alexander Lind (Sc 1929)**, who had been working in insurance in Singapore before the war, joining the RNVR in 1939 and then SOE in December 1941. In February 1942 he commanded a motor launch working with Davis to insert guerilla groups behind Japanese lines, but was ordered to Sumatra just before Singapore fell.

The crossing from Sumatra to Ceylon in the *Sederhana Djohanis* was over 1,700 miles, took 38 days and was an epic in its own right. The 65-foot boat was purpose-built for coastal trading and unsuited to ocean voyages. Short of both food and water, strafed by Japanese aircraft and desperately trying to avoid Japanese ships in seas they now completely controlled, they finally sighted Ceylon and were picked up by a British freighter. One officer remembered the importance of Davis's 'majestic self-assurance and great physical strength' in this ordeal, while Lind's part in sailing and navigating the boat was also vital. He

returned to service in the Royal Navy, finishing as Flag Officer under Admiral Cunningham and returning with him to Singapore on the day of the Japanese surrender.

Davis remained in the SOE Malaya section known as Force 136. Its initial goal was to restore contact with guerilla forces in the Malayan jungle, including survivors of the original stay-behind parties. Davis was adamant that he should lead the first mission to establish that contact, despite the fact that a white European would stand out like a sore thumb among the local population. On 24 May 1943 he and five Chinese agents made a blind landing from a Dutch submarine on the Perak coast and hacked their way inland through the jungle to establish a camp. Having embedded his agents into the area, Davis was picked up by submarine in late June and returned to Colombo.

Alex Lind (right) and John Davis (behind him with beard) escaping from Sumatra on the Sederhana Djohnanis.

In August 1943 he returned to Perak for what turned out to be the rest of the war, organising and training the guerillas in subversive warfare with the help of the local MCP leader Chin Peng, who became a firm friend. In December 1943, as personal representative of Mountbatten, Davis signed an agreement with the MCP and other elements of the anti-Japanese resistance, promising arms and money in return for stirring up labour disputes and sabotaging Japanese communications.

The problems of bringing under one operational command all the anti-Japanese forces in Malaya were considerable, as there were not only internal political differences between the MCP and others, but also scattered groups elsewhere in the jungle commanded by British

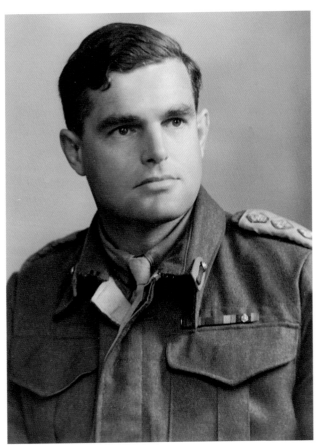

John Davis.

officers, some of whom had been there since 1942. The Japanese were now becoming increasingly successful in uncovering resistance, and in March 1944 Davis's camp was overrun, arms supplies and wireless sets lost and many of his agents arrested. SOE in Ceylon lost contact and feared he must be dead, but he had escaped deeper into the jungle with Chin Peng's guerillas.

In February 1945 another SOE operative found out that Davis was alive; wireless contact was re-established and arms and training officers brought in. Davis was awarded the DSO for his outstanding leadership under dangerous and difficult conditions, promoted full Colonel and given control of all Force 136 personnel and operations in Malaya. His task now was to organise the resistance in advance of a planned Allied landing, but this was overtaken by the dropping of the atomic bombs and Japan's surrender.

His final role as the most trusted guerilla leader in Malaya was to initiate the process of Japanese disarmament and the peaceful disbandment of the guerillas. He then joined the Malayan Civil Service and found himself developing successful counter-insurgency strategies against his former allies when the Communists under Chin Peng staged a violent insurgency against British rule from 1948–60.

When Davis died in 2006, aged 96, a tribute from Chin Peng, friendship now restored, was read at his funeral: 'I remember John as an implacable leader in the most harrowing of circumstances. On one occasion in Perak an arms drop went terribly wrong. Parachutes landed in the wrong place and we came under heavy Japanese machine-gun fire. I looked across at John and he appeared calm and in control.' Davis not only endured huge danger in the jungles of Malaya, at any moment liable to betrayal and Japanese torture and execution, but also proved himself a born leader and organiser of resistance forces.

Desmond Hubble (PH 1923) became a director of the family business in London in the 1930s, and joined the Intelligence Corps when war broke out. He went as a cipher officer to the Belgian Congo, where the task was to subvert Vichy French colonies in Africa, but he returned to England in 1942 to be recruited into SOE for the same kind of work.

In late 1943 he moved into SOE's RF Section, set up to liaise with de Gaulle and the Free French in creating a unified resistance movement inside France for sabotage and intelligence-gathering. Hubble's recruiter to RF Section was Wing Commander Frederick Yeo-Thomas, famous as 'The White Rabbit', who parachuted into France twice on missions in 1943 and February 1944, when he was arrested in Paris by the Gestapo. Yeo-Thomas became a friend and tried to persuade Hubble, as a married man with three children, not to volunteer for dangerous operational work. Hubble however wanted to achieve something special in his life before the war came to an end and volunteered for one of the 80 Jedburgh teams dropped into France in June 1944 to co-ordinate the local resistance with allied invasion strategy and arrange supplies of arms.

Hubble's Jedburgh team, codenamed 'Citronelle', supported the Ardennes Maquis in the area of Charleville-Mezieres. On the night of 5 June 1944 he parachuted into a field near Thilay in military uniform and was picked up by a reception committee. He was taken to a farm where he announced, to huge excitement, that the invasion was happening as he spoke. Over the next week he began his role of organising and training the Maquis in the nearby forest of Manises to assist Allied ground forces when they eventually liberated the area. On 6 June the Ardennes Maquis had rashly issued a mobilisation order calling on young men of the area to come and join them. This proved to be a fatal error, based on an over-optimistic view of

Desmond Hubble working for SOE in Sierra Leone, 1941.

the likely progress of the invasion forces, and it was a threat which the still powerful German forces in the area could not ignore. German planes tracked the path of Maquis recruits into the mountainous, pine-covered forest between Revin and Fumay, overlooking the River Meuse. Hubble and the other Allied officers with Citronelle must have viewed events with considerable alarm.

On the morning of 12 June, about 3,000 German troops, including Waffen SS, created an armoured cordon round the area and entered the forest, where the first clashes occurred with groups of maquisards, who were seriously outnumbered and unable to compete with the enemy's superior training and firepower. Over 100 were captured and taken to a location in the forest, where graves had already been dug, and were then shot four or five men to each grave. Three-quarters of them were under 25 years old and the youngest was only 16, a tragedy of huge proportions for the local community. When the Germans attacked, Hubble was away from the main Maquis encampment on a reconnaissance mission with an American officer, Victor Layton. They ran into a German patrol and, while Layton escaped, Hubble was captured still in his army uniform. As a British officer with potentially important intelligence information he avoided the immediate fate of the maquisards and was taken to local Gestapo headquarters, where

Desmond Hubble depicted in a sketch done in Buchenwald in September 1944, just before his execution.

but some women prisoners crawled along to the men with cups of water, including Violette Szabo, celebrated heroine of the film *Carve Her Name With Pride*.

The next day the men parted company from the women and were driven across the German border, Hubble now shackled to Yeo-Thomas. Just before Saarbrucken, they turned into the grim hutted camp of Neue Bremm, surrounded by watchtowers and barbed wire and notorious as a torture camp, where prisoners were held for a short time to try to break them before transfer elsewhere. The 37 prisoners were chained in five-man groups and locked in a tiny hut – 37 men in an area less than ten feet square, sweltering in the heat of summer. Hubble's British uniform seemed to inspire particular hatred among the guards as they punched and kicked him. They stayed there four days and witnessed many scenes of SS brutality towards helpless prisoners. Hubble commented to Yeo-Thomas that 'if this is an example of German culture, the sooner the bastards are wiped out the better.'

They left by train on 15 August. Hubble had with him a small bundle of personal effects including a pipe and pocket chess set given him by his mother. At about midnight the prisoners' carriage was shunted into a siding within a large barbed wire compound about five miles north of Weimar. They had arrived at Buchenwald, built as a concentration camp in 1937. Up to 1941 the camp housed only 10,000 prisoners, but by the time Hubble and his party arrived numbers had grown to over 80,000, including Jews and many captured resisters from all over Europe. Total SS disregard for prisoner welfare had resulted in appalling living conditions and a very high death rate by 1944, and formal executions were commonplace. Yeo-Thomas described the sinister atmosphere on their arrival 'as though some unseen danger stalked around us'.

he was interrogated and then transferred to prison in Paris.

On 8 August, only two weeks before the liberation of the city, a train filled with captured SOE agents from all over France left Paris for Germany. All of them had been tortured while in Gestapo custody and were now chained. Much of what subsequently happened has been recounted by Yeo-Thomas, who was particularly distressed to find there his friend Hubble. Within an hour of leaving Paris the train came under Allied air attack and was disabled. The temperature in the carriages increased rapidly,

Hubble and the others were stripped, disinfected, showered and heads shaved. They were then issued with a pair of wooden clogs and a distinctive blue-and-white striped prison uniform. Formal registration followed, with an identity number and a red cloth triangle to sew on their clothes, indicating they were political prisoners. They were then marched to one of the huts, Block 17, filled with bunk beds up to the ceiling. Hubble and Yeo-Thomas teamed up again to share a bunk bed. An SOE prisoner who had preceded them warned that they were in 'one of the worst concentration camps, that life was dreadful, the death rate appalling and that they must be very careful'. Step by step they became accustomed to an immense unfolding horror.

They shared what small possessions they had, including Hubble's stick of shaving soap, and Yeo-Thomas tried to maintain a rigorous group discipline. They also held a chess tournament, using Hubble's pocket set, and a bridge competition with home-made cards. It is not difficult to imagine the sense of dread which Buchenwald must have aroused, all of them already weakened by months of brutal ill-treatment, but the comradeship in the group helped to raise spirits. Yeo-Thomas and Hubble were sketched by a French inmate and spent much time talking about their plans for life after the war. Yeo-Thomas recalled that 'Hubble and I became inseparable. We resolved to do all in our power to remain cheerful and to boost the morale of those around us. We were truly happy together, enjoying little jokes, reminiscing, sharing everything. Hubble would talk about his children, his family'.

Then on 9 September, three and a half weeks after their arrival in Buchenwald, the blow fell. An announcement over the camp loudspeaker ordered Hubble and 15 other members of the group to report to the main gate. There seemed no reason for it beyond a possible routine examination and, after a few brief words with the others, they marched off. An uneasy Yeo-Thomas asked a German prisoner if he could explain the group's summons and was told: 'I do not think you will see your comrades again.' Not until three days later, on 12 September, did any news come. Two other prisoners working in the execution block reported that the 16 had been held in the cellars of the crematorium for two days and nights, during which they were brutally beaten. Then at 5.30pm on 11 September they were taken out in groups and hanged by nooses from hooks let into a wall, suffering slow strangulation over the five to ten minutes they took to die. The bodies were then immediately burned in the ovens of the crematorium. Hubble's notebook fell from his body as he died and was later returned to his family.

Yeo-Thomas and just six of the original 37 survived. He returned the pipe and chess set to Hubble's children, and wrote to Hubble's mother: 'Desmond was one of the finest men I have ever met and one of the bravest. He never faltered, never weakened and no man could have had a better friend than he turned out to be. As long as I live, I will never forget him. He did his duty quietly and without fuss. His family can be very, very proud of him.' News of what happened to Hubble and the others only reached London in April 1945.

On the outskirts of Revin, on a small winding road into the forest overlooking the valley of the Meuse, stands a monument on which is inscribed '*Aux Mortes du Maquis des Manises*'. On it are inscribed over 100 names, all male and grouped to show family ties composed mostly of those killed by the Germans in the mass executions in the forest. One name stands out because it is English, Desmond Ellis Hubble, honoured with equal respect here and at the memorial service held every year.

CHAPTER 10:

MEDITERRANEAN SOLDIERS
AND AIRMEN

When France fell and Italy entered the war in June 1940, the Mediterranean became the only battleground on which British land forces could engage the enemy. The initial strategic imperative of preserving Britain's position in the Middle East, her oil supplies and the Suez Canal meant that the Mediterranean became fiercely contested with fighting stretching from Gibraltar to Greece, from Iraq to Tunisia and the committed involvement of all three services. In 1943 the invasion of Sicily and then Italy opened the way to the eventual liberation of Europe, but became one of the hardest-fought and most gruelling campaigns of the war in which 20 Tonbridgians died, adding to the similar number killed in North Africa.

One unlikely bomber pilot in the Middle East was the Reverend Walter Mason (JH 1922), ordained in 1934 and a curate in Pimlico before departing for missionary work in Africa. He had learned to fly at university, so was called up and sent to Egypt as a pilot of Blenheim light bombers

Outside the Mess tent at ATS Camp, Norton Priory, July 1939. Jimmy Sowrey second from left.

Jimmy Sowrey 1941, seated on a Hurricane.

operating against Italian forces in Libya. Mason was known as 'The Friar' by his fellow officers, and at one point conducted his wing leader's marriage, but he was a fine pilot who insisted he should take part in bombing raids as well as reconnaissance and must have been one of the few priests in a combat role. At sunrise on 29 June 1940, nine Blenheims bombed the airfield at Tobruk, where two squadrons of Italian fighters were stationed, but enough fighters managed to get off the ground to massacre the slow and vulnerable bombers. Mason's plane was shot down in flames.

The range involved in the flight from England meant that many of the fighter reinforcements for Egypt and Malta had to come via West Africa or be flown in from carriers. The Sowrey brothers were among the first Hurricane pilots to arrive in the Western Desert. John Sowrey (FH 1933) was a Cranwell cadet who flew Lysanders in France in 1940 dropping supplies to troops, but then converted to Hurricanes. In May 1941 he embarked on a troopship to Takoradi on the Gold Coast, where Hurricanes were re-assembled for flying across Africa to Egypt. This was a challenging journey in a single-engined fighter with minimal navigation equipment and had to be done in several

stages. He found himself being guided across Africa by Flight Lieutenant Peter Farr (WH 1932), his Tonbridge contemporary, and on arrival in Cairo he found his brother, Jimmy Sowrey (FH 1935), another Hurricane pilot had also just arrived. A massive party resulted, somewhat tempered by the Provost Marshal, who wanted to halt proceedings on the grounds of them being improperly dressed. It was to be the last time he would see his brother.

Jimmy Sowrey had been one of the founding cadets of the Air Training Section, attending the camp at Tangmere with Bill Brown in July 1939. He had flown Hurricanes in defence of London in the winter of 1940/1 before transfer to the Middle East. His experience in England availed him little as, only two weeks after his fortuitous meeting with John at the Cairo party, he was shot down in flames by three ME109s on 24 June 1941. Five months later one of the surviving Battle of Britain pilots, Joseph Hobbs (JH 1929), was also shot down and killed, and both are buried at Halfaya Sollum.

John Sowrey remained with the Desert Air Force until July 1942. Life in the desert was a lot more primitive than England. He slept in a tent with sacks and petrol tins for beds, but sometimes under the aircraft on a lilo, until his was punctured by camel thorn. It was very cold in winter, especially at night, and very hot in summer with plenty of flies, but, in spring, rain filled the wadis with beautiful flowers for a short time before the arid desert returned. Action was initiated from hastily improvised airstrips, from which the biggest rocks would be cleared, and maintenance of the planes was challenging, especially when sudden dust storms grounded aircraft. Officers and NCOs messed together, but it was only on infrequent leave in Cairo that real parties and female company could be enjoyed. During the retreat from Gazala to Alamein in 1942 they heard that the NAAFI at one airstrip was to be blown up, so they sent over a lorry to collect beer and cigarettes; one pilot subsequently found that you could keep beer cold in the flare chute of the Hurricane.

The skies were generally of an intense blue, with no clouds to escape into, but Sowrey was blessed with exceptional eyesight enabling him to spot enemy aircraft at great distance, although he yearned for a Spitfire to take on the ME109s. He had his first success on 15 June 1941 when he shot down two ME109s near Halfaya. His squadron was almost continually in action in the Western Desert and for a time against Vichy French forces in Syria. They moved from one airstrip to another as Eighth Army advanced and more generally retreated along the coast. The regular RAF barb at army officers they met was to ask them which retreat they were currently in. In June 1942 Sowrey was leading the wing when they met a formation of Stukas head on. He must have collided with one, as he found himself upside down and out of control, but managed to bale out, fortunately landing among friendly troops who returned him to the squadron two days later. When asked in later life what it was like when his aircraft was hit, he was unable to answer, for he saw more than enough horrific sights of friends going down in flames. He destroyed seven enemy aircraft in 18 months of continuous operations

before becoming an instructor. He returned to action in 1943 in the Mediterranean and then back in England as a Squadron Leader, flying Spitfires escorting bombers deep into Germany. For his long and sustained period of combat flying he was awarded the DFC in 1945 and retired from the RAF as an Air Commodore in 1968.

Peter Farr, who had led John Sowrey across Africa, had been flying transport aircraft in the Middle East since 1938. By 1941 he was therefore a veteran of desert air routes, carrying troops around and leading reinforcement aircraft on the long journey from West to East Africa across a landscape which to new arrivals appeared endless and threatening. In October 1941 he became a flight commander in a Wellington bomber squadron operating from advanced landing strips in the desert against enemy airfields and troops in support of Operation Crusader, the Eighth Army's advance through Cyrenaica. He saw his direct Welldon contemporary Roger Maggs (WH 1932), serving in the same squadron, shot down and killed on 5 March 1942. Farr was awarded the DFC for 'displaying courage and fearlessness in the face of the enemy' and eventually retired from the RAF in 1972 as an Air Vice-Marshal.

There was plenty to dislike about fighting in the desert. It was a vast tract of largely inhospitable land: stony scrub, almost bereft of trees and water, with boiling daytime temperatures and often freezing nights. The water provided in cans tasted so strongly of disinfectant that even the whisky was lost in it, the Egyptian flies were particularly agile and vicious, the dust covered everything, and there was little cover from shellfire. Major John Kirkaldy (FH 1925) used the names of School Praes, learned in his novi bumph test, as a mantra during shelling to take his mind off the possibility of sudden death. Twice he was buried under sand and dug out just in time, a memory which caused him to wake up screaming and sweating in later life.

John Sowrey, Western Desert 1942.

The campaign in North Africa lasted from 1940 until May 1943. The turning point was El Alamein in October 1942, a victory which caused the church bells to ring in Britain for the first time since the invasion scare of 1940, and one which cost the lives of five OTs and one member of staff, Captain Hector Chadwick. Two of the casualties, Major Deryck Boyd-Moss (PH 1926) and Major Denis Ward (PS 1926), had joined Tonbridge the same term, were professional soldiers in the Royal Tank Regiment, and were both killed within a day of each other. Boyd-Moss's father had been killed at Gallipoli and he had benefited from a War Memorial Fund bursary to come to Tonbridge as one of the last of Stokoe's boys.

Rapid pursuit of Rommel followed, but the German resistance hardened, and not until April 1943 was the final assault on Tunis launched and the war in Africa ended on 7 May. The fierceness of the fighting is shown by the fact that seven Tonbridgians were killed in this last two-week period, three of them in the same Royal West Kent battalion, including Sidney Keyes. Captain Hugh Walker (FH 1933) had a narrow escape in his first action with his Churchill tank squadron. In the attack on Tunis his tank lost its drive so could not be steered. Walker manoeuvred forwards and backwards down a road, under fire from German shells, then backed down into a minefield where Stukas attacked and blew off his tracks. Fifteen of the squadron's 18 tanks were lost that day, but Walker survived.

Working in an Egyptian hospital was Major John Crofton (JH 1925). Crofton had qualified with a first from Cambridge and served with a field ambulance south of Dunkirk in May 1940, learning how to operate at great speed and under huge pressure, eventually being evacuated through Brittany where he had to deal with the aftermath of an ammunition train hit by German bombers; 'I did not get all the blood off me until we landed in Portsmouth,' he later said. Sent to the Middle East,

he operated on wounded servicemen in both Egypt and then Malta, but also worked with tuberculosis patients. This became the basis of a lifetime's work. TB was then a leading cause of death but in 1950, building on his wartime work, Crofton discovered a treatment with the drug streptomycin, which meant that TB could now be successfully treated for as little as ten pounds per patient, a godsend in poorer countries. As Professor of Respiratory Diseases in Edinburgh, Crofton became a medical figure of great international stature and was consulted on TB until he died in 2009.

Meanwhile the island of Malta was under siege. Flying Officer Neville King (JH 1927) was one of its defenders, a fine rugby player at Tonbridge, who had joined the Metropolitan Police and by 1941 was a station inspector, coping with the worst of the Blitz. He decided he wanted to see more action and volunteered for the RAFVR, his courage and quick reactions making him a natural fighter pilot despite being nearly 30. He joined 603 Squadron, which embarked their Spitfires on USS *Wasp* in the Clyde in March 1942 and sailed for the Mediterranean. On the morning of 20 April these 47 Spitfires took off from the carrier, a hazardous operation in itself, and landed in Malta. King immediately found himself in the middle of the most intense fighting, regularly engaging enemy fighters and bombers, accounting for at least three enemy planes and having once to crash-land his damaged Spitfire. On 8 July he shot down an enemy bomber at low level but, as he turned away, his wing-tip touched the sea and he was lost. His ground crewman recorded in his diary: 'King failed to bale out. I nearly cried when I knew because he's the greatest guy I've met yet and that's saying a lot.'

Also based on Malta were Blenheim light bombers used to attack Axis shipping. Pilot Officer Alistair Ramsay (DB 1921) was a navigator in one of the crews. He had won the DFC on 4 July 1941 when 105 Squadron had taken part in a celebrated low-level raid on the German port of Bremen. Ramsay was navigating the plane of Wing Commander Hughie Edwards, awarded the VC for pressing home his attack at 50 feet despite the terrifying flak. Transferred very soon after to the equally hellish environment of Malta, Ramsay's squadron was called on again and again to attack enemy ships. On 1 August he launched a low-level attack on a tanker off Lampedusa and was shot down into the sea. The pilot survived but Ramsay died of his wounds and is buried in Sicily.

The preparations for the invasion of Sicily began immediately after the fall of Tunis. The plan included an airborne assault on the Ponte Grande, an important bridge near Syracuse, with troops landed by gliders. John Palmer (FH 1933), who had played in the 1936 Hockey XI before training as an architect, was one of the glider pilots. He was turned down by the RAF as they had too many volunteers, but after further strenuous efforts to escape from his army enlistment, including an irate letter to the War Office, he joined the newly formed Glider Pilot Regiment in January 1942 as one of their first volunteers. After training as a pilot, he was sent to North Africa in early 1943 to prepare for the assault on Sicily.

Glider pilots were a special breed of men, not only trained to fly but also expected to fight as infantry when they had landed. These gliders were towed behind transport aircraft and, even in the most benign conditions, posed considerable challenges for the pilot. Once the tow rope was released, the pilot had to nurse down his heavy, cumbersome machine somewhere near the objective and land lightly enough to disgorge safely the troops he was carrying. For the Sicily landings Palmer flew an American Waco glider, but his training on it was minimal and included less than

Staff Sergeant John Palmer (FH 1933), Glider Pilot Regiment.

an hour's night flying. His commanding officer was full of apprehension, realising that his men were desperately under-prepared for such a hazardous operation. Towed behind a Dakota, Palmer, carrying 20 infantry, took off on a night so dark that he could not even see the Sicilian coast when his tow rope was released, and the winds were so strong that keeping formation on the three-hour flight was very difficult. Palmer did well to land his glider not far from the objective as over half either landed in the sea or crashed miles away.

An early casualty in the invasion of Italy was Major Nigel Oswald (HS 1928), who had won the MC in Tunisia for re-establishing an abandoned position under enemy fire, but was killed at Salerno on 11 September. The subsequent fighting up both coasts of Italy and into the mountains was desperately tough. Gyles Longley (JH 1932) remembers stepping on a German anti-personnel mine, which sprung into the air at head height but miraculously failed to explode. Even today, when he steps on a twig and hears that little snap, his memory goes back to that moment. He won the MC at Salerno on 16 September 1943, while serving with 44th Reconnaissance Regiment, on the same

Nigel Oswald (HS 1928), killed at Salerno.

day as his great friend and step-cousin Roy Follit (PH 1931) was killed nearby while attached to 5th Hampshires, a battalion commanded by Lieutenant Colonel Richard Ward MC (MH 1919). Cassino, lynchpin of the German Gustav Line, held up the Allied advance in 1944 and cost four Tonbridge lives, including Anthony Graff (PH 1934), killed during the fiercely contested crossing of the River Garigliano and buried in the war cemetery below the iconic monastery.

One movingly descriptive account of the campaigns in Africa and Italy was provided by another doctor, Lieutenant Colonel Cedric Prowse (Sc 1917), School Captain in 1922 and in the cricket and rugby first teams. Gazetted to the RAMC in 1940, he landed in North Africa in November 1942 as part of Operation Torch and saw action all through the Tunisian campaign with 18th Casualty Clearing Station (CCS), providing the first emergency surgical treatment for wounded men close to the battlefield. He moved with this unit to Italy and stayed with them through that first terrible winter. He had by then been in the front line of battlefield medical care for 15 months.

By coincidence a colleague at 18th CCS was Lieutenant Colonel Hoadley Gabb (HS 1922), who had practised in East Sussex after winning squash and fives blues at Cambridge. Prowse described him as 'our specialist in anaesthesia but also the one who decided priorities for surgery'. Gabb had joined 18th CCS in 1939 and was militarily senior to Prowse who mused on their reversed roles because of 'my considerable seniority to Hoadley at school, where I had been School Captain when he was a new boy'. Gabb was transferred to command 8th CCS at Anzio, and later found himself treating his wounded younger brother Geoff (HS 1937), a subaltern in the Buffs who had won the MC.

Prowse wrote an evocative account of his experiences coping with the consequences of modern warfare. The CCS was stretched to the limit, not just by wounded soldiers but by various kinds of sickness, including venereal disease and malaria, and the harrowing treatment of injured Italian children who had stepped on mines. He recalled the 'poor boy who suddenly bled profusely from the stump of his amputated leg. I found a suitable vein in his good leg and poured in blood while Ernie tied the femoral artery in the other. The haemorrhage was controlled and colour returned to the boy's ashen cheeks.' Their first base in October 1943 at Termoli was in a school, damaged by shellfire, without running water inside the building, and very cold in winter. Prowse wrote: 'Every corner held a stretcher. Orderlies kneeled over them giving pain relief or a drink. MOs gauged fitness for surgery or for travel. Padres comforted the fearful and murmured last rites. Noble sights, sad sights, horrifying sights, all there to be seen and so few to attend to so many.' He was proud that 18th CCS had attended to over 5,000 casualties during December 1943 alone, often

Cedric Prowse greeting the Governors on Skinners' Day, 1923.

involving complex surgery for skeletal damage, burns and severe abdominal wounds. He noted his use of the new wonder drug penicillin for the first time 'with good but not spectacular results', and was also sent to Bari to cope with the aftermath of a ship blowing up with a cargo of mustard gas shells.

In January 1944, exhausted after a particularly gruelling four months in the Italian winter, 18th CCS was pulled out of the front line for a rest. Prowse was now promoted and given command of the medical division of 94 General Hospital in Naples, a more comfortable billet with better facilities. While there he visited another hospital where he found wounded who had passed through Hoadley Gabb's hands at Anzio. 'The chest wounds from Gabb's CCS all do well,' the physician in charge told him, a remark Prowse took as a compliment to himself as well, for he had taught Gabb his routine for the early treatment of chest wounds. Prowse, Gabb and John Crofton stand as witness to those many other Tonbridge doctors whose job was to save lives and who managed to retain their humanity among so much carnage.

Hoadley Gabb (left) and Cedric Prowse (right) at 18th CCS, North Africa.

NORMAN HEATLEY

Norman Heatley (PS 1924) saved more lives than any other Tonbridgian in the war, playing a crucial role in the discovery of penicillin, the first practical antibiotic. He was the best scientist of his year at Tonbridge, remembering his schooldays with affection, before going to Cambridge for his first degree and a PhD in biochemistry. In 1936 he moved to Oxford to work with Ernst Chain and Howard Florey in the School of Pathology, where he spent the rest of his working life.

Alexander Fleming had discovered penicillin by accident in 1928, but not until 1938 was serious research resumed at Oxford. When Florey and his team recognised the potential of penicillin for combating bacterial infection, they faced the problem of how to manufacture it in sufficient quantities to be of practical use in treating humans. That was Heatley's major contribution. He was a great improviser and used his practical skills to see a means of cultivating, extracting and purifying the penicillin, growing it on porcelain bedpans and biscuit tin lids he had collected for his laboratory, which effectively became the first penicillin factory and the means for the first experiments on humans.

He had also worked closely with Florey in the first successful experiments on mice in 1940, recording prosaically in his diary: 'After supper with some friends, I returned to the lab and met the professor to give a final dose of penicillin to two of the mice. The 'controls' were looking very sick, but the two treated mice seemed very well. I stayed in the lab until 3.45am, by which time all four control animals were dead.' On returning home he realised that in his haste he had put his underpants on back to front, which he also recorded in his diary, adding that 'it really looks as if penicillin may be of practical importance'. In early 1941 the first human patients were treated and the results published in *The Lancet*. Florey and Heatley then flew to America to organise mass production of the new wonder drug, which began by 1943 in time for its use in Sicily and Italy. Penicillin made a huge difference in the war in the treatment of infected wounds, saving an estimated 15 per cent of lives (and many limbs from amputation), while future millions around the world also benefited from one of the greatest medical advances of the 20th century.

Heatley is often regarded as the unsung hero of the discovery of penicillin. He said modestly of himself that 'I am not a very good scientist but I am good at improvising'. A colleague, however, made clear his importance: 'without Fleming, no Chain or Florey; without Florey, no Heatley; without Heatley, no penicillin.'

Norman Heatley PS, 1928.

CHAPTER 11:

THE END IN SIGHT

On 6 June 1944 Peter Bathurst (PS 1940) was walking to Tonbridge station to catch a train to Charterhouse when he heard the news of D-Day. Above him there was a constant rumble of bombers passing overhead on their way to Normandy. That afternoon, as Tonbridge subsided to a heavy defeat, he had the satisfaction of bowling out a future England captain, Peter May. Across the Channel many Tonbridgians, particularly those who had left during the war years, were experiencing battle for the first time. Sandy Smith was at Pegasus Bridge, wounded and holding on to positions dearly won the previous night; Desmond Hubble was with his Maquis group in the Ardennes, a sense of exhilaration abroad at the prospect of liberation; Pierre Jeannerat (PS 1914) was on Sword Beach, a war correspondent with the *Agence Francaise Independent*, returning to his homeland with the Free French forces. Others had a wide variety of roles that day.

At about the time Sandy Smith was landing by glider at Pegasus Bridge, Murray Christie (SH 1933), a platoon commander in 9th Battalion, Parachute Regiment, was parachuting into France, tasked with one of the night's more difficult jobs of destroying the four heavy guns of the Merville Battery immediately to the east of Sword Beach. Flak broke up the aircraft formations and made the drop chaotic, leaving the battalion scattered over a wide area, but the guns were destroyed and Christie moved with 9 Para to hold the high ground to the east of the River Orne. For nearly a week the exhausted battalion held out against relentless attacks from German troops and armour, a stubborn defensive action which allowed the whole Normandy bridgehead to be consolidated. On 11 June Christie led a counter-attack at the point of the bayonet to re-take a position, but was killed the next day by a shell just before the battalion was withdrawn. His grave can be found in the beautiful cemetery at Ranville, alongside so many other airborne troops whose desperate endeavours did so much to ensure the success of the invasion.

Stuart Hills had heard the planes carrying the airborne forces pass overhead as he crossed the Channel that night in his Landing Craft Tank (LCT), keyed up with anticipation at the prospect of his first action. The crossing had been rough and many of the soldiers seasick but, as dawn broke, he viewed the vast armada around him, thousands of ships of every size and shape, an awe-inspiring and unique moment. His DD Sherman tank of the Sherwood Rangers was meant to be launched two miles from Gold Beach, coming ashore with its own propeller, the driver under the waterline and the commander peering over a supposedly waterproof canvas screen. Sea conditions, however, were so bad, with the wind whipping up white tops to the waves, that the LCT brought them in much closer. Gradually the heavy ramp of the LCT was lowered and Stuart could see the narrow strip of beach, the enemy pill-boxes he was tasked to engage and the spouts of shells in the water around.

His was the leading tank, poised at the top of the ramp and clearly silhouetted. A shell slammed into the water just in front as he gave the order to go. The tank lumbered in and managed about 60 yards before it started sinking, probably a result of the earlier shell perforating the unarmoured plates beneath it. Frantically the crew scrambled into the dinghy, all their personal effects gone, to be picked up later by a launch, and next day were told to paddle into Gold with just the bedraggled clothes they stood up in. The Naval Beachmaster watched this 'invasion force' come ashore and declared that 'there would be consternation in Berlin'.

Gold Beach saw other Tonbridgians come ashore that day. Lieutenant Colonel George Fanshawe (PH 1915), commanding the 86th Field Regiment (Hertfordshire Yeomanry), became stuck on a sandbank in his landing craft and had to

Stuart Hills beside a Sherman tank, Normandy, 2002.

wade under fire for 300 yards in waist deep water. He recalled that in training for D-Day, a staff officer suggested that they were expecting 90 per cent casualties, but 'the divisions which followed should be all right' – a remark not calculated to improve morale. Artillery was to be a vital resource in the fierce battles which followed, and Fanshawe was awarded the DSO in December 1944. One of his young officers to land with him on D-Day was Stephen Perry (JH 1933). In early August Perry's troop of 25-pounder self-propelled guns (SP) was deployed near Jurcques when a German Tiger tank was spotted. Perry jumped into one SP and began a fierce and deadly duel, which ended when his eleventh round brought a cloud of smoke from the Tiger, a cool and corageous action recognised by the award of the MC.

The 4/7 Royal Dragoon Guards was another Sherman tank regiment to land on Gold. With them was a troop commander, Charles Pillman, who was killed on D-Day, while Clarence Hampton (MH 1927), the regimental signals officer, was wounded a few days later. The regimental doctor, Captain Samuel Hood (WH 1932), was a Cambridge Scholar who, with war approaching, forsook a certain First at Cambridge to complete his clinical qualifications as a doctor and join the army as soon as possible. In subsequent heavy fighting around Cristot he went back time and again under heavy fire to collect wounded men from both sides in his half-track, some of those recovered from shot-up tanks suffering terrible burns, but on 13 June, while attending to another wounded man, a sniper shot him dead.

Further west two Tonbridgians were helping American forces on D-Day. Alistair Birrell (HS 1936) was commanding an LCT carrying seven Sherman tanks and their American crews to Omaha Beach. He had left Plymouth on 5 June and rendezvoused at the Isle of Wight with the vast armada crossing the Channel on this historic but

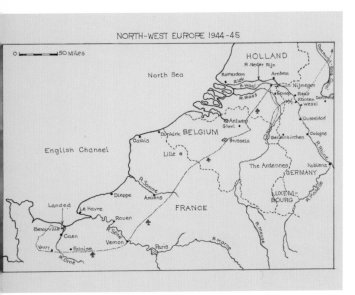

Route taken by John Hoare's RE Field Company, 1944–5.

General Montgomery crossing the Seine at Vernon on 'Goliath' bridge.

rough night. He had only been given his command a week previously and his American troops were also going into action for the first time. As he landed them at about mid-day the fighting had moved from 'bloody Omaha' to the heights beyond, and he watched the tanks move off the beach towards the battle. He often wondered about their fate.

Above him Dick Law (JH 1934), a Fleet Air Arm pilot, was flying Seafires spotting for the guns of American warships off Omaha. Venturing too close to a shore battery, he was shot down and crash-landed in no man's land behind Omaha, from where he was rescued by a very large American soldier, who offered him a swig from his water bottle containing a very acceptable vin rose. Later he was to win the DSC in the Far East, beating off the final kamikaze attack of the war.

A little further east John Hoare (FH/SH 1934) came ashore on Sword Beach. He had become a regular soldier in the Royal Engineers after leaving Tonbridge, which he still remembers fondly for his good education and the professionalism of the OTC. By early 1944 he was second-in-command of a Field Company RE, training on the Humber

to build Bailey bridges, one of the great British inventions of the war. Hoare moved under fire on D-Day to Pegasus Bridge, which he found intact after the glider assault of the previous night, and in the next three days his company built two more bridges across the Orne Canal, each about 300 feet across, to increase the flow of troops and equipment into the eastern part of the bridgehead. As the Allies broke out of Normandy, so Hoare and his Field Company followed close behind the leading infantry. Under German artillery fire they bridged the Seine at Vernon in two days with a 700-foot span, which needed a convoy of over 300 vehicles to bring up the parts. Further bridges followed in Belgium and Holland, including a massive structure across the River Maas. The skills and courage of these field companies, often under fire, were extremely important in preserving the momentum of the advance.

As the invasion forces moved slowly inland, so the Normandy campaign became the most costly fought by the British Army since the Great War, the casualty rate comparable to the Somme, especially among junior officers. The reason for this was partly the tenacity of the German defence, but also the ideal defensive country of the Normandy bocage. It was broken country, pieces of high ground descending into valleys and criss-crossed by numerous streams, with few main roads but many narrow lanes sunk beneath high banks topped by hedgerows. Tanks and infantry working together were regularly subjected to the close-range ambush fire of Spandau machine-guns, mortars and Panzerfaust anti-tank weapons from enemy positions almost impossible to spot.

In an attack on Fontenay on 25 June, Stuart Hills's tank was in the lead, moving down a narrow, sunken lane. The infantry was moving cautiously in single file and suddenly went to ground as they heard the sound of an incoming shell, which exploded with a blinding flash just in front of Hills's tank, shattering the driver's periscope. Three of the infantry stayed down and then a machine-gun opened up, the infantry scattering and bullets hitting the tank like the rat-tat-tat of a hammer. Hills put two shells into the enemy machine-gun position, enabling the infantry to move forward again. The infantry may have been more vulnerable to small-arms fire but tank crews feared the direct hit from an armour-piercing shell which invariably caused the Sherman to

The Normandy bocage – narrow lanes, high banks, stout hedges.

catch fire, giving the crew only a second or two to escape before the ammunition inside exploded.

One infantry casualty in this fighting was Arthur Woodland (PH 1937), a recent 1st XV centre, killed near Tilly-sur-Seulles. Another was Private David Pipe (PS 1938), who had only left school in 1942. He served in a machine gun team of 8th Middlesex in the terrifying battles through the bocage and died of wounds on 24 August just as the Allies broke out of Normandy into the wider fields beyond. Long after the war John Wrightson, who had fagged for Pipe in Parkside and remembered him as someone who treated his juniors kindly, was returning from a holiday in France when he stopped by chance at the Tilly-sur-Seulles cemetery. He walked down a long line of headstones and suddenly found himself staring at Pipe's name. It took his mind back over the years to those shouts of 'Boy', to racing down the corridor of Parkside cubicles until he had reached Pipe's and then to the chore for which he had been called – shining his shoes, posting his mail, carrying his books or whatever. Every time John hears on Remembrance Sunday Binyon's 'they shall grow not old', he remembers Pipe, who reached only his 20th birthday.

In Normandy and the pursuit which followed, several Tonbridgians provided determined leadership. Richard Anderson (Sc 1921) came from 1st King's Own Royal Regiment to take over command of 2nd Infantry Brigade in October, winning the DSO in 1944, a bar to the DSO in 1945 and ending his distinguished army career as a Lieutenant-General. Bill Roberts (Sc 1926) took over 5th Wiltshires in August 1944 under very difficult circumstances after its previous CO had been killed and the battalion decimated in the assault on Mont Pincon. He too won the DSO in 1944, for his leadership in Normandy, and a bar in 1945 for gallantry during the Rhine Crossing. Dennis Talbot (DB 1922), last noted in a daring escape following the fall of Calais in 1940, took over command of 7th Hampshires in July 1944, leading them until the end of the war, winning an MC in 1944 and a DSO in 1945 and ending his career as a Major-General.

One of the reasons for the ultimate success of the Normandy campaign was the overwhelming air superiority the Allies enjoyed. This was the work of the Second Tactical Air Force (TAF) formed in June 1943 to support the army's preparations for the invasion and the subsequent advance. Among those Tonbridgians who served in the TAF was Wing Commander Ivor Dale (DB 1919) commanding 21 Squadron, equipped with Mosquito fighter-bombers for low-level daylight attacks. At 39 years old he was one of the oldest squadron commanders in the RAF, earning him

the nickname of 'Daddy' Dale. Flying the light and rapid Mosquito at low level called for considerable flying skills, which Dale revealed in various daring attacks. On 18 February 1944 he led one of three Mosquito squadrons which succeeded in breaching the walls of Amiens Prison to release French Resistance fighters sentenced to execution, an operation codenamed 'Jericho' in emulation of Joshua's Old Testament feat. Then on 31 October 1944 he led an equally dangerous raid on Gestapo headquarters in Aarhus University, Denmark. The Danish Resistance had requested this to kill Gestapo officers and destroy incriminating records held on the resistance. Each Mosquito carried two 500lb bombs, and the mission had to be conducted at very low level across the North Sea and into Denmark, but total surprise was achieved and it was

Ivor Dale's Mosquito squadron attacking Gestapo HQ Aarhus, Denmark, 31 October 1944.

Snowballs at Judde, 1939. John Bryan front. Standing behind left to right: Neville West, Paul Pilditch, Geoffrey Sims.

John Bryan's grave, Bretteville-sur-Laize. 'Courage held his squadron for it was first radiant in his own soul.'

superbly executed by Dale with the loss of just one aircraft. All the targeted buildings were destroyed and several Gestapo personnel killed, including its head. Dale was awarded the DFC in August 1944, but was killed on 2 February 1945 when his Mosquito crashed near Sittard after engine failure.

Above the D-Day beaches in his Typhoon roamed John Bryan (JH 1936), the son of a clergyman and 17 years younger than Dale. He was a natural pilot who flew Hurricanes from 1942, and then Typhoons against enemy transport in France with such success that he destroyed or damaged 28 locomotives, two minesweepers, and an E-Boat, as well as two enemy aircraft. He rose quickly through the ranks, from Flying Officer in 1942 to Squadron Leader in 1943 and Wing Commander in 1944, when he was still only 22

years of age. By 1943 he was regarded as one of the finest ground attack pilots in the RAF and in August was given command of 198 Squadron, flying rocket-firing Typhoons against ground targets in the invasion build-up. He was awarded the DFC and bar in 1943 for 'his high standard of leadership and setting an inspiring example', and continued flying through the winter without much rest. In May 1944 he was again promoted to command 136 Wing with three Typhoon squadrons under him. He led them from the front on D-Day and in the hectic days which followed, was frequently called in by ground forces to break up concentrations of enemy armour and artillery. On 10 June 1944 he was attacking an enemy column south of Caen; he dived down to about 600 feet and executed a steep starboard

Airborne division preparing to board planes for operation Market Garden.

turn, when flak set his aircraft on fire, and it dived straight into the ground.

On 12 June 1944 the Germans launched at London their first salvo of V1 Flying Bombs, christened 'doodlebugs'. The destruction they and the later V2s wrought was enormous, killing over 9,000 people. It was a nasty shock to a population which imagined after D-Day that the war was as good as won. The worst single disaster came on the morning of Sunday 18 June in the Guards Chapel. It was packed for morning service, conducted by the Bishop of Maidstone, and, as the congregation finished the opening hymn, they heard a distant buzzing which turned into a roar directly overhead. The doodlebug exploded on the roof of the Chapel which collapsed onto the congregation below, piling up rubble ten feet deep. It killed 121 people and seriously injured many more, most of them serving or retired soldiers and their families. Only the Bishop was totally unhurt, protected by the altar from which he was conducting the service. One of the dead was Lieutenant Harold Dods (PS 1923) of the Scots Guards, a minor county

cricketer for Lincolnshire, where he farmed, and who often returned to play against the school. A second fatality was the Reverend Ralph Whitrow (DB 1910), Chaplain to the Brigade of Guards and uncle of the Tonbridge actor, Ben Whitrow. Ralph had served on the Western Front before being ordained, was a Canon of Winchester Cathedral and had only recently taken up his appointment with the Guards. The disaster was a reminder that the war could reach out well beyond the fighting front to claim its victims.

By September 1944 Belgium had been liberated and Montgomery believed that he would be able to establish a foothold over the Rhine for a drive into the Ruhr. Operation Market Garden involved the use of British and American airborne troops to seize vital bridges over the Rhine to enable the main body of armour and infantry to cross. The British 1st Airborne Division was tasked with the capture of the furthest bridge at Arnhem. The operation was launched on 17 September but it greatly underestimated the difficulties involved and turned into a costly if gallant failure.

Arnhem Drop, painting by Peter Stainforth.

1st Airborne landed by both parachute and glider. Staff Sergeants John Palmer (FH 1933) and Marcus Southey (PH 1935) were among the glider pilots involved. They were both veterans of the night landings on Sicily in July 1943, and this time Palmer was carrying into action elements of 1st Parachute Brigade. His Horsa glider was towed by a Stirling bomber and landed successfully west of Arnhem on the designated landing zone. Palmer now took on the role of infantryman, fighting with a platoon of glider pilots. On the next day he was riding on a lightly armoured Bren carrier, when it took a direct hit from a tank. Southey survived the fighting to become a prisoner.

Captain John Howard (Sc 1933), a journalist with the *Scottish Daily Express* before the war, was wounded at Alamein with the Royal Sussex before transferring to the 10th Parachute Battalion. He dropped by parachute, but his battalion failed to reach the Arnhem road bridge because of strong German armoured forces blocking their way and had to pull back within the Oosterbeek perimeter, where the remnants of 1st Airborne had dug in to make their final stand. Howard was wounded and left behind when the surviving troops pulled back across the Rhine, but managed to evade capture and was hidden by some Dutch people. On 20 October he tried to swim across the Rhine back to British lines but must have drowned and, along with Palmer, is commemorated at Groesbeek, where over 1,000 airborne troops with no known grave are named. 'We live in the hearts of friends for whom we died' runs the inscription on the memorial.

Peter Stainforth at 1st Parachute Brigade reunion, 2008.

The task of ensuring that the road and rail bridges at Arnhem were free of explosives fell to 1st Parachute Squadron, Royal Engineers, including Lieutenant Peter Stainforth (HS 1935), from the same Hill Side year as Sidney Keyes. He had his baptism of fire in Tunisia, where he was wounded, and then fought in Sicily and Italy. After landing at Arnhem, Stainforth's job was to search the railway bridge for explosives, but the Germans blew it up just as he arrived. He and his small group of sappers then tried to re-join the fighting in the town, but ran into a large party of SS troops with whom an intense firefight followed at very close quarters. Stainforth remembers sprinting for cover, spraying his Sten gun behind him but, with two yards to go before he reached a thick clump of trees, he felt a bullet smack into his side. After lying for some hours in a ditch, badly wounded and heavily dosed with morphine, he was carried into a nearby house where he was later captured by German troops and spent the rest of the war in prison camp.

It is sometimes difficult for schoolboys to remember that housemasters too are family men.

At the end of summer 1944, the Reverend M.S. Page ('Pagga') retired from the staff after 20 years as housemaster of Parkside. He was an astute and avuncular housemaster and his wife Marjorie was a very kindly support, who always wrote comforting postcards to the mothers of sick boys. Some of her letters to the van Heek family survive, showing how sympathetic she was in their unenviable predicament. The Pages also had to suffer the fact that 25 of their Parkside charges had been killed in the war, including, in February 1944 in Italy, Mike Birnie (PS 1937), the son of the widowed Parkside assistant housekeeper.

The Page's son, Michael, had been a Marlborough scholar, where he also captained the 1st XV, and then taught at Glasgow Academy. He was 32 years old, married with three young children, and at Arnhem a Major in command of HQ Company of the 156th Parachute Battalion. He was clearly much loved by his men, one of whom summed him up as 'a large, dependable, caring man who was the bedrock of the unit'. The battalion suffered heavy casualties and the remnants were withdrawing to Oosterbeek, under heavy fire from German tanks and infantry. Page led a bayonet charge through the German positions to reach a hollow just outside the Oosterbeek perimeter, where he organised defensive deployment and planned the next move. As he moved around to encourage his men, he momentarily raised his head above the rim of the hollow and was shot through the forehead by a German sniper. He was later buried in the cemetery at Arnhem, where Bernard van Heek (PS 1938), repaying the Pages' kindness to him, was able regularly to visit his grave.

During Arnhem, the value of a Tonbridge classical education was shown. Brian Burnett (WH 1934) had landed on D-Day with the 25-pounder guns of 90 Field Regiment and won an MC in the campaign. During the attempt to relieve the

Rhine Crossing, March 1945. Gliders being towed.

airborne troops at Arnhem, the road there was often cut by the Germans and Burnett had to fire his guns in both directions to try to keep it open. Then came a moment when he had not the slightest idea where the enemy was. Driving down the road in a Jeep, he came across a Dutch Catholic priest. Unable to converse in Dutch, English or French, he tried the priest in Latin and was immediately rewarded: '*Ubi sunt Germani?*' (where are the Germans?) to which the priest replied '*Germani egressi sunt*' (the Germans have left).

The last phase of the war followed the Allied crossing of the Rhine on 23 March 1945. Captain Frank Harbord (MH 1936) died in this operation. He had been wounded in Normandy when commanding a troop of 591 Para Squadron Royal Engineers, dropping as a pathfinder during the early hours of D-Day to clear landing zones for the gliders which followed. Now he was crossing the Rhine in a glider himself, but German shell-fire bracketed their landing-zone and destroyed his glider.

Peter 'Pan' Mitchell (MH 1938) was two years below Harbord in Manor. He was a talented artist who contributed many cartoons to the MH magazine *Holly Leaves* and also had a reputation as a devil-may-care character. Once Mitchell built a four-foot bomb in his study, using biscuit tins and bullets filched from the armoury, from which he extracted the powder to fill his bomb.

He hid it under the lino floor until it was ready, when he wrapped it in a raincoat and summoned his admiring acolytes to follow him. Out they trooped into the countryside, where he hauled the bomb up and over a tree branch with a cord, raised his 'barge' in salute and let go the cord. The bomb went off with an almighty explosion, scattering foliage, while his companions whooped with excitement.

Such a character was likely to be up in the thick of any action, and by April 1945 Mitchell, although wounded twice, was the only surviving platoon commander in the 1st Rifle Brigade after months of continuous action. On 2 April he won the MC for 'great courage and dashing leadership' in leading his platoon under heavy fire to clear first a wood and then some farm

Lt Peter Mitchell (MH).

buildings occupied by elite German parachute troops. Six days later, just short of Bremen, he was killed leading his platoon against strong German positions, less than a month before the end of the war. The Rifle Brigade history records the loss of an officer 'whose name has appeared with distinction in all the recent battles'. John Powell (MH 1938), his study companion when the bomb was being built, heard the news in a letter from home, unable to believe that such a seemingly indestructible person had died. 'They had got Pan,' he wrote later, 'Pan the invincible, Pan the happy-go-lucky nut. It took a long time for the ache to go. The memory of him never has.'

Pan Mitchell was the third-to-last Tonbridgian to be killed in the war. Following him two days later was Sub-Lieutenant Tom Little (PS 1938), who was killed in the Mediterranean when his torpedo boat hit a mine, and finally Denis Elmore (SH 1937), Stuart Hills's opening partner at Lord's in 1942, killed on 19 April 1945 just outside Bremen when his tank received a direct hit. A few days later word came through that the German forces would surrender the next morning, 8 May, VE Day.

Just before VE Day Lieutenant Colonel Walter Brice (PS 1923), commanding 176 Anti-Aircraft Regiment, was ordered to move his batteries to the area of Celle. He was briefed there about a concentration camp lying about a mile from his HQ, called Bergen-Belsen, and asked to guard the Celle jail, where about 60 SS guards from the camp were being held before being removed for trial. On 27 April Brice was dusted against typhus and entered Belsen a few days after its liberation. Even 40 years later he could recall the horror of that moment, the piles of decomposing corpses, the smell of filth and disease, the desperate state of the survivors. It was testimony, if any were needed, to the nobility of the cause for which all had been fighting.

HAMBURG AND TONBRIDGE

Hitler's coming to power in 1933 posed political, economic and above all racial problems for some German families. Those with the means to do so chose emigration, and this brought to Tonbridge in 1936 two German boys from Hamburg.

Walter Eberstadt (Sc 1936) came from a prosperous German Jewish banking family in Hamburg. 1933 brought his father's business career in Dresdner Bank to a standstill, and threatened worse, so the family emigrated to England in 1935. Walter spent three years in School House, mainly it seems because his father liked Sloman, and a personal history written in later life offers some astute observations on Tonbridge life. Not surprisingly he found the year-group hierarchies, the obsession with sport and the fagging strange, but he accepted his new way of life without too many questions, as he wanted to advance up the ladder himself. His random memories included

John Knott having grapenuts and double cream for breakfast each morning, singing 'Eternal Father Strong to Save' in School House prayers, and admiring Gilbert Hoole on parade in his polished cavalry boots and bemedalled uniform jacket. He was academically able, and Sloman in his final report wrote of 'a well-balanced mind likely to flourish at Oxford', which is where he went in 1939 to read PPE at Christ Church.

Hans Hoffman (FH 1936) also came from Hamburg, where his father managed a coffee trading firm. In 1934 he moved his business to England because of the imposition of currency controls, the takeover of Hoffman's hockey team by the Hitler Youth and, above all, the future threat posed by his paternal grandmother being Jewish. Hamburg folk are said by other Germans to put their umbrellas up when it rains in England, and this affinity helped persuade his father to move

School House, 1939. Walter Eberstadt back row, far left. John Knott and Harold Sloman seated centre. On John Knott's left, Bill Brown and then Tom Wood. On Mrs. Sloman's right, Charles Pillman. Harold Mitchell third row from the back, fourth from left.

here. Hoffman had limited English on arrival at Tonbridge but had a happy and successful three years, throwing himself enthusiastically into cricket and rugby, and finishing in the same Economics Sixth as Eberstadt, before leaving to study accountancy in the summer of 1939.

Eberstadt completed one year at Oxford before to his great surprise and disgust, he was interned as an 'enemy alien' in the frenzied days of June 1940, along with other mainly German Jewish refugees. Internment came as a great emotional shock to one by now steeped in English ways, and an act he found hard to forgive. On his release later that year, he joined the Pioneer Corps before being commissioned in 1942, when the War Office graciously decided aliens could become officers. In June 1943 he was allowed to transfer to a combatant unit and joined the Ox and Bucks Light Infantry.

Hoffman was also interned as an enemy alien in that same camp at Kempton Park, but was then moved to Canada. On the boat, the ship's captain, clearly believing the internees were confirmed Nazis, paraded them on deck to show them where another liner had been torpedoed and 'our German friends' had murdered women and children. By the winter of 1940 the British realised their mistake in interning people with every reason to be anti-Nazi and Hoffman, like Eberstadt, joined the Pioneer Corps, returning to England to build military camps and other non-combatant tasks. Eventually in 1943 he too was accepted for combat and enlisted in the 21st Independent Parachute Company, an elite pathfinder force within the Parachute Regiment. He was strongly advised to change his name for possible operations behind German lines and, having grown to love cricket at Tonbridge, chose Compton after his hero Denis. He fought in Tunisia and Italy, before parachuting into southern France in August 1944 in advance

of the Allied invasion, Operation Dragoon, to prepare drop zones for the main airborne brigade. He did the same in Greece in October 1944, parachuting on to Megara airfield near Athens, where he was involved in heavy street fighting against Communist partisans as the Greek Civil War erupted, costing his company more casualties in those three weeks than in all their other actions combined.

Meanwhile, on 28 June 1944, Eberstadt landed in Normandy and was posted to the 1st Worcesters as a platoon commander, holding the line near the heavily contested Carpiquet airfield. In August, leading a charge across open ground

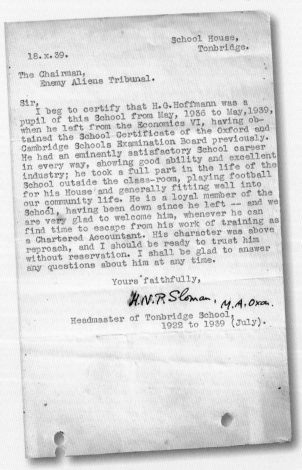

Testimonial from Harold Sloman to Chairman, Enemy Alien Tribunal in support of Hans Hoffman.

to the edge of a wood held by German troops near Mont Pincon, he was shot through the chest and evacuated to hospital in England. When fit again in October 1944, he worked for Radio Luxembourg, broadcasting to Germans behind the combat zone, and decided to change his name to Everitt, picked at random from the London telephone directory.

A week after VE-Day he was sent back to Hamburg to help run the radio station. He had left Hamburg ten years previously as a 14-year-old Jewish boy and now returned as Captain Walter Everitt, British officer. The sensitivities were a constant challenge in attempting to re-educate the German population, and Walter was conscious not to abuse the authority he now had. 'Victory,' he mused 'goes to the head, defeat to the heart.' He also visited his old school and found that half his classmates had been killed in the war. One special day there was a performance of Mendelssohn's *Violin Concerto* given by Yehudi Menuhin in a displaced persons' camp, not a dry eye in the audience or orchestra at this symbolic watershed of a banned Jewish work being performed by a Jewish soloist, seemingly a moment of atonement for the past and hope for the future.

Eberstadt found that his mother's family had not been so lucky. Her parents remained in Germany until 1937, when they moved themselves and their business to Amsterdam, living there in increasingly uncomfortable and threatening conditions. The Eberstadts in England received some news of them, but in October 1943 they were arrested and taken to Westerbork camp. From here they were deported to Bergen-Belsen in February 1944, where they died later that year from disease and starvation. Walter's brother-in-law and his young son were arrested in France and deported to Auschwitz in 1943. In April 1945 Walter was able to visit Belsen, the full horror of what his grandparents and so many other friends

had endured being graphically revealed to him. In July 1946 he was demobilised and returned to Oxford, finally achieving naturalisation as a British subject; later he emigrated to the USA to start a successful business career, his name now restored to its original Eberstadt. In 1986 he was awarded the OBE for furthering British financial interests in New York over a number of years.

Michael Compton, as he remained, volunteered to work for the Allied Control Commission in Germany and was posted to Lubeck, where he acted as chief interpreter at the Military Court. He too visited his devastated home city of Hamburg and found his old house destroyed in those apocalyptic fire-storm raids in August 1943. He finally left the army in 1946 to join his father in his successful coffee agency.

Walter Eberstadt, 1943.

CHAPTER 12:

THE GATE OF REMEMBRANCE

It had been a long calvary from Thane Ladefoged on 13 December 1939 to Denis Elmore on 19 April 1945, marked by 300 crosses. On Sunday 14 July 1946, a memorial service was held in Chapel for all those who had lost their lives, attended by the families of the dead, masters, boys and Old Tonbridgians. Outside in the ante-Chapel, surrounded by red and white roses, the inscribed roll of honour stood near the names from the Great War. As the congregation emerged from Chapel on that bright summer's day, they would have seen that wonderfully timeless view of The Head and the School beyond, encompassing the sense of continuity and partnership between the living, the dead and those as yet unborn, which is the essence of a great school.

Some in Chapel that July day would have remembered a similar commemoration in 1925, when the Gate of Remembrance was dedicated. The decision taken after the Great War to create permanent cemeteries for the war dead in France and other countries, rather than repatriating them, increased the demand for symbols of remembrance in this country to act as a focus for individual grief. The design of the Tonbridge memorial was by Henry Wilson, whose works can be found all over Britain. It took the form of a Gate of Remembrance at the entrance to Chapel, through which all succeeding generations

must pass as they process into the nave. It was a design heavy in symbolism, presenting the idea of duty and sacrifice, with a central bronze group depicting St George, a youth, and two Angels standing triumphant over the dragon. Above St

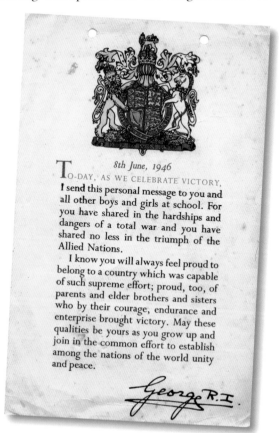

8th June, 1946

To-day, as we celebrate victory, I send this personal message to you and all other boys and girls at school. For you have shared in the hardships and dangers of a total war and you have shared no less in the triumph of the Allied Nations.

I know you will always feel proud to belong to a country which was capable of such supreme effort; proud, too, of parents and elder brothers and sisters who by their courage, endurance and enterprise brought victory. May these qualities be yours as you grow up and join in the common effort to establish among the nations of the world unity and peace.

George R.I

Victory message to schools from HM The King.

George was the Mother and Child, typifying all mothers who have given their most priceless possession, and the Son descended from the Cross, welcoming the dead to his embrace. On the gate piers were inscribed the names of the dead and the paradoxical inscription 'They gave us peace by their warfare and by their death life.'

On 10 October 1925 the Gate of Remembrance was unveiled by General Ironside, who was received on a gloriously fine day by an OTC Guard of Honour, and dedicated by the former Bishop of Birmingham, Henry Wakefield (PH 1891). At the end of the service the whole congregation then passed in procession through the Gate, while wreaths were laid by the President of the OT Society, Herbert Marzetti, and the Captain of the School, Leslie Rowan. After the service, General Ironside addressed the School

with the prophetic message that 'we should learn to work hard and to play the game, as those others had done, so that we might be ready if the call came to us in our turn to defend our country.'

One matter of regret and mystery remains in the commissioning of this memorial. If you drive out to the Ypres Salient's furthest extent at Passchendaele, you will visit the largest British war cemetery in the world at Tyne Cot, with its 11,000 graves, designed by Sir Herbert Baker (JH 1875). Baker, one of the foremost artistic figures in the School's history, captained both the XI and XV before training as an architect. In 1892 he went to South Africa, where he worked for Cecil Rhodes and had the opportunity to develop his grand imperial style of architecture. Collaboration followed with Sir Edwin Lutyens on the design of government buildings in New Delhi, and in

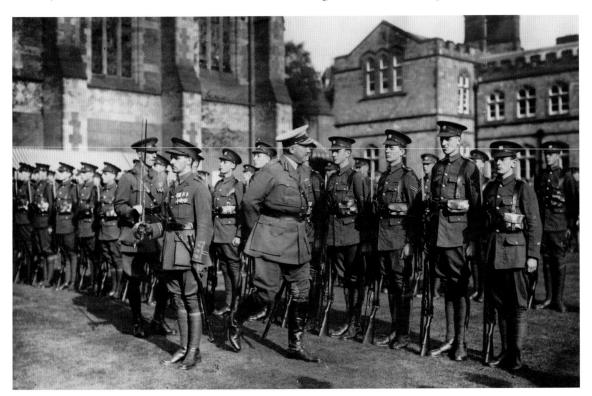

Maj.-Gen. Sir Edmund Ironside inspecting the OTC Guard of Honour at the unveiling of the Gate of Remembrance, 10 October 1925.

1917 Baker was asked by Sir Fabian Ware, head of the IWGC, to work with Lutyens, Kipling and the garden designer, Gertrude Jekyll, on creating cemeteries and memorials in France and Belgium. The result was that perfect fusion of architecture and landscape, with the uniform style of stone walls, iron gates and carefully planted trees and flowers setting off to perfection those mesmerising ranks of headstones in the setting of an English country garden, which future generations still regard with wonder. Apart from Tyne Cot, the South African Memorial at Delville Wood and the Indian Memorial at Neuve Chapelle were Baker's main contributions.

In 1918 Baker put forward a proposal to the Tonbridge War Memorial Committee for a cloister at the west end of Chapel. The Governors however intervened to block Baker's scheme and in his memoirs he wrote: 'Tonbridge has no memorial which expresses the magnitude of the sacrifice made. A scheme which I proposed was rejected, a small cloister, through which the

boys must pass before entering the Chapel.' The Governors probably baulked at the cost, more than double that of Wilson, but Tonbridge's loss was Winchester's gain as Baker created there a charming memorial cloister which Kipling regarded as his masterpiece.

Tonbridge remembered its dead not only through a physical memorial but also through a scheme to provide a Tonbridge education for the sons of fallen OTs. One who benefited from this was Deryck Boyd-Moss (PH 1926), whose father had been killed at Gallipoli, and who was to perish himself at Alamein. The War Memorial Fund which paid for all this was established in 1918 and administered by a management committee. From its inception until his death in 1942 the staff representative on this fund was Henry Stokoe.

Stokoe was a remarkable Tonbridge institution who had bought Park House from the Reverend Joseph Little in 1890 to become its housemaster for a remarkable 41 years until his retirement in 1931. It is even rumoured that

Tyne Cot Cemetery and Memorial, designed by Sir Herbert Baker.

he sent a letter to the Headmaster, Joseph Wood, saying 'I have purchased Park House and will be joining your staff next term.' In his early days Stokoe was known as 'The King', a nickname deriving from his initials 'H.R.', but also from the commanding manner in which he surveyed his kingdom. Humphrey Ellis (FH 1921) described a figure of imposing dignity. 'For the outsider,' he wrote, 'it was enough to see Stokoe mount his bicycle from the rear; the left foot planted firmly on the step, a strong take-off with the right and then the trunk (one would not particularise further with such a man) lowered with matchless dignity into the saddle. He never wobbled or departed a hair's-breadth from the upright. That was true of him in all things – a man to respect, revere and obey.'

From the start of the Great War, Stokoe meticulously recorded service details of Tonbridge boys in a growing number of notebooks surrounding him in his study, issuing each year a new War List. Tragically one of the early casualties was his own son, Bertram Stokoe (PH 1908), who left Oxford to volunteer and was killed on 12 October 1915, when a British rifle grenade exploded prematurely in front line trenches near St Eloi and a splinter punctured his carotid artery. Bertram was buried in the Elzenwalle Brasserie Cemetery on the road to Kemmel. It is a small battlefield cemetery not much visited, set in farmland with just 150 graves. After the war, as the Imperial War Graves Commission embarked on its huge task of creating and maintaining the 'silent cities'

Henry Stokoe presenting cups on Sports' Day, 1922.

known so well to visitors and pilgrims today, groups of relatives began to seek the graves of loved ones, a very different journey from those made by school parties today. Henry Stokoe made that journey to Ypres soon after the war through countryside still littered with blackened tree trunks, dumps of rusty barbed wire and piles of unexploded shells. The road out of Ypres through the Lille Gate to Kemmel was barely passable, and marked by regular clumps of crosses, but finally Stokoe was able to stand silently before the grave of his son.

Henry Stokoe's greatest legacy, however, is a large, handsomely bound book published in 1923 and entitled *Tonbridge School and the Great War*. Other schools have books

CAPT. H. B. STOKOE.
King's Own Yorkshire Light Infantry.
PARK HOUSE. 1913.
Killed in Action at St Eloi.
AGED. 21.
Oct 12th 1915.

Captain Bertram Stokoe (PH 1908), killed in action at Ypres 12 October 1915.

commemorating their war dead, but there is none better than this in illustrating the devastating effect of the war on as close a community as a school. It is the most prodigious work of meticulous record-keeping, research and editing. Not only does it have photographs and extensive biographies of all those 415 Tonbridgians who died, but also the full military records of 2,000 or more who served. It became an immense labour of love for Stokoe, a fitting memorial not only to his son, but all those others he had known personally and in many cases with great affection.

When the Second World War ended, an exhausted country stopped well short of creating the many new symbols of remembrance which followed the Great War. There was a fund for stone tablets with the names of the dead to be placed in Chapel alongside the Gate of Remembrance, and a list published in the 1946 School Register, but there was no Henry Stokoe to produce a full record of service and sacrifice. The 1918 memorials had expressed the idea that war on such a scale should never be allowed to happen again, but it had happened again and, in the harsh days of post-war austerity, the overwhelming feeling in school and country this time seemed to be one of trying to forget.

Elsewhere existing war cemeteries were used to bury the dead, and names added to 1914–18 memorials, but the IWGC (later the Commonwealth War Graves Commission) did construct over 500 new cemeteries and 36 new memorials, using the same principles as in 1919. Where Tonbridge graves of the Great War are largely concentrated across the Channel, the more truly global nature of the second conflict means that they can be found in every corner of the world – from Taiping in Malaysia to Catania in Sicily, from Imphal in Burma to Tilly-sur-Seulles in Normandy, from Massicault in Tunisia to Kanchanaburi in Thailand – and on

large new memorials like those at Alamein and Singapore. In 1920 Churchill, in justifying the government's decision not to repatriate the dead, had commented that 'in periods as remote from our own as we are from the Tudors, the graveyards in France will remain an abiding memorial to the glory of the British Army and the sacrifices made in the great cause.' At Cassino or Kohima or Arnhem it is also easy to share that belief.

At Tonbridge itself a tragic event was to create the need for a new war memorial. On 17 September 1998 the Edwardian Chapel, and with

War Memorial Gate, Tonbridge School Chapel, 2010. Mother and Child tondo on far wall.

it the Gate of Remembrance and the 1939–45 memorial, was consumed by a devastating fire, and it was to be seven long years before the magnificent new Chapel, designed by Donald Buttress, rose from the ashes. A moving and eloquent memorial was designed, using some miraculously recovered parts of the original, but also creating a greater equality of commemoration between the two wars. The figures of St George, the youth and the two angels standing triumphantly over the dragon have been re-cast and now protect the handsome new slate wall panels with the names of the 1939–45 war dead. The alabaster tondo of Mother and Child somehow survived too, the figure of the Son descended from the Cross stands above a new entrance gate, and the restored bronze tablets with the names of the 1914–18 dead stand on either side of the door into the nave. It is a fitting and moving Via Sacra still passed by all who enter Chapel daily.

But there is one other place where remembrance has a special meaning for Tonbridge. The Air Forces Memorial at Runnymede, commemorating those 20,000 airmen lost on operations from this country with no known grave, overlooks the Thames field where Magna Carta was signed by King John in 1216 and further beyond to the towers of Windsor Castle and the planes taking off from Heathrow. Thirty-six Tonbridgians are commemorated in this moving and eloquent shrine, many more than in any other single place except Chapel. The names are arranged by date and rank in rows of stone tablets along the cloister enclosing the shrine. Here are Roly Leahy and Dick Hood, Kenneth Ward and Pip Lefevre, Arthur Rose-Price, Harold Coates and the Harwood-Smith brothers of Manor House, all of them lost without trace in the sea, buried unknown in the earth or consumed by the fires which engulfed their aircraft. As I moved round the cloister on a crisp, sunny January day, the shouts of boys playing football in a nearby field seemed

Runnymede Cemetery.

to be reaching out to what these once were on the fields of Tonbridge. On the great north window of the shrine, looking over the quintessential English landscape they once defended, comforting and inspiring words from the 139th Psalm, sometimes called the Airman's Psalm, are engraved: 'If I take the wings of the morning and remain in the uttermost parts of the sea, even there also shall Thy hand lead me; and Thy right hand shall hold me.'

In this place, close to the seat of English liberty, everything important for which that 1939–45 generation fought is represented. When Her Majesty Queen Elizabeth II dedicated this memorial in 1953, she reminded us that 'as only free men can, they knew the value of that for which they fought and that the price was worth paying.' Small comfort for those who mourned but, as the years roll by, their children and their School can honour a generation who gave their all.

ROLL OF HONOUR

Burial or cremation place or memorial commemoration stated where known.

KIA – killed in action
DOW – died of wounds
KOAS – killed on active service.

Three hundred OTs and two members of Common Room are listed by calendar year of Tonbridge entry and in alphabetical order within that year.

1897
Meyrick, F.C. (JH) Planter Malaya
Presumed killed Feb 1942 when SS Giang Bee Sunk

1899
Bartram, R.S. (DB) Capt. RE.
Died Harrogate 19 Jan 1943

1900
Tapply, A. (Sc) Pte Home Guard
Died 4 Feb 1943

1901
Christie, C.S. (MH) Min of Shipping
Died in Hull from accident 15 April 1942

1902
Leslie-Smith, C. (Sc) Brig Army Recruiting *Died 27 Feb 1942 Cheltenham*

1903
Igglesden, R.S. (JH) Capt S Staffs
Died 11 Oct 1944 Ashford

1904
Malden, C.C. (MH) Maj-Gen Dir Military Training *KOAS 25 March 1941 Frant*

1905
Montague, P.J.A. (JH) Brig RA
Died 29 Nov 1940 Stoke

1906
Ferry, E.L. (HS) Lt National Defence
Died 12 May 1941

Platt, E.N. (HS) Capt RAOC
Died 28 Aug 1944 Coulsdon

1907
Eales, H.G. (PS) ARP
KIA 25 Dec 1941 Hong Kong

1908
Fraser, E.G. (DB/MH) Lt Col Suffolk R
DOW 23 May 1940 Leigh, Kent

1910
Whitrow, Rev. R.H. (DB) Capt Chaplain Bde of Guards *Killed by VI 18 June 1944 Winchester*

1911
Moysey, R.A.L. (DB) Burmese Gov
Died 1943 Tavoy Island

Porter, W. (FH) Brig RE OBE CBE
Died 7 Oct 1943 Woking

1912
Hay, A.W. (PH) Capt Straits Sett VF
POW *Died 21 Oct 1944 Kanchanaburi*

Winkworth, J.S. (MH) Lt RAOC
Died 11 March 1943 Cape Town

1913
Paul, C.C. (FH) Lt KAR
Died Somaliland 8 June 1945 Hargeisa

1914
Burdekin, H.B. (PS) Civilian
Killed by V1 23 July 1944 Reigate

Kortright, M. (DB) Maj Suffolk R
KIA 29 May 1940 Dunkirk

Symons, H.E. (Sc) F/L RAFVR
KIA 28 May 1940 Runnymede

1915
Cooper, E.S.C. (Sc) F/L RAFVR
KOAS 18 Dec 1944 Chipstead

Rice, R.B. (JH) Lt Col RA
KIA 9 May 1943 Medjez-el-Bab

1916
Aston, G.T. (PS) Maj RA
KIA 4 Aug 1943 Brookwood

Jupp, J.E. (PH) W/O HKRNVF
Died as POW 12 Oct 1942 Yokohama

Kerbey, G.H. (DB) Pte HKVDF
KIA 24 Dec 1941 Sai Wan

1917
Bouchier, H.S. (JH) S/L RAFVR
KIA 14 Nov 1944 Choloy

Ferguson, G.K.R. (HS) Coder RN
HMS *Whitaker*
KIA 1 Nov 1944 Plymouth

Ievers, E.O. (DB) F/O RAFVR
KIA 29 April 1942 Kirkby Wharfe

1918
Burrows, R.M. (MH) Maj AIF
Died Melbourne 2 Aug 1942

Colman, C.H.A. (Sc) S/L RAF
KIA 4 Jan 1941 Tangmere

Wills, R.D.J. (PH) Engineer
Killed in Blitz 20 April 1941 Rochester

1919
Bouch, J.C. (HS) Maj RA
KIA 26 Feb 1942 Singapore

Brown, H.S. (FH) Sgt Pilot FMSVAF
KOAS Singapore 16 May 1941

Dale, I.G.E. (DB) W/C RAF DFC
KIA 2 Feb 1945 Sittard

Davies, P.E. (FH) S/L AAF
KIA 6 June 1945 Bombay

Staniland, C.S. (FH) F/L RAF
KOAS 26 June 1942 Keddington

1920
Burch, R.J. (DB) Lt Cdr RN DSO
HMS *Narwhal*
KIA 1 Aug 1940 Portsmouth

Laurie, F.G. (DB) Civilian
Killed in Blitz 27 Feb 1941 Sodbury

Sankey, R.C. (PS) P/O RAFVR
KOAS 2 July 1940 Stoke

Wrangham, S.D.A. (JH) Lt E Yorks R
Died 14 May 1942 Somersham

1921
Blackden, V.Q. (JH) W/C RAF
KIA 10 April 1941 Lemsterland

Hankey, S.D. (Sc) Doctor
Died of typhus China Jan 1944

Humphrey, R.S.M. (DB) Lt RNVR
HMS *Hyacinth*
KIA 7 April 1941 Portsmouth

Linay, I.L. (DB) Lt RNVR HMML
125 *KIA 2 Nov 1942 Chatham*

Musson, G.B. (MH) F/O BOAC
KOAS 14 Sept 1942 Malta

Ramsay, A.S. (DB) P/O RAFVR DFC
DOW 1 Aug 1941 Catania

Skinner, R.M.P. (FH) Lt Cdr RN
HMS *Dunedin*
KIA 24 Nov 1941 Portsmouth

1922
Barrell, K.G. (MH) Maj. Lincs R
KIA 23 Sept 1943 Salerno

Brown, M. (MH) Capt. RA
KOAS 13 April 1942 Leicester

Ellis, A.W. (Sc) Maj. RA
KIA 11 April 1945 Greece

Knights, D.M. (FH) Lt RWK
Died Oxford 4 July 1942

Mason, Rev. W.R.P.K. (JH) F/O RAF
KIA 29 June 1940 Alamein

Oclee, H.D. (MH) Maj. Loyal R
KIA 23 April 1943 Massicault

Orton, J.E. (DB) Capt. FF Regt IA
Died 27 Sept 1940 Rawalpindi

Percy, M.F. (PS) Sapper RE
Died 6 Feb 1940 Shirley

Reinhold, D.M. (PH) Maj. RAC
KIA 23 Dec 1941 Alamein

Ward, E.A.C. (PS) Capt. Hampshire R
DOW 2 Oct 1944 Crowborough

Willis, G.G.L. (HS) Lt Col CLY DSO
KIA 17 July 1943 Catania

1923
Adye, A.F.C. (DB) Maj. RHA
KIA 31 May 1940 Dunkirk

Charles, G.P. (JH) W/C RAF OBE
KIA 13 Jan 1942 Benghazi

Curzon (formerly Cohen), R.K. (Sc)
F/O RAF
KIA 13 June 1940 Runnymede

Dods, H.W. (PS) Lt Scots Gds
Killed by V1 18 June 1944 Donington

Elgar, C.M. (Sc) P/O AAF
KIA 15 Aug 1941 Runnymede

Forbes, D.K. (DB) Lt RNVR HMS
Lanka
KIA 7 Dec 1942 Portsmouth

Glendinning, J.E. (MH) F/O RAFVR
KIA Norway 22 Dec 1943 Runnymede

Hallam, J.S. (DB) Lt KRRC
KIA 4 Jan 1943 Alamein

Hood, H.R.L. (DB) S/L RAF DFC
KIA 5 Sept 1940 Runnymede

Hubble, D.E. (PH) Capt. SOE Croix
de Guerre *Executed Buchenwald 11 Sept
1944 Bayeux*

Selous, E.M. (JH) Sarawak Admin POW
Died Kuching 2 March 1945 Borneo

Smythe, E.A. (FH) Capt. RASC
KIA 28 May 1940 Lille

Sparke, C.L. (HS) F/O RAFVR
KIA 11 Dec 1942 Villeneuve

Stevens, B. (MH) Capt. RAC
KOAS 14 Nov 1940 Chiddingfold

1924

Bedell, P.E. (PS) F/O RAFVR
KIA 7 Dec 1941 Singapore

Bennett, P.J. (PH) Lt Singapore VDF
POW Died 2 July 1943 Kanchanaburi

Day, J.H. (HS) P/O RAF
KIA 20 May 1940 Mont Huon

Dumas, G.J.P. (JH) Cpl RASC
KOAS 12 Oct 1940 Horsell

Heywood, J.H. (HS) Maj. Gold Coast R
KIA 5 March 1944 Rangoon

Irvine (formerly Nachman), R.N.
(DB) Lt R Berks
KIA 11 June 1944 Rangoon

Orton, C.T. (DB) Capt. R Warwicks
DOW 28 May 1940 Dozinghem

Spence, M.G. (HS) Capt. Leicester R
DOW 23 Oct 1944 Lier

Withers, G.G. (MH) Lt Loyal R
KIA 4 Feb 1942 Singapore

1925

Bolster, R.V.C. (DB) P/O RAFVR
KIA 28 June 1941 Hamburg

Brettell, G.S. (HS) Lt RNVR HMS
Hecla
KIA 12 Nov 1942 Plymouth

Elgar, C.R. (Sc) S/L AAF
KOAS 22 May 1943 Bobbing

Harrison, D.S. (Sc) P/O RAFVR
KIA 28 Sept 1940 Tangmere

Higgins, D.D. (MH) Maj 4/5 Mahrattas
IA KIA 24 March 1944 Imphal

Jacobs, J.R.M. (JH) Capt SAF
KIA 24 Oct 1942 Alamein

Monypenny, J.B.S. (DB) S/L RAF
KIA Kiel 20 July 1940 Runnymede

Moon, A.J. (HS) Lt RAMC
KIA SS Lancastria 17 June 1940 Dunkirk

Musson, R.G. (MH) W/C RAF
KIA 24 Aug 1943 Heanton Punchardon

Peal, H.D. (HS) Capt. RHA
DOW 7 June 1942 Knightsbridge, Libya

Smyth, J.P.S. (DB) W/C RAF DFC
KOAS 22 Oct 1942 Heliopolis

Solano, A.L.H. (PS) S/L RAF
DOW 25 Feb 1941 Alamein

1926

Banner, M.S. (Sc) Lt RA
KIA 22 March 1942 Singapore

Bartholomew, J.W.F. (DB) P/O
RAFVR *KIA 12 Nov 1940 Sevenoaks*

Blackden, W.A.S. (JH) F/L RAFVR
KIA 14 Nov 1944 Runnymede

Boyd-Moss, D.F. (PH) Maj. RTR
KIA 28 Oct 1942 Alamein

Cave, W.O. (Sc) Maj. Gold Coast R
KIA 3 April 1944 Rangoon

Edwards, G.M. (Sc) Sgt RAFVR
KIA 4 May 1942 Runnymede

Forbes, W.H. (PH) Lt RN HMS
Glorious
KIA 8 June 1940 Plymouth

Lean, G.W. (MH) P/O RAFVR
KOAS 23 Jan 1943 Bridgewater

Nottidge, J.J. (HS) P/O RAFVR
KIA 13 Aug 1941 Berlin

Ward, D.E. (PS) Maj. RTR
KIA 27 Oct 1942 Alamein

Witney, P.N. (HS) Capt. RAMC
KIA Hong Kong 25 Dec 1941 Stanley

1927

Adcock, D. (PH) F/L RAFVR
KIA 11 Aug 1944 Middelkerke

Barclay, D.P. (PS) S/L RAF
KIA 28 April 1941 Alamein

Body, J. (PS) P/O RAFVR
KIA 12 Aug 1940 Darlington

Darby, O. (DB) Lt FMSVDF
KIA 17 March 1942 Taiping

Farrell, P.A.L. (HS) F/O RAF
KOAS 7 April 1940 Terlincthun

Hovenier, A.P. (PH) F/O RAFVR
KIA 29 Nov 1940 Runnymede

King, N.S. (JH) P/O RAFVR
KIA 8 July 1942 Malta

MacDonald, R.A.S. (PH) Sub/Lt RN
HMS *Penzance*
KIA 26 Aug 1940 Chatham

McComas, H.N. (FH) P/O RAFVR
KIA 16 July 1942 Boulogne

Neve, C. (DB) P/O RAFVR
KIA 22 Aug 1942 Runnymede

Spence, G.L. (HS) 2/Lt Gordons
KIA 17 June 1940 Cherbourg

Tree, T.N. (HS) P/O RAFVR
KIA 27 April 1942 Trondheim

Tulloch, C.H.L. (HS) F/O RAFVR
KIA 24 Nov 1941 Runnymede

1928

Benn, D.F.H. (HS) Sgt RMP
KIA 25 May 1940 Le Grand Luce

Biggleston, D.H. (FH) Lt RA
KIA 1 July 1942 Alamein

Body, S. (PS) P/O RAFVR
KOAS 9 Sept 1940 Birkenhead

Brown, N.C. (Sc) Pte Singapore VDF
POW Died Kuching 19 June 1945 Labuan

Canney, P.J.C. (HS) W/C RAF
KIA 25 Feb 1942 Trondheim

Chapman, L.B. (PH) Lt RTR
DOW 25 March 1945 Reichswald Forest

Dare, H.W.J. (FH) F/L RAFVR
KIA Hamburg 2 Aug 1943 Runnymede

Dickson, F.O. (DB) F/L RAF
KOAS 5 April 1940 Runnymede

Godby, A. (PH) Lt RAC
KOAS 15 Dec 1942 Chislehurst

Hammond, L.P. (Sc) Capt. 4/15
Punjabs, IA
DOW Burma 29 Jan 1944 Maynamati

Jackson, F.J.P. (JH) Capt. RA
DOW 29 June 1944 Ranville

La Fontaine, G.C. (SH) Lt Beds and
Herts R *KIA 6 May 1943 Massicault*

Lambert, H.A. (JH) Maj. 3/9 Jat R IA
KIA Imphal 5 May 1944 Rangoon

Misselbrook, S.T. (Sc) W/C RAF
DSO *KIA Brest 13 Dec 1941 Runnymede*

Oswald, N.A. (HS) Maj. Queens R
MC *KIA 11 Sept 1943 Salerno*

Pilditch, F.S. (JH) Lt RE
KIA 19 March 1945 Reichswald Forest

Sanderson, L.E. (DB) F/O AAF
KIA 19 Nov 1940 Cambridge

Wheelwright, I.S. (WH) P/O AAF
KIA 30 May 1940 Runnymede

Willis, J.G.E. (JH) P/O RAFVR
KIA 28 April 1941 Chatelaillon

1929
Briggs, J.L. (HS) F/Sgt RAFVR
KIA 28 Aug 1941 Rotterdam

Davis, G.S. (Sc) Surg. Lt RNVR HMS
Mourne
KIA 16 June 1944 Plymouth

Day, D.A.S. (Sc) Capt. Wiltshire R
KIA 22 Feb 1944 Taukkyan

Elliott, T.P.N. (PS) Maj. RA MC
KIA 11 Sept 1944 Geel

Graham, J.O. (Sc) Capt. 1/8 Punjab IA
KIA 3 Jan 1942 Taiping

Hall, F.C. (Sc) Lt E Surrey R
KIA 3 Dec 1942 Medjez-el-Bab

Hansen-Raae, H.W. (PH) Maj. RWK
MC *KIA 14 May 1944 Cassino*

Hobbs, J.B. (JH) F/L RAFVR
KIA 7 Dec 1941 Halfaya Sollum

Jackson, G.H. (WH) P/O RAF
KIA 2 Sept 1940 Bergen-op-Zoom

Long, J.T.C. (MH) F/L RAFVR
KIA 10 July 1942 Runnymede

Meredith, K.E. (DB) Maj. Dorset R
KIA 11 July 1944 Bayeux

Mole, N.B. (Sc) F/L RAF
KIA Norway 24 Sept 1940 Runnymede

Thwaites, E.H.T. (PS) S/L RAF AFC
DOW 17 Aug 1940 Durnbach

Tibbits, W.G. (DB) F/O RAFVR
KIA 25 Feb 1944 Runnymede

Ure, R.R. (MH) Capt. RA
KIA 18 Feb 1944 Cassino

Vaughan, E.H. (FH) Lt RN
HMS *Curacoa*
KIA 2 Oct 1942 Chatham

Walker, C.J.R. (Sc) P/O RAF
KIA 6 Nov 1940 Ootmarsum

Wix, H.M. (FH) Capt. RA MC
DOW 17 June 1943 Nicosia

1930
Brooks, G.N. (FH) Sgt Pilot RAFVR
KIA 7 Nov 1940 Albania

Clark, H.M. (PH) P/O RAFVR
KIA 12 Aug 1941 Strijen

Coningham, W.D.M. (PH) Capt. Duke
of Well R *KIA 30 March 1942 Rangoon*

Darby, J. (DB) Maj. 3/1 Gurkha R
KIA 28 May 1944 Imphal

Firminger, L.D. (MH) Sgt Obs
RAFVR
KIA 22 July 1942 Runnymede

Gardner, D.L. (PS) 2/Lt RA
KIA 22 May 1940 Dunkirk

Jacoby, M. (MH) F/O RAFVR
KIA 30 Sept 1941 Kiel

Johnston, R.R. (Sc) P/O RAFVR
KIA 9 April 1943 Runnymede

Lehmann, A.R.J. (MH) Capt. DCLI
KIA 8 Oct 1944 Assisi

Mason, J.E. (PH) Maj. N Staffs
KIA 30 May 1944 Anzio

Montague, R.P. (JH) Capt. RA MC
KIA 30 July 1943 Catania

Munro, K.M. (PH) Capt. Buffs
KIA 1 Feb 1945 Taukkyan

Nicolson, E.J.B. (WH) W/C RAF VC
DFC *KIA 2 May 1945 Singapore*

Sawyer, C.W.R. (Sc) F/O RAF
KOAS 12 April 1941 Silloth

Street, P.A. (JH) Sgt Pilot RAFVR
KIA 7 March 1944 Bromley Hill

1931
Arbib, J.H.V. (MH) Lt RA
KIA 21 Sept 1943 Salerno

Bellhouse, W.K. (Sc) Capt. RA
KIA 3 June 1944 Imphal

Briginshaw, O.O'N. (SH) P/O RAF
KIA 10 Sept 1940 Runnymede

Coates, H.K. (HS) F/O RAFVR
KIA 4 Sept 1943 Runnymede

Coote, M.A. (MH) F/O RAFVR
KIA 24 May 1942 Chatham

Cunningham, J.C. (PS) P/O RAFVR
KIA 30 May 1941 Great Bookham

Follit, W.R. (PH) Capt. Hants R
KIA 16 Sept 1943 Salerno

Hughes-Hughes, W.A. (JH) Sgt
RAFVR *KIA 9 Dec 1941 Runnymede*

Jenkins, M.T.E. (SH) P/O RAF
KIA 16 June 1940 Alamein

Johnson, E.I.C. (DB) P/O RAF
KIA 24 Jan 1941 Chorleywood

Lefevre, P.W. (PH) S/L RAF DFC
KIA 6 Feb 1944 Runnymede

Lyle, P.A. (HS) Lt R Sussex
KIA 27 Oct 1942 Alamein

Stevens, A.O.L. (MH) P/O RAFVR
KIA 7 Nov 1940 Felixstowe

Welford, J.H. (WH) F/O RAF
KIA 26 May 1940 Minster

Young, R.N.D. (JH) Capt. Irish Gds
KIA 23 Feb 1944 Anzio

1932
Bromham, J.W.T. (MH) P/O RAFVR
KIA 7 Sept 1941 Kiel

Crofton, R.M.E. (JH) Flt Sgt RAFVR
KOAS 28 Sept 1942 Beck Row

Gain, A.P. (PH) Lt RTR
KIA 4 July 1942 Alamein

George, G.C. (FH) Lt Lincs R
KIA 27 Jan 1944 Minturno

Harwood-Smith, K. (MH) Sgt
Obs RAFVR
KIA 8 Nov 1941 Runnymede

Hood, S.C.H. (WH) Capt. RAMC
4/7 RDG
KIA 13 June 1944 Tilly-sur-Seulles

Jenkins, P.R.E. (SH) P/O RAF
KIA 6 Aug 1942 Kirkby Wharfe

Kerry, J.G. (HS) S/L RAFVR DFC
KIA 5 Oct 1942 Lille

Ladefoged, T.A.N. (MH) Sig. RNVR
HMT Sedgefly
KIA 13 Dec 1939 Portsmouth

Latham, M. (WH) Maj. 3/1 Gurkhas
KIA 11 May 1944 Imphal

Maggs, R. (WH) F/O RAFVR
KIA 5 March 1942 Alamein

Mitchell, J.G. (SH) P/O RAFVR
KIA 22 June 1940 Reichswald Forest

Shaw, R.T. (PH) Lt Queens R
DOW 19 Dec 1942 Fayid

Thomas, J. (JH) Lt RN HMS *Porpoise*
KOAS 15 April 1942 Alexandria

Wingate, D.L. (JH) P/O RAF
KIA 22 Aug 1940 Runnymede

1933
Bailey, J.C.L.D. (Sc) P/O RAFVR
KIA 2 Sept 1940 Maidstone

Blackman, R.D. (MH) Steward RN
KOAS 17 Dec 1940 Chatham

Cardwell, D.F. (HS) Capt. R Sussex
KIA 27 May 1940 Strazeele

Christie, M.W. (SH) Lt Para
KIA 12 June 1944 Ranville

Firminger, J.R.A. (MH) Lt RNVR
GM *KIA Sicily 23 Aug 1943 Plymouth*

Foster, N.A. (FH) Sub Lt RN(FAA)
KOAS 2 Sept 1942 Port of Spain

Franklin, J.B.G. (WH) 2/Lt 2/11Sikhs,
IA *KIA 25 Aug 1941 Basra*

Gooch, A.H.N. (JH) F/L RAF
KIA 18 July 1943 Runnymede

Hall, J.W. (Sc) Sgt Northants R
DOW 9 April 1943 Medjez-el-Bab

Healey, E.F.G. (WH) F/L RAFVR
DFC DFM
KIA 13 Jan 1943 Apeldoorn

Hill, A.R. (PH) F/O RAFVR
KOAS 17 Jan 1941 Johannesburg

Howard, J. (Sc) Capt. Para
KIA 20 Oct 1944 Groesbeek

Keable, N.H.C. (HS) P/O RAFVR
KIA 5 Aug 1941 Noordwijk

Lees, R.S.M. (JH) F/O RAFVR
Died 6 Aug 1944 Shrewsbury

Palmer, J. (FH) Staff Sgt Glider Pilot R
KIA 18 Sept 1944 Groesbeek

Paterson, A.G. (Sc) Sgt RA *Drowned
when POW transport sunk 1942 Alamein*

Rendall, M.G. (PH) F/O SAAF
KOAS 5 Nov 1943 Vereeniging

Sharps, R.H. (MH) Lt RN HMS
Quilliam
KIA 19 Nov 1943 Chatham

Sorenson, T.G. (Sc) F/O RAFVR
KIA 14 Oct 1944 Nederweert

Steuart-Richardson, J.D. (WH) F/L
RAF DFC *KIA 28 Dec 1940 Tonbridge*

Turner, J.H. (WH) Lt RN HMS
Cormorant
KOAS 25 Sept 1942 Gibraltar

Ure, J.N. (SH) F/O RAFVR
KIA 23 Aug 1943 Runnymede

Wallis, R.G. (Sc) F/O RAFVR
KIA 18 April 1943 St Valery

Waring, J.E.L. (HS) F/L RAFVR
KOAS 25 Aug 1944 Halstead

Wood, E.I.C. (PS) Sgt Obs RAFVR
KIA Essen 9 March 1942 Uden

1934
Brown, R.W.B. (JH) Sgt Obs RAFVR
KIA 6 April 1942 Charleroi

Burr, J.O. (Sc) Mid RN (FAA) HMS
Raven
KOAS 22 April 1940 Haslar

Coleman, P.B. (Sc) P/O RAFVR
KOAS 20 Dec 1940 Hawarden

Dickson, C.C. (WH) P/O RAFVR
KIA 17 Feb 1942 Taukkyan

Elliott, J.D. (SH) 2/Lt KRI Hussars
KIA 27 May 1942 Alamein

Ephraums, M.J. (Sc) Capt. R Marines
MC KIA 3 Oct 1943 Sangro River

Gilliam, B.E. (WH) Capt. RA
KIA 12 May 1944 Cassino

Graff, A. (PH) Lt Ox and Bucks
KIA 20 Jan 1944 Cassino

Harwood-Smith, N.H. (MH) P/O
RAFVR *KIA 10 Aug 1940 Runnymede*

Lee, R.M. (JH) P/O RAFVR
KIA 11 July 1942 Runnymede

Mieville, G.N.C. (HS) P/O RAFVR
KOAS 22 July 1941 Runnymede

Nottidge, D.R. (SH) Pte RWK
KIA 17 Dec 1942 Tabarka Ras

Pillman, C.H. (Sc) Lt 4/7 RDG
KIA 6 June 1944 Bayeux

Ponder, P.G. (HS) Lt E Lancs
KIA 25 Aug 1944 Taukkyan

Rose-Price, A.T. (JH) F/O RAF
KIA 2 Sept 1940 Runnymede

Rothwell, J.H. (FH) P/O RAF
KIA 22 Feb 1941 Poynings

Salmon, P.J. (PH) Lt HAA IA POW
Murdered Ballale Island 1943 Singapore

Sloman, H.G. (PH) Sgt Pilot RAFVR
KIA 15 Sept 1941 Hamburg

Smith, L.G.J. (HS) Sgt Pilot RAFVR
KOAS 29 Feb 1940 Woking

Turner, C.M.S. (WH) Lt RWK
KIA 30 April 1943 Massicault

Vicary, A.J. (SH) Motor engineer
Killed in Blitz Birmingham 13 Nov 1940

Wallace, R.A. (FH) Cpl RAFVR
POW Died Borneo 6 April 1945 Singapore

Wood, P.G.C. (PS) P/O RAFVR
KIA Cologne 31 Aug 1941 Rheinberg

1935

Atkinson, A.J. (HS) Mid RN HMS
Gloucester
KIA 8 July 1940 Plymouth

Crowther, A.R. (JH) Flt Sgt RAFVR
KIA 5 Sept 1943 Durnbach

Dunkels, C.O. (FH) P/O RAF
KIA 29 Aug 1940 Rheinberg

Farquhar, D.G. (MH) F/O RAFVR
DFC KIA 19 Nov 1944 Jonkerbos

Franklin, D.H. (WH) Lt 3/3 Gurkhas IA
KIA 11 April 1944 Imphal

Keyes, S.A.K. (HS) Lt RWK
KIA 29 April 1943 Massicault

Kingsley, A.R. (MH) F/O RAFVR
KIA 10 May 1943 Malta

Ladefoged, A.F.N. (Sc) P/O RAFVR
KOAS 1 Dec 1941 Great Bircham

Law, D.C. (JH) F/O RAFVR
KIA 12 Sept 1944 Vitry-les-Nogent

Leman, D.F. (FH) LAC RAF
KOAS 27 Dec 1941 Montgomery USA

Lloyd, M. (PH/Sc) F/O RAFVR
KIA Cassel 22 Oct 1943 Rheinberg

Moffatt, J.D. (PS) P/O RAFVR
KIA 17 Sept 1942 Malta

Marriner, J.E.D. (SH) LAC RAFVR
KIA 4 Jan 1941 Teverham

Porter, A.R. (SH) F/O RAF
KIA 29 June 1943 Runnymede

Sowrey, J.A.F. (FH) P/O RAF
KIA 24 June 1941 Halfaya Sollum

Wood, T.R.R. (Sc) F/O RAFVR DFC
KIA 3 June 1942 Becklingen

1936

Boddam-Whetham, A.J.T. (PS) P/O
RAFVR *KIA 25 Oct 1941 Netheravon*

Booker, G.D. (SH) Pte REME
Died 8 April 1945

Borradaile, G.C. (SH) Sgt RAFVR
KIA 30 Jan 1944 Berlin

Bryan, J.M. (JH) W/C RAFVR DFC and
bar *KIA 10 June 1944 Bretteville-sur-Laize*

Bryden, R.A. (Sc) P/O RAFVR
KOAS 4 May 1942 Annan

Harbord, F.G. (MH) Capt. RE Para
KIA 24 March 1945 Reichswald Forest

Hawes, A.G. (HS) LAC RAFVR
KOAS 19 April 1942 Monkton

Healey, J.B. (WH) Sgt Pilot RAFVR
KIA 9 Sept 1941 Cleveleys

Hudson, L.A. (PH) F/L RAFVR
KOAS 15 Feb 1945 Chester

Johnson, T.D.L. (HS) App MN SS
Sulaco KIA 19 Oct 1940 Tower Hill

Lloyd-Morgan, P. (SH) Sub Lt
RN(FAA) HMS *Illustrious*
KOAS 2 Jan 1944 Lee-on-Solent

Leahy, G.R. (PH/Sc) F/O RAFVR
KIA 1 Dec 1942 Runnymede

Lendon-Smith, L.J. (PS) Lt RWK
DOW 30 April 1943 Oued Zarga

Maddex, J.D. (MH) F/O RAFVR
KOAS 17 Nov 1943 Cambridge

Maling, E.L. (WH) O/S RNVR HMS
Ganges
Died 18 Oct 1941 Shotley

Reed, J.H. (MH) Flt Sgt RAFVR
KIA 1 July 1943 Greece

Rumsam, P.D. (HS) Sgt Pilot RAFVR
KOAS 23 Feb 1943 Hampstead

Senior, E.R. (Sc) P/O RAFVR
KIA 21 June 1942 Runnymede

Ward, K. (WH) P/O RAFVR
KIA Berlin 1 Sept 1943 Runnymede

Young, C.D. (Sc) F/L RAFVR
KOAS 16 Oct 1944 Wokingham

1937
Allford, C.A.W. (PS) Lt Rifle Bde
KIA 9 Oct 1944 Florence

Birnie, J.R.M. (PS) Lt Green Howards
KIA 4 Feb 1944 Minturno

Cantin, R.C.H. (WH) Sgt RAFVR
KIA 27 Nov 1943 Sage

Crofts, J.A.L. (MH) 2/Lt Welsh Gds
*Killed by enemy action 30 June 1944
Ewhurst*

Elmore, J.D. (SH) Lt Notts Yeo
KIA 19 April 1945 Becklingen

Greville-Smith, J.N. (HS) F/O
RAFVR 1941
KIA 22 Feb 1944 Cagliari

Halfhead, P. (Sc) Pte Hampshire R
KIA 2 Aug 1944 Hottot-les-Bagues

Mitchell, H.O. (Sc) F/O RAFVR
KOAS 17 Nov 1943 Mitcham

Montgomery, D.R. (SH) Staff Sgt
Glider Pilot R
KIA 24 March 1945 Reichswald Forest

Pillman, R.H. (Sc) 2/Lt 4/7 RDG
KOAS 16 April 1944 Bournemouth

Stainbank, R.E. (WH) F/O RAFVR
KIA 12 Sept 1944 Vitry-les-Nogent

Woodland, A.L. (PH/JH) Lt DLI
KIA 11 July 1944 Hottot-les-Bagues

1938
Greig, R.T. (Sc) F/O RAFVR
KIA 3 Jan 1945 Malta

Little, T.E. (PS) Sub Lt RNVR HMMTB
710 KIA 10 April 1945 Portsmouth

Mitchell, P.A.N. (MH) Lt Rifle Bde
MC KIA 8 April 1945 Becklingen

Pipe, D.J.A. (PS) Pte Middlesex R
KIA 24 Aug 1944 Tilly-sur-Seulles

1939
Muffett, G.A. (SH) A/G RAFVR
KIA 6 Sept 1943 Durnbach

Common Room
Browning, O.C. (1935–38) Maj. RA
KIA 2 Nov 1943 Sangro River

Chadwick, H.G. (1937–42) Capt.
RAC *KIA 25 Oct 1942 Alamein*

ROLL OF HONOUR	1939	1940	1941	1942	1943	1944	1945	Total
Army		15	7	24	22	43	11	122
Royal Navy	1	7	3	7	3	3	1	25
Royal Air Force		34	35	30	23	16	6	144
Civilian		1	2	3	1	2	1	10
TOTAL	1	57	47	64	49	64	19	301

LIST OF SUBSCRIBERS

Tonbridge School, honouring all who served 1939–45

Tim Haynes, Headmaster
Jonathan Cohen QC, Chairman of Governors
Roy Brown (HS 1961), Chairman Tonbridge School Foundation
Professor Colin Seymour-Ure (PH 1952), President Old Tonbridgian Society
Hugh Carson (MH 1960), Master of The Skinners' Company

The date given is of entry to the School as a boy or as a member of Staff.

Michael G. Adams	SH 1946	Deryck Ball	PS 1937	The Binnie Family	
Richard Adamson	MH 1992	James Ball	FH 2004	Donald A.L. Birrell	HS 1938
Adam Aiken	HS 1994	Nicholas Ball	FH 2008	N.A. Birrell	HS 1936
Tim Akroyd	FH 1984	Graham R Barnes	JH 1968	B.A.S. Blackie	PS 1940
Michael Allen	MH 1945	Martin Barraud		J.S. Blackie	PS 1936
Charles Allison	HS 1969	Dr John J. Barrett	HS 1956	William Blair	FH 2009
The Alvey Family		Colin Basford	Sc 1945	Thomas Bodger	WH 1989
James Amiss	JH 1996	Dr Sam Bass	PS 1977	Sir John Bond	PS 1955
Jonathan Amiss	JH 2005	David Batten	HS 1950	Charles Booth	Sc 1973
John P. Anson	HS 1944	John Bazalgette	Sc 1950	Rex Comyn Boucher	HS 1942
James Anstice	HS 2008	Michael J. Beaman		Douglas Bourne	SH 2004
Ian E. Aplin	WH 1939	Patrick Beaumont	Sc 1935	Cameron Bourne	SH 2006
Neil Arnott	MH 1963	Josh B. Beech	PS 2007	Peter Bourne	MH 1963
Jonathan Arscott	PH 1983	Carolyn Belcham	PH Matron	John Bowis	FH 1958
Judy Arscott		The Very Revd James Bell		Geoffrey M.R. Bowler TD	PS 1965
Richard Arscott	PH 1988		Chaplain 1983	Peter Bowring	
Stephen Arscott	PH 1981	John A. Bell		David Bowyer	JH 1954
Richard Arthur	MH 1986	Henri P. Benardout	Sc 1950	I.D. Boyce	JH 1958
Major Piers L. Ashfield	HS 1991	Nigel Benn	JH 1943	Penny Brandling-Harris	CR 2000
Tom Attenborough	PH 1985	Grahame Berkeley	HS 1955	A.W. Brice	PS 1952
Robert Austin	CR 1949	Robin Berkeley OBE	HS 1951	Edward Brice	PS 1949
Nicholas ter Averst	HS 1989	John Berry	SH 1996	Paddy Brice	FH 1982
H.M. Axten	WH 1942	Henry Berry	PS 2003	Toby Black	WH 2008
Sue Bailey		Tony Biddle	Sc 1943	Roger Brooke	Sc/FH 1944

James Brown	FH 2004	Ian A.E.W. Cleveland	Sc 1938
N.J.R. Brown	PH 2005	Martin R.V. Clinch	MH 1952
T.B.J. Brown	PH 2009	Dr M.J. and	
Thomas Brown		Mrs C. Clugston	CR 1978
William Brown		Charles Coldman	CH 1997
Dr Sean Buchanan	JH 1983	John and Nicola Coldman	
Richard Buckingham	JH 1990	Tom Coldman	MH 2007
Theo C. Buffini	PS 2010	B.G. Monty Collyer	WW 2003
Robert Burder	PH 1944	Robert Colvill	FH 1955
Maurice Burnett	WH 1936	Martin Colvill	FH 1954
David L. Burt	MH 1943	Charlie Compton	JH 2001
George Bush	Sc 2001	Ed Compton	JH 2004
M.H. Bushby	CR 1954	M.S. Connell	PS 1952
C.J. Butler	CH 1994	Dr Alec Cook	
Andrew Butler	JH 1947	Richard Cooper	JH 1943
R.J. Butler	Sc 1978	Dr Stephen Cooper	
Richard Butterworth	Sc 1944	James Coppin	WW 1996
André Calder	PH 1983	Brigadier Robin Cordell	
Philip Callow	PH 1991	SH/WW 1971	
Dr Katharine Campbell		Jeremy Cowdrey	PH 1973
(daughter of Lord Douglas)		Sir Sherard Cowper-Coles	
	DB 1906		PS 1968
Matthew Camp	PS 1988	Adam Cox	WH 1976
Mr and Mrs R.L. Campin		James Cranfield	Sc 1982
Peter Canney	JH 1957	Colin Crang	JH 1952
Cameron Carr	CH 2010	Rodney Crang	JH 1949
J.D.H. Cave	Sc 1942	John Crates	PH 1953
James Champness	JH 1997	Edmund Crawford	SH 1940
Andrew D.C. Chapman	SH 1962	Hamish Crawford	JH 1940
Keith L.M. Chapman	MH 1936	Hugh Crawford	JH 1941
Richard H. Chapman	JH 1949	James E.B. Crease	MH 1941
Alex Charlton	JH 1971	Dr Matthew Cripps	SH 1972
Chris Charlton	SH 1989	William Crispin	FH 1990
Mrs J.C. Charlton		Tim Crofton	FH 1980
David T.W. Cheng	FH 2006	Jeremy Cronk	HS 1997
The Chester Family		Julian and Eileen Cronk	
Nicholas S. Child	PH 1951	Philip Curtis	WH 1979
Dr Ben Chishick	SH 1966	Richard Dalzell	HS 1954
Gerald Chishick	Sc 1963	James Dammers	SH 2005
Jonathan Chishick	Sc 1964	Matthew Dammers	SH 2007
Hugh Chivers	MH 1993	John Darby	HS 1952
Alex N.H. Chong	MH 2008	Jonathan Davie	JH 1959
Nicholas A.C. Clark	MH 1980	Henry E. Davies	JH 2001
John Clay	PH 1970	Oscar Davies	PS 2010
John A. Clemence CBE TD		Peter Davies	FH 1975
	JH 1950	Robert Davies	
Aaron C.D. Clements-Hunt		Robin Davies	PS 1951
	HS 2010	Anthony E. Davis	PS 1962

James Davis	MH 1990
Tom Davis	Sc 1971
James Day	PS 1967
John H. Day	PS 1936
Nicholas de Brett	PS 2007
Olivier de Brett	PS 1999
P.H.C. de la Fuente	Sc 1948
Luke J.L. Deacon	FH 2006
Tim Denham	PH 1960
Simon and Kay Denton	
John Dickinson	OH 2006
Squadron Leader Clive 'Dizzy'	
Disdel RAF	JH 1977
Anthony Dod	MH 1972
Bill Dod	MH 1979
Henry Dodds	PS 1970
Peter Dodge	MH 1973
Captain Peter Doresa MC	
	Sc 1938
Charles Doubleday-Potts	SH 2009
William Doubleday-Potts	SH 2008
Peter Dunkley	HS 1972
The Eakins Family	
John Earle	SH/FH 1943
Walter Eberstadt OBE	Sc 1936
Stephen R.R. Edlmann	FH 1967
Hugh Edmonds	PH 1962
M.A. Edmondson	
Conrad Edwards	FH 1937
Ollie Edwards	WW 2008
Ted Elgood	HS 1941
François and Jane Eliet	
James Elliott	PH 2001
Robbie Elliott	PH 1995
Duncan Elliott	HS 1991
Tom Elliott	PH 2005
Andrew J. Ellott	JH 1979
David Emms	Sc 1938
John Emms	Sc 1966
James Engelbach	MH 1967
Michael Engelbach	MH 1962
D.H. Evans	MH 1939
Fergus Evans	FH 1983
Henry Evans	Sc 2003
J.W.H. Evans	MH 1971
Mark Evans	MH 1975
Revd Norman Evans	SH 1944
Paul Evans	HS 1978

Christopher Everett		
Headmaster 1975		
Guy Faller	FH 1972	
D.W.H. Farmer	PS 1949	
Bernard Farrant	MH 1965	
Dr David J.D. Farrow	PS 1951	
Samuel Fearn	JH 2009	
Adrian M. Feather	MH 1957	
Andrew Featherstone	PS 1962	
Guy Featherstone	HS 1998	
Squadron Leader J.C.L. Fell		
MH 1948		
Forbes Fenton	Sc 1979	
Lewis W. Ferrett	HS 2001	
M.H. Fisher	MH 1944	
N.P. Florence	PS 1948	
Mark Fone	JH 1978	
Mr and Mrs D. Forbes-Nixon		
Bertie Ford	WH 2009	
Harry Ford	WH 2007	
John Foster-Powell		
I.W. Fotheringham	JH 1942	
Patrick Francis	PH 1966	
Peter J. Fuller	PS 1945	
Cosmos Fung	MH 2007	
William Gamon	MH 2000	
Malcolm Garrard	JH 1970	
Steven Gee	PH 1966	
Edward Gerrard	HS 2008	
John Gibbs	FH 1956	
Brian Gibson	FH 1963	
C.G. Gibson	HS 1955	
Mark Gibson	HS 1979	
Justin Gilbert	PH 1983	
Clayton Gillespie	WH 2008	
Todd Gillespie	WH 2010	
Adam Gillett	WH 2001	
Edward Gillett	WH 1999	
Hugo Goodson	PS 2007	
Rory Goodson	PS 2009	
David Goodwin	JH 1950	
J.E. Gordon	PS 1953	
Richard Gracey	PS 1950	
A.A.K. Graham	WH/FH 1943	
Hugh Granger	SH 2007	
Jamie Grant	MH 2002	
Ian Grason	WH 1957	
James O.C. Green	MH 2010	

David Greenslade	Sc 1947	
Major A.I.M. Gregor		
MacGregor	JH 1944	
Mrs W.P. Griffith		
Owen Griffiths	HS 1990	
M. Haddleton	JH 1947	
Dr Noel Hadfield	MH 1933	
Douglas J. Hadler	SH 1951	
Stephen P. StJ. Hall	WW 1983	
Joshua Hancock	WH 2009	
Peter Hancock	PH 1955	
J. Hankinson	SH 1940	
Niel Hare	SH 1938	
Robin L.A. Hare	HS 1966	
Eric Hargreaves	CH 2009	
Freddie Harris	SH 2007	
R.T.M. Harrison	SH 2006	
W.S.M. Harrison	SH 2003	
Air Commodore R.E.E.		
Hart OBE	Bursar 1994	
Mr and Mrs R.B. Harvey		
Joshua Hawkins	MH 1991	
Nicholas Hawkins	MH 1992	
Richard Hawkins	MH 1988	
Joshua J.A. Cronin	HS 2010	
E.C. Heathcote	MH 1958	
Roger and Betty Hedley-Jones		
In Memory of		
Bernard Van Heek	PS 1938	
Matthew and Andrew Hemmings		
PS 2003 and PS 2007		
Chris Henshall	CR 1996	
Andrew Heywood		
R.M. Hickman	MH 1944	
Lieutenant Colonel A.J. Hicks		
Kieran B. Hicks	PH 1990	
Michael Hicks	FH 1962	
Dennis Hill	PS 1941	
Gordon F. Hill	PS 1942	
Tim Hill		
Ian Hinton	PH 1944	
John H. Hoare	FH/SH 1934	
Richard Hoare	CR 1995	
Charles Hoblyn	HS/WH 2004	
Harry Hoblyn	FH 1973	
Richard Hoblyn	FH 1971	
Anthony G.P. Hobrow	PS 1968	
David Hodge	JH 1953	

Henry Hofman	MH 2004	
Anthony Holman	WH 1955	
Brigadier J.C. Holman CBE		
WH 1951		
Ian Hooper	Sc 1955	
Richard Hough	PH 1979	
T. Howden	Sc 1950	
Andrew Huang	MH 2009	
Jonathan Hubbard	PS 1960	
Humphrey R.O. Hubble	WH 1935	
A.B.E. Hudson MBE	PS 1952	
Duncan Huleatt-James	FH 2007	
Alastair Hume	FH 1956	
Brian Hunt	WH 1946	
James Hunt	WH 1998	
William Hunter	Sc 1957	
Jolyon Hutchings	FH 2007	
The Lord Ironside	MH 1938	
D.R.H. Jackson	WH 2008	
Dr I.R.H and		
Mrs J.M. Jackson	CR 1989	
Ian Jackson	MH 1951	
Richard Jackson	FH 1957	
Peter Jeffrey		
Alexander W.O. Jenkins	SH 1989	
Sir Brian Jenkins	MH 1949	
Chris Jenkins	MH 1967	
C. Grant Jenkins	FH 1963	
Andrew F. Jenner	SH 1971	
Steve and Diana Jennings		
Henry Jobber	WW 2010	
C.J.W. Johnson	MH 1921	
Matthew Noble	PS 2011	
Major R.M. Johnson	Sc 1941	
Thomas Noble	PS 2010	
Dr C.L. Joiner	WH 1940	
A.D.B. Jones	JH 1942	
Gregory Jones	CH 2010	
Ekasith Jotikasthira	FH 1984	
Ziad Kassem	PS 1968	
Clement Keevil	JH 1933	
Julian Keevil	JH 1962	
Peter Keevil	FH 1997	
Philip Keevil	JH 1960	
David Kemp	PS 1942	
G.C.K. Kemp	FH 2000	
Peter Kemp	PH 1987	
Will Kemp	WH 1985	

George A. Kendrick	FH 2005	Jacob MacKenzie	PS 2010	John Mew	SH 1942
Kim N.R. Kennedy	WH 1971	Nicholas MacKichan	Sc 2007	Stephen Middleton	HS 1943
L.E. King		Peter Mackinnon	FH 1952	James Miles	MH 1996
Martin King	CR 1975	Andrew MacLaren	MH 1957	Andrew Millard	Sc 1976
O.B. King	JH 2007	David Macnamara	WH 1970	Paul Miller	PH 1958
Dr J.M.G. Kirkaldy	FH 1961	Richard Macnamara		Trevor Mills	PH 1963
Roger Kirkpatrick	SH 1941		WH/WW 1970	Andrew Mitchell	JH 1953
John Kitching	MH 1948	Malcolm MacNicol	PS 1941	Brian Mitchell	FH 1951
James Lambert		Simon R. Mair	SH 1968	Ian M. Mitchell	Sc 1976
S.J.B. Langdale	WH 1950	Tim Mair	SH 1970	A.H.V. Monteuuis	HS 1960
Nick Langford	PH 1974	Alan and Julia Maltby	PS 1956	Greville Moore	WH 1940
Alexander Langridge	OH 2001	R.P.G. Le Marchand	WH 1959	Colonel Ian Moore CBE	Sc 1954
James Lark	FH 1970	William Marle	Sc 1971	Mrs M. Moore	
Aaron H.Y. Lau	Sc 2010	William Marle	Sc 2001	Peter Moore	OH 1996
C. Laughton-Scott		Andrew Marrs	SH 1956	Michael Moreland	SH 1936
The Lavers Family		Dr Timothy C. Marrs	SH 1959	Peter Moreland	SH 1935
Ashley Law	Sc 1988	A.G. Marsden	WH 1934	Andrew Lloyd Morgan	
Diana E. Law		Wing Commander		MBE DSC	SH 1937
Jonathan Law	WW 1974	N.G.S Marshall	SH 1937	Gerry Morgan	PH 1961
Stuart Law	JH 1966	Sir Peter Marshall	SH 1938	H.D.T. Moss	HS 1953
Hugo Lawrence	PH 1988	David Martin	PS 1982	W. Peter B. Moss	WH 1950
James Leahy	PH 1974	David Marwood	WH 1936	D.G. Moxon	PS 1956
Sir John Leahy	Sc/PH 1941	Dion Mason		Oliver Moynes	WH 2010
David Leask	MH 1953	Anthony Massey	SH/WW 1973	Richard Munton	
Charles Ledsam	HS 1962	Beverley Matthews	CR 2000	William E. Musker	HS 2002
Graham Lee	MH 1938	Dr David Matthewson and		Andrew R. Musson	Sc 1954
Simon Lee	WH 1974	Miss Carole Wanless		Martin Musson	WH 1947
Andy Leeds	MH 1996	Tom Matthewson	SH 2008	Richard Musson	WH 1958
Mr and Mrs B.M. Leek		Andrew H. Mayer	FH 1962	Charlie Naismith	PS 2005
Alexander van Leeuwen	WH 2009	Lord Mayhew of Twysden	Sc 1943	Harry Naismith	PS 2008
Benjamin van Leeuwen	WH 2008	Major Ian Mayman DL	JH 1943	Tom Naismith	HS 2006
D.M.A. Legrand	FH 1957	Dominic McCarthy	JH 1980	James R.O. Nakajima	HS 2008
In Honour of A.U. Lind and		David McClure Fisher	PS 1952	Luke Naylor-Perrott	WH 2010
A.W. Lind	Sc 1928 and 1965	Roger McCrann	MH 1949	S.C. Nazmi	MH 1987
J. Llewelyn		John McGowan	SH 1943	Peter Neill	HS 1994
Peter Logsdon	PH 1958	John N.M. McLean	JH 1967	Matthew Newlands	
J.F.J. London	MH 1978	Dominic McMullan	PH 1992	Mark Newnham	MH 1978
William Long	PS 2006	Charlie McNeilage	OH 2007	Andrew Newton	JH 1967
O. Gyles Longley CBE MC		James McNeilage	OH 2005	O.P. Nicholas	WH 1945
	JH 1932	Rory McNeilage	OH 2011	J.A. Nicholson	MH 1991
Nick Lord	CR 1983	Tom Meade	WH 2005	P.G. Nicholson	Sc 1947
A. Lowrie		Nicholas Meimarides	CH 1994	M. Nieman	PS 1972
Ian Lucas	CR 2000	Edward Mellor	PS 2005	George E.M. Nodder	PH 2003
Anton Luck	MH 1968	John Mellor	PS 2002	James Nolan	MH 1981
E.W.B. Lyndon-Stanford		Peter and Juliet Mellor		Mark D. Northwood	HS 1975
	FH 1949	Dominic Merchant	PH 2008	David R. Nottidge	SH 1934
Dr John Lynn		Paul Merchant	WW 2003	Jonathan O'Brien	PS 1980
Christopher Mack	Sc 1988	A.G. Meredith	PH 1950	V.R. O'Connell	CR 1975

Christopher O'Donovan MH 2002
Michael O'Dwyer MH 1983
Richard O'Grady MH 2008
T.G. Oatley WH 1982
Duncan Odds PH 1998
J.D.R. Oliver PH 2008
David Ollington JH 1943
K.L. Osborne JH 1935
William Osman SH 2008
R.J. Packer WH1978
Barrie R.K. Pain SH 1938
Charles Paine PS 1954
Kenneth Palmer Sc 1944
Rex Palmer Sc 1945
H. Colin Panes Sc 1952
M.F. Parkes SH 2010
Dr and Mrs Parry
Victor E.G. Parry FH 2010
Ian Parsons PS 1960
Richard Partridge MH 1970
Chris Passmore Sc 1972
Stephen Passmore Sc 1973
Alasdair Paterson PS 1966
J. Stuart Paton HS 1939
Andrew Payne HS 1970
Richard Peel FH 1978
Freddie Pelly JH 1999
Charles B Penruddocke WH 1957
John Peters
A.J.N. Peterson PH 1985
Mark Pexton WH 2003
Matthew Pexton WH 2005
James Pigot WH 2005
David M Pigott CH 2003
Nicholas Pike
Mark J. Plant Estates Bursar
Kenneth R. Pointon MH 1946
Lieutenant Colonel Sebastian
    Pollington RTR PH 1980
Aly Popat MH 1998
John Powell MH 1938
Peter Pragnell PS 1973
Brian D. Price MH 1953
Cindy Price
Richard Price HS 1974
Mr and Mrs Anthony Proctor
Hector Proud HS 1984

Nicholas R.B. Prowse PS 1950
Sebastian J. Pudney FH 2007
Andrew Pullman WH 1974
Lieutenant Colonel
    J.R. Rahilly SH 1934
Charles Rainer WH 1940
Robert Ramage JH 1943
John Ramplin PH 1944
Stanley E. Randall SH 1930
Janet and Stephen Rapicano
Christopher Rash MH 1978
Edward Rash MH 1985
Guy J.E. Rash MH 1979
William Rash MH 1983
F.C. Raven SH 1949
R.H. Rawlins Sc 1973
Tim Read Sc 1971
Jonathan Reed MH 1964
William J. Reeve PS 1960
David and Faith Reich SH 1957
Nigel Reid MH 1971
Captain Rob Reynolds PS 1995
Tom and Caroline Rider
Jonathan Rigden PS 1944
Brian P. Roberts-Wray HS 1949
Alastair J. Roberts MH 2007
David Roberts WW 1976
Jonathan A. Roberts MH 2001
Mark W. Roberts MH 2004
Phillip Roberts Sc 1962
Richard Roberts PS 1953
David Robins CR 1969
James Rogers PH 1995
Robert Rogers SH 1963
Charles Rosenmeyer SH 1962
Michael Ross-Collins
A.G. Rossi-Ashton PS 1940
Ruth Rouse
    (niece of John Palmer) FH 1933
Alexandra L. Rowan
Charles Rowe
J.G.C. Rowe PH 1992
J. Rowland PS 1985
Mr and Mrs C.J. Rudge
Dr John Ruston MH 1968
Michael Ryan PH 2002
Anthony B. Rye PH 1945
Joffy Sale PH 1976

Commander David Salmon
    SH/FH 1943
Derek C.N. Salmon WH 1939
Sefton B. Samuels SH 1980
M.D. Sanders PH 1949
Richard Sankey PS 1982
Josh Saville HS 2007
Theo Saville HS 2008
Richard Sax Sc 1952
Jeremy Sayers WH 1952
Revd Roger Scoones FH 1961
M.J.H. Scott PH 2010
Richard Scott PH 1968
David Seex JH 1974
Dr Anthony Seldon HS 1967
Mr and Mrs Sergeef
Michael Sharp MH 1937
Henry Shaw MH 2008
Mei Wah B. Shek
Gabriel X.J. Sherliker MH 2005
Edward Shields CH 2010
Charles Shildrick SH 1952
Lieutenant Colonel David
    Sievwright Sc 1959
A.E.B. Simpson MH 1985
Mel Sims
Sir Andrew Judd Foundation
David J.M. Slade PS 1986
Mr and Mrs E.J.
    Smalman-Smith CR 1961
C.H. Smith WW 1984
Jeremy Smither
Kenneth Somer PS 1943
Michael Somers FH 1956
David M. Sowrey PH 1979
John Sowrey FH 1933
David Spackman FH 1970
Brigadier Martin
    Speller CBE JH 1964
Peter Stainforth HS 1935
Crispin P. Stephens PH 1988
Dr Charles Stephenson PH 1944
Dan Stevens MH 1996
C.J. Stewart FH 1956
C.P. Stewart FH 1990
Richard Stocks Sc 1953
Ian A. Stoker HS 1956
Andreas Stradis OH 1999

Athamos Stradis	OH 2002	
Peter Strawson	WH 1957	
Peter F. Strouvelle	JH 1933	
Joe Stuart-Smith	WH 1948	
Mrs R.H. Stubington		
Simon R. Stubington	PH 1976	
Henry J.H. Sturgess	PS 1996	
John P. Sudlow	Sc 1939	
W.R. (Bill) Sylvester	JH 1950	
John Symons	SH 1939	
Lieutenant Colonel Richard D.B. Talbot CD	WH/Sc 1955	
Ian Tapply	WH 2001	
Revd Hugh Taylor	HS 1957	
Ian Taylor TD	Sc 1957	
John R. Taylor	HS 1942	
R.F. Teubler	WW 1975	
C.H. Thomas		
Edmund Thompson	WH 2009	
George Thompson	WH 2005	
M.R. De Courcy Thompson	Sc 1963	
P.C. Thompson	WH 1955	
Andrew and Christine Tivenan		
Brian Toll	SH 1969	
Ned Towle	FH 1963	
Sara Tozzi	Governor	
Paul S. Trotman	Sc 1953	
Tunbridge Wells Fire Protection Ltd		
Harry G. Twitchell	PS 1935	

Graham Tyler	HS 1978	
James Underhill Foundation Director		
Konrad van Halewyn	MH 2009	
Siegmar Vetter		
Guy James Vigar	Sc 1970	
Brigadier A.C. Vivian	PS 1946	
N.P. Wakeling	HS 2000	
Hugh Walker	FH 1933	
Andrew Wallace	WH 2006	
Chris Walsh	PH 1989	
Michael Walsh	WH 1994	
Roger Ward	HS 1952	
Cosmo Warner	PS 2007	
Andrew Warrener	SH 1970	
Vaughan Watson	FH 1986	
David Watts	WH 1943	
Mark Wauton	SH 1970	
Dan Webb	SH 2006	
Robin F. Wells	WH 1972	
Josh West	HS 2003	
Sam West	HS 2000	
Dr John Weston	JH 1950	
Julian Weston	HS 1961	
Fred Wheadon	WH 2007	
Ben Wheatley	WW 2002	
Jonathan Wheeler	PH 1986	
W.A. White	JH 1996	
Richard Whittle	JH 1953	
Mrs K. Whyte		

Brigadier John B. Wilks CBE	PH 1944	
Dan Willett	HS 1995	
Max Willett	HS 1997	
Charlie Williams	FH 1984	
Martin B.M. Williams	FH 1960	
Neil Williamson	JH 1957	
Jeremy Wilmot	FH 1982	
Sir Sandy Wilson	HS 1954	
Matthew Wilson	Sc 1972	
J.G. Wiltshier	PH 1947	
Colonel R.F.M. Windsor CBE DL	PH/JH 1940	
Derek See-Kit Wong	PH 1983	
Helenka Wood		
David Woodcock	PH 1979	
N.G. Woodcock	WW 1982	
James Woodman	Sc 1997	
Michael Woodman	Sc 1996	
Philip Woodman		
Tim Wooff	HS 1979	
Flight Lieutenant Gareth Wright	WW 1993	
Leslie Wright	JH 1938	
J.R. Wrightson	PS 1942	
G.J. Yeoman	SH 1958	
Anthony Young	SH 1952	
Ben Young	MH 2007	
Freddie Young	MH 2009	
R.J.Q. Young	SH 1956	

GLOSSARY

Tonbridge School abbreviations and terms

Boarding Houses

Sc	School House
JH	Judde House
HS	Hill Side
PH	Park House
PS	Parkside
FH	Ferox Hall
MH	Manor House

Day boy Houses

WH	Welldon House (founded 1932)
SH	Smythe House (founded 1932)
DB	All day boys grouped alphabetically before 1932 (A-K and L-Z)

Other school terms

Army Class	For those wishing to enter the Services
Blue Book	Annual report of Old Tonbridgian Society
Bumph test	School knowledge test which had to be passed by all novi
Certificate A	Proficiency exam taken in the OTC
Cras	School cross-country race
Ferdie	Name given to bag for carrying books, devised by 'Ferdie' Eames, housemaster of Hill Side
Gate of Remembrance	1914–18 Chapel War Memorial (destroyed in 1988 fire)

Grubber	Tuck shop
The Fifty	1st XV rugby pitch
The Head	1st XI cricket ground
Novi	New boys
OT	Old Tonbridgian
OTS	Old Tonbridgian Society
OTC	Officers' Training Corps (Junior Training Corps or JTC from 1941)
Prae	School or House praeposter (prefect)
Sanatorium	Medical Centre
School Certificate	Public exam predecessor of O/Level and GCSE (Higher School Certificate equivalent of A/Level)

Military abbreviations and terms

AAF	Auxiliary Air Force
AFC	Air Force Cross
A/G	Air Gunner
AIF	Australian Imperial Forces
Anzacs	Australian and New Zealand soldiers
App	Apprentice (Merchant Navy rank)
ARP	Air raid precautions
Bde	Brigade
BEF	British Expeditionary Force
BOAC	British Overseas Airways Corporation

CCS	Casualty Clearing Station
C-in-C	Commander-in-Chief
CIGS	Chief of the Imperial General Staff
CLY	County of London Yeomanry, Royal Armoured Corps
CO	Commanding Officer
Croix de Guerre	French gallantry medal
CWGC	Commonwealth War Graves Commission
DCLI	Duke of Cornwall's Light Infantry
DD tank	Duplex drive tank – designed to 'swim' ashore with its own propeller
DFC	Distinguished Flying Cross
DFM	Distinguished Flying Medal
DLI	Durham Light Infantry
DOW	Died of wounds
DSO	Distinguished Service Order
FAA	Fleet Air Arm
FF Regiment	Frontier Force Regiment, Indian Army
F/L	Flight Lieutenant
FMSVAF	Federated Malay States Volunteer Air Force
FMSVDF	Federated Malay States Volunteer Defence Force
F/O	Flying Officer
F/Sgt	Flight Sergeant
GC	George Cross
GM	George Medal
GOC	General Officer Commanding
HAA	Heavy Anti-Aircraft Regiment
HAC	Honourable Artillery Company
HKVDC	Hong Kong Volunteer Defence Corps
HKRNVF	Hong Kong Royal Naval Volunteer Force
IA	Indian Army
IWGC	Imperial War Graves Commission (est 1917 – name changed to Commonwealth WGC in 1960s)
KAR	King's African Rifles
KIA	Killed in action
KOAS	Killed on active service
KRRC	King's Royal Rifle Corps
LAC	Leading Aircraftman
LCT	Landing craft (tank)

MBE	Member of the British Empire
MC	Military Cross
MCP	Malayan Communist Party
ME109	Messerschmitt 109 (German fighter plane)
Mid	Midshipman
ML	Motor Launch
MN	Merchant Navy
MTB	Motor Torpedo Boat
OTU	Operational Training Unit
P/O	Pilot Officer
POW	Prisoner of war
RA	Royal Artillery
RAF	Royal Air Force
RAFVR	Royal Air Force Volunteer Reserve
RFC	Royal Flying Corps
RAMC	Royal Army Medical Corps
RAC	Royal Armoured Corps
RASC	Royal Army Service Corps
RAOC	Royal Army Ordnance Corps
RDG	Royal Dragoon Guards
RE	Royal Engineers
REME	Royal Electrical and Mechanical Engineers
RHA	Royal Horse Artillery
RMP	Royal Military Police
RTR	Royal Tank Regiment
RMS	Rendering mines safe (Royal Navy bomb and mine disposal)
RN	Royal Navy
RNVR	Royal Navy Volunteer Reserve
RWK	Royal West Kent Regiment
SAF	South African Forces
SAAF	South African Air Force
SOE	Special Operations Executive
SSVF	Straits Settlement Volunteer Force
S/L	Squadron Leader
TAF	Tactical Air Force
UXB	Unexploded bomb
VC	Victoria Cross
VE Day	Victory in Europe
VJ Day	Victory over Japan
VI	German flying bomb or 'doodlebug'
W/C	Wing Commander
W/O	Warrant Officer
Yeo	Yeomanry

INDEX

Regular = in text
Bold = contribution
Italics = image / artist

ACKNOWLEDGEMENTS

In particular I would like to thank the late Bevil Mabey (WH 1930), one of that remarkable wartime generation, who donated a substantial sum to help cover publishing costs.

I have also received well over 100 contributions from Old Tonbridgians or their children about war experiences in the services and at school. I am sorry not to be able to mention them all but the following have been particularly helpful and forthcoming:

Michael Atkins, Deryck Ball, Alan Bennett Jones, Alistair Birrell, Donald Birrell, Brian Blackie, Rex Boucher, Reymie Bousfield, John Brown, Maurice Burnett, Ian Cleveland, Tom Davis, Victor de Waal, Peter Doresa, Walter Eberstadt, Michael Engelbach, Roger Ephraums, David Farrow, Michael Fisher, Neil Florence, Michael Graham, David Kemp, John Hoare, Richard Johnson, John Kirkaldy, Andrew Law, Robin Lind, James Leahy, John Leahy, Gyles Longley, Malcolm MacNicol, Peter Marshall, Patrick Mayhew, Guy Meredith, Grenville Moore, Andrew Musson, Richard Musson, Geoffrey Oswald, Keith Osborne, Barrie Pain, Chris Passmore, Stuart Paton, John Powell, Nicholas Prowse, Tim Read, William Rouse, Richard Scott, Michael Sharp, John Sowrey, Gordon Stainforth, Peter Stainforth, Peter Steer, James Stewart, Tim Thomas, Hugh Walker, David Watts, Dennis Williams, John Wilks, Sandy Wilson, Rodney Windsor, Leslie Wright, John Wrightson and Bryan Wolfe. I should also like to mention Miriam Nicholls, Jacquie Isaac and Katharine Campbell, the daughters respectively of Harold Newgass, Desmond Hubble and Sholto Douglas, and Chris Compton, son of Michael Compton. Sue Scott, Stephen Matthews and Zon Harper, cousin, stepson and great-nephew respectively of David Legge, were also very helpful.

Bill Brown not only agreed to write the Foreword but provided some evocative photographs from his collection. Ian Taylor has been indefatigable in helping me to research Tonbridge soldiers. Air Commodore Graham Pitchfork has given considerable help and advice on Tonbridgians in the RAF. Bernard van Heek's wartime scrapbook, which he donated to the school archives, has also been a fascinating source of information. Robin Lucas, of 141 Squadron and one of the remaining 'Few', was very helpful about Ted Wolfe.

James Underhill, Judith Edwards and Cindy Price from the Foundation Office have taken on many of the tasks associated with production, while Bev Matthews in the Smythe Library has helped me enormously with material in the school archives. Peter Carpenter kindly contributed an essay on the poetry of Sidney Keyes. Graeme Gales took the photo of Bill Brown and gave other photographic help. Tim Haynes, Ceri Jones, Jonathan Smith and John Gibbs have also been very supportive and helpful.

I would also like to thank Neil Burkey, Chris Fagg, Michael Jackson and Matthew Wilson at Third Millennium for their professional guidance and encouragement, and for producing such a high quality book. Roddy Paine's Photographic Studio digitised many of the photos from the school archives and elsewhere. Various other individuals and institutions have also helped with photographs and information, including the Imperial War Museum, the Commonwealth War Graves Commission, the Fleet Air Arm Museum, the Royal Engineers Library, Tony Banham and the Hong Kong War Diary, Richard Hide and the Hong Kong Escape, Dulwich College, the War Graves Photographic Project, Philip Harvey, and the Gurkha Museum. The school histories of David Somervell and Barry Orchard have both been invaluable as has been the 1861–1945 School Register edited by H.D. Furley. Above all a love both of Tonbridge and of history has been nurtured in many ways and by many different people over the last 38 years, for which I will always be grateful.